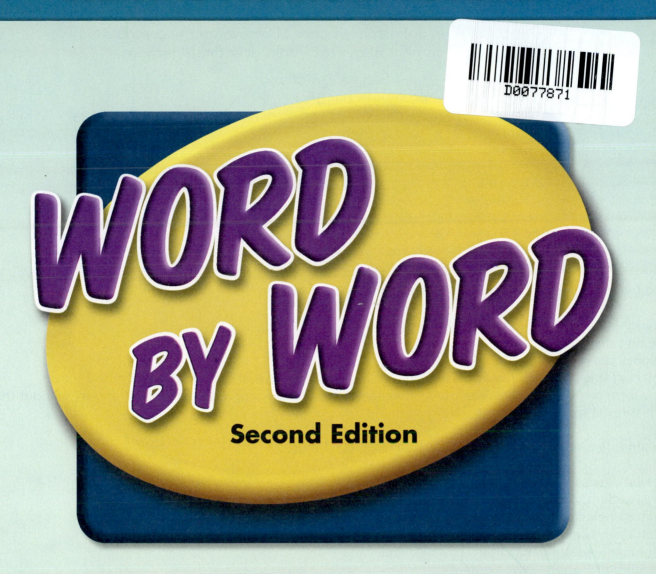

WORD BY WORD

Second Edition

Steven J. Molinsky • Bill Bliss

Contributing Authors
Robert Doherty
Ann Kennedy

Illustrated by
Richard E. Hill

PEARSON
Longman

Dedicated to Janet Johnston in honor of her wonderful contribution to the development of our textbooks over three decades.

Steven J. Molinsky
Bill Bliss

Word by Word Beginning Vocabulary Workbook, second edition

Pearson Education, 10 Bank Street, White Plains, NY 10606

Editorial director: Pam Fishman
Vice president, director of design and production: Rhea Banker
Director of electronic production: Aliza Greenblatt
Director of manufacturing: Patrice Fraccio
Senior manufacturing manager: Edith Pullman
Marketing manager: Oliva Fernandez
Associate Paging Manager: Paula Williams
Text design: Wendy Wolf
Cover design: Tracey Munz Cataldo, Warren Fischbach
Realia creation: Warren Fischbach, Paula Williams
Illustrations: Richard E. Hill
Contributing artist: Charles Cawley

ISBN 0-13-189229-0
Longman on the Web
Longman.com offers online resources for teachers and students. Access our Companion Websites, our online catalog, and our local offices around the world.

Visit us at longman.com.

Printed in the United States of America
7 8 9 10 – V082 – 13 12

CONTENTS

A WHAT'S THE WORD?

| apartment | family | phone | zip |
| area | first | social security | |

1. What's your ____family____ name?
   Montero.
2. What's your _____ name?
   Carla.
3. What's your _____ number?
   937–873–2690.
4. What's your _____ number?
   394–23–9582.
5. What's your _____ number?
   4B.
6. What's your _____ code?
   10024.
7. What's your _____ code?
   937.

B WHAT'S THE ANSWER?

__d__ 1. What's your last name?
_____ 2. What's your first name?
_____ 3. What's your address?
_____ 4. How do you spell that?

a. 132 Madison Street.
b. M-I-L-L-E-R.
c. James.
d. Miller.

_____ 5. What's your apartment number?
_____ 6. What's your place of birth?
_____ 7. What's your date of birth?
_____ 8. What's your social security number?

e. Los Angeles.
f. 583–79–5397.
g. March 19, 1986.
h. 2C.

C YOUR APPLICATION

Fill in the form with your personal information.

Name: _____
       LAST   FIRST   MIDDLE
Address: _____
        NUMBER   STREET   APT. #
       _____
       CITY   STATE   ZIP CODE
       _____
       E-MAIL ADDRESS   TELEPHONE   SEX: ☐ M ☐ F

1

A WHICH GROUP?

| brother | father | mother | son |
| daughter | husband | sister | wife |

- __daughter__
- _____
- _____
- _____

- _____
- _____
- _____
- _____

B HIS NAME OR HER NAME?

| His | Her |

1. What's your wife's name?

____Her____ name is Ellen.

2. What's your brother's name?

_____ name is Robert.

3. What's your mother's name?

_____ name is Donna.

4. What's your husband's name?

_____ name is Donald.

5. What's your grandfather's name?

_____ name is Patrick.

6. What's your granddaughter's name?

_____ name is Susan.

C WHO IS WHO?

__e__ **1.** My father's daughter is

_____ **2.** My mother's father is

_____ **3.** My father's mother is

_____ **4.** My daughter's son is

_____ **5.** My grandmother's daughter is

_____ **6.** My grandson's father is

a. my grandson.

b. my son.

c. my mother.

d. my grandmother.

e. my sister.

f. my grandfather.

D WHICH WORD DOESN'T BELONG?

1.	mother	grandmother	(son)	daughter
2.	son	husband	brother	mother
3.	baby	grandmother	grandfather	father
4.	sister	brother	sibling	wife
5.	husband	son	children	daughter

A WHICH GROUP?

Look at page 3 of the Picture Dictionary. Write each word in the correct column.

_____aunt_____

_____

_____

_____

_____

_____

_____

_____

_____

_____

_____

_____

_____

_____

B WHO ARE THEY?

Look at page 3 of the Picture Dictionary and complete the sentences.

1. Walter is Alan's _____grandfather_____.

2. Frank is Jennifer's _____.

3. Alan is Timmy's _____.

4. Helen is Linda's _____.

5. Walter is Nancy's _____.

6. Nancy is Linda's _____.

C WHICH WORD?

1. He's my (aunt (uncle)).
   What's (her   his) name?

2. (She's   He's) my daughter-in-law.
   Where does (he   she) live?

3. (His   Her) name is David.
   Is he your (niece   nephew)?

4. Is she your (niece   nephew)?
   Yes. (His   Her) name is Julie.

5. Is he your (uncle   aunt)?
   No. He's my (cousin   sister-in-law).

6. Is (he   she) your son-in-law?
   Yes. His (wife   sister) is my daughter.

D WHAT'S THE WORD?

1. Is she your aunt?
   Yes. She's my father's ___sister___.

2. Is he your grandfather?
   Yes. He's my father's _____.

3. Is she your mother-in-law?
   Yes. She's my wife's _____.

4. Is he your brother-in-law?
   Yes. He's my wife's _____.

5. Is he your nephew?
   Yes. He's my brother's _____.

6. Is she your niece?
   Yes. She's my sister's _____.

(continued)

E AT LINDA AND TOM'S WEDDING

Sue and Larry are at Linda and Tom's wedding. Write the correct words to complete the conversation. Then practice the conversation with a friend.

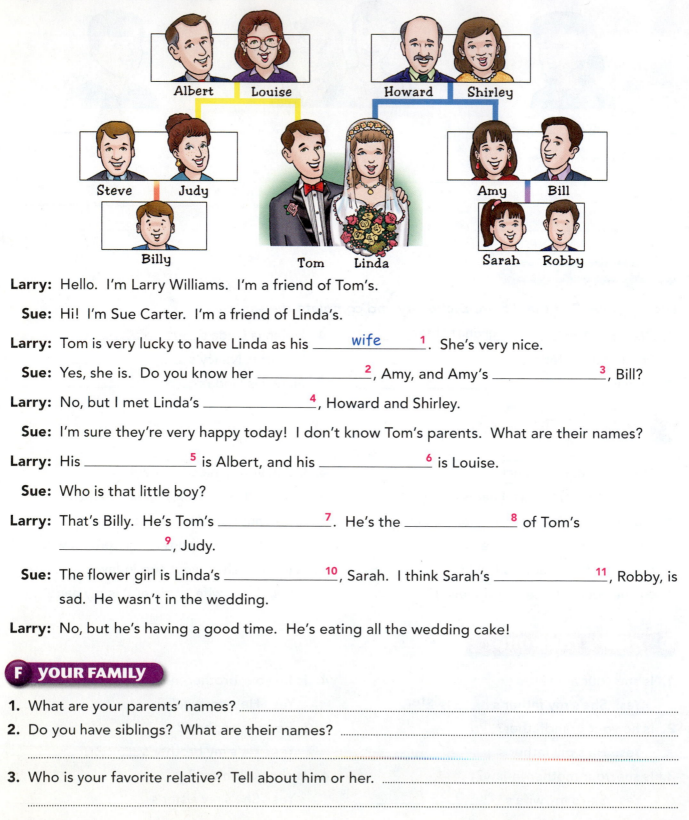

Larry: Hello. I'm Larry Williams. I'm a friend of Tom's.

Sue: Hi! I'm Sue Carter. I'm a friend of Linda's.

Larry: Tom is very lucky to have Linda as his _____wife_____ 1. She's very nice.

Sue: Yes, she is. Do you know her _____ 2, Amy, and Amy's _____ 3, Bill?

Larry: No, but I met Linda's _____ 4, Howard and Shirley.

Sue: I'm sure they're very happy today! I don't know Tom's parents. What are their names?

Larry: His _____ 5 is Albert, and his _____ 6 is Louise.

Sue: Who is that little boy?

Larry: That's Billy. He's Tom's _____ 7. He's the _____ 8 of Tom's _____ 9, Judy.

Sue: The flower girl is Linda's _____ 10, Sarah. I think Sarah's _____ 11, Robby, is sad. He wasn't in the wedding.

Larry: No, but he's having a good time. He's eating all the wedding cake!

F YOUR FAMILY

1. What are your parents' names? ....

2. Do you have siblings? What are their names? ....

....

3. Who is your favorite relative? Tell about him or her. ....

....

....

A MATCHING

Study page 5.

_d_	**1.** chalk	**a.**	speaker
____	**2.** thumb	**b.**	basket
____	**3.** work	**c.**	case
____	**4.** book	**d.**	board
____	**5.** waste	**e.**	tack
____	**6.** loud	**f.**	book

B WHAT DO YOU USE?

> a calculator   chalk   a keyboard   a pencil   a ruler   a thumbtack

1. What do you use to write on the board? _____chalk_____

2. What do you use to write on paper? _____

3. What do you use to type on? _____

4. What do you use to put papers on a bulletin board? _____

5. What do you use to draw straight lines? _____

6. What do you use to add and subtract numbers? _____

C WHERE ARE THEY?

Look at page 4 of the Picture Dictionary. Complete the sentences.

> bookcase   chalkboard   desk   monitor   pencil sharpener   table

1. The keyboard is next to the _____monitor_____.

2. The screen is next to the _____.

3. The globe is on the _____.

4. The globe is next to the _____.

5. The printer is on the _____.

6. The binder is on the _____.

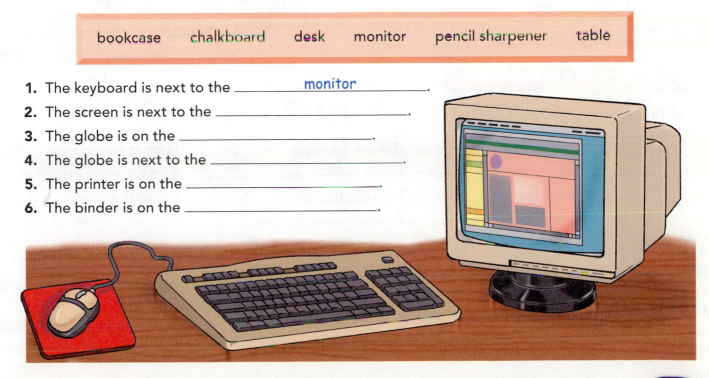

A THE TEACHER'S INSTRUCTIONS

1. Copy the ((word)   book).
2. (Look   Pronounce) up a word.
3. Take out a piece of (board   paper).
4. Put the (words   shades) in order.
5. (Hand in   Correct) your mistakes.
6. Help (a book   each other).
7. Repeat your (homework   name).
8. (Match   Answer) the words.
9. Take your (seat   hand).
10. Work in a (partner   group).

B WHAT'S THE WORD?

answer	blank	groups	name	seat	word
answers	dictionary	lights	paper	together	work

1. Work _____ together _____.
2. Unscramble the _____.
3. Spell your _____.
4. Fill in the _____.
5. Look in the _____.
6. Mark the _____ sheet.
7. Do your own _____.
8. Go over the _____.
9. Take your _____.
10. Turn off the _____.
11. Break up into small _____.
12. Write on a separate sheet of _____.

C WHAT'S THE SEQUENCE?

Put the actions in the best order.

1. ___ Put your book away.
   _1_ Open your book.
   ___ Close your book.
   ___ Study page 5.

2. ___ Correct your mistakes.
   ___ Go over the answers.
   ___ Do your homework.
   ___ Bring in your homework.

3. ___ Collect the tests.
   ___ Check your answers.
   ___ Pass out the tests.
   ___ Answer the questions.

4. ___ Go to the board.
   ___ Stand up.
   ___ Erase the board.
   ___ Write on the board.

5. ___ Look at the screen.
   ___ Turn on the lights.
   ___ Lower the shades.
   ___ Turn off the lights.

6. ___ Listen to the answer.
   ___ Ask a question.
   ___ Raise your hand.
   ___ Ask another question.

D WHAT ARE THEY DOING?

Write a sentence to describe the action.

1. _He's signing his name._

2. _____

3. _____

4. _____

5. _____

6. _____

7. _____

8. _____

E LISTENING

Listen and choose the best word to complete the instructions.

1. a. question
   b. name
   c. question

2. a. board
   b. hand
   c. test

3. a. screen
   b. question
   c. test

4. a. shades
   b. homework
   c. board

5. a. book
   b. work
   c. word

6. a. groups
   b. notes
   c. lights

7. a. together
   b. class
   c. piece of paper

8. a. answer sheet
   b. sheet of paper
   c. answer

9. a. dictionary
   b. blank
   c. book

A WHERE ARE THEY?

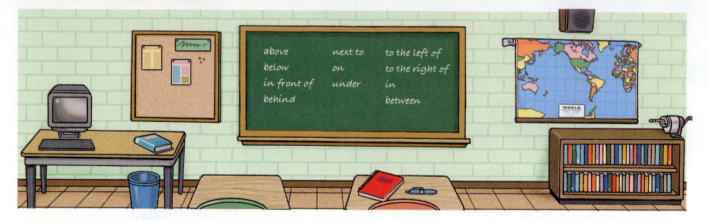

1. The pencil is ((in)   on) the pencil sharpener.
2. The loudspeaker is (above   below) the map.
3. The keyboard is (in front of   behind) the monitor.
4. The pen is (to the left of   to the right of) the notebook.
5. The board is (behind   between) the bulletin board and the map.
6. The book is (under   on) the table, and the wastebasket is (on   under) it.

B LISTENING

Listen and write the number next to the correct item.

☐ clock	☐ globe
☐ dictionary	☐ pen
☐ map	1 pencil
☐ monitor	☐ bulletin board

C LIKELY OR UNLIKELY?

Put a check in the best column.

	Likely	Unlikely
1. There's a pen in the pencil sharpener.	_____	✓
2. There's a clock above the door.	_____	_____
3. There's a teacher in front of the classroom.	_____	_____
4. There's a student on the desk.	_____	_____
5. There's a map to the left of the chalkboard.	_____	_____
6. There's a bookcase under the teacher's desk.	_____	_____

A EVERY MORNING

| brushes | get | have | shaves | washes |
| combs | get | puts on | takes | |

Every morning Jennifer and Jonathan _____get_____ [1] up early.

She _____ [2] her teeth, _____ [3] her face, and _____ [4] makeup.

He _____ [5] a shower, _____ [6], and _____ [7] his hair.

They _____ [8] dressed and _____ [9] breakfast.

B MATCHING

_f_ 1. take   a. my teeth
___ 2. brush   b. lunch
___ 3. comb   c. dressed
___ 4. wash   d. my face
___ 5. get   e. my hair
___ 6. eat   f. a shower

C CROSSWORD: What Do We Do?

Across
1. We have ____.
4. We eat ____.

Down
2. We make the ____.
3. We take a ____.

²B R E A K F A ³S T

D WHAT'S THE SEQUENCE?

Put these actions in the best order.

___ go to bed
1 get up
___ make lunch
___ make breakfast
___ cook dinner
___ get dressed

E LISTENING: Everyday Sounds

Listen to the sounds. Write the number next to the activity you hear.

___ shaving
___ brushing teeth
___ making dinner
1 taking a shower
___ taking a bath

A CHOOSE THE RIGHT WORD

1. She goes to _____ every day.
   a. store
   b. work
   c. bus

2. We're doing our _____.
   a. school
   b. cat
   c. laundry

3. They're cleaning their _____.
   a. apartment
   b. work
   c. lunch

4. When do you come _____ from work?
   a. house
   b. home
   c. to home

5. He's feeding his _____ now.
   a. dinner
   b. laundry
   c. dog

6. I'm busy. I'm washing the _____.
   a. laundry
   b. bus
   c. dishes

B WHICH WORD DOESN'T BELONG?

1. I'm eating _____.   a. breakfast   b. the dishes   c. dinner
2. I'm brushing my _____.   a. baby   b. teeth   c. hair
3. I'm cleaning my _____.   a. house   b. work   c. apartment
4. I'm washing my _____.   a. bath   b. face   c. hair
5. I'm feeding my _____.   a. baby   b. cat   c. breakfast
6. I'm going to _____.   a. bed   b. bus   c. work
7. I'm taking a _____.   a. school   b. bath   c. bus
8. I'm getting _____.   a. dressed   b. undressed   c. dog

C A BUSY DAY

Complete the telephone conversation between Dave and Bob.

do	feeding	go	iron	studying	take

Bob: Hi, Dave. This is Bob. What are you doing?

Dave: I'm _____studying_____[1] English. How about you?

Bob: I'm _____[2] the cat.

Dave: Are you going to _____[3] to work soon?

Bob: Yes. I'm going to _____[4] the bus to work in a little while. What are you doing later?

Dave: I'm going to _____[5] the laundry and _____[6] my clothes.

Bob: You're going to be very busy today!

Dave: You're right. I am!

A WHICH WORD?

1. They're watching ((TV)   the dishes).
2. He's writing a (computer   letter).
3. She's planting (the guitar   flowers).
4. I'm (using   writing) the computer.

5. I'm listening to the (radio   newspaper).
6. He's (practicing   exercising) the piano.
7. You're reading a very good (TV   book).
8. She's playing the (guitar   computer).

B LISTENING

Listen to the sounds. Write the number next to the activity you hear.

	practicing the piano	1	swimming
	watching TV		using the computer
	listening to music		playing the guitar

C WHAT ARE THEY DOING?

Write a sentence to describe the action.

1.    _He's swimming._

3. 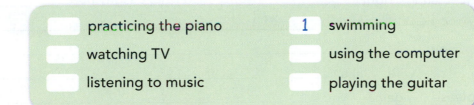   _____

2.    _____

4.    _____

D JOURNAL

What leisure activities do you like to do?

I like to ....
....
....

11

A WHAT'S THE RESPONSE?

_e_ **1.** Thanks.

____ **2.** What's new?

____ **3.** How are you doing?

____ **4.** I'd like to introduce my wife.

____ **5.** May I please speak to Mary?

a. I'm fine.

b. Yes. Hold on a moment.

c. Nice to meet you.

d. Not too much.

e. You're welcome.

B WHAT'S THE ORDER?

1. here   Robert   now.   isn't   right _____ Robert isn't here right now.

2. that?   please   you   Can   repeat _____

3. are   doing?   you   How _____

4. to   my   introduce   I'd   wife.   like _____

5. that   Can   say   please   again?   you _____

6. I   to   Maria?   Can   speak   please _____

C WHICH WORD?

1. Hello. ((I'm)   My) Eduardo.

2. Nice to (meet   introduce) you.

3. May I (say   ask) a question?

4. Sorry. I don't (understand   repeat).

5. See you (afternoon   soon).

6. What's (new   fine) with you?

7. May I (see   speak) to Janet?

8. Can you please (tell   say) that again?

9. I'm sorry. George isn't (here   near) right now.

D LISTENING

Listen and choose the best response.

1. (a.) Good morning.
   b. Good afternoon.

2. a. Fine.
   b. Not much.

3. a. Good morning.
   b. Good night.

4. a. I'm okay.
   b. Hello.

5. a. Nice to meet you.
   b. I'd like to introduce Tom.

6. a. Good-bye.
   b. Good afternoon.

7. a. Excuse me.
   b. See you later.

8. a. Hello.
   b. I'm okay.

9. a. See you later.
   b. Nice to meet you, too.

10. a. See you soon.
   b. Hi.

11. a. Fine, thanks.
   b. You're welcome.

12. a. Yes. Hold on a moment.
   b. Not too much.

A WHAT'S THE WORD?

| foggy | humid | raining | smoggy | sunny | windy |

1. It's a beautiful _____sunny_____ day today!
2. Don't forget your umbrella. It's _____.
3. It's hot, and the air is wet. It's a very _____ day.
4. The leaves are blowing off the trees. It's very _____ today.
5. It's _____ in our city because there are so many cars and trucks.
6. Be careful when you drive home! It's hard to see because it's so _____.

B ASSOCIATIONS

__c__ 1. snowstorm
_____ 2. thunderstorm
_____ 3. lightning
_____ 4. drizzling
_____ 5. heat wave
_____ 6. hailing
_____ 7. sleeting

a. flashes of light in the sky
b. very hot for several days
c. cold winds and snow
d. small balls of ice
e. warm rain and noises in the sky
f. snow mixing with cold rain
g. light rain

C WHICH WORD?

1. The (weather   temperature) is going to be twenty-five degrees Celsius today.
2. I don't think we should go to the beach. It's going to be very (warm   cool) today.
3. Yesterday was sunny, but I think today is going to be (cloudy   sunny).
4. There's often lightning during a (thunderstorm   thermometer).
5. It's hot, windy, and very dry. Do you think we're going to have a (snowstorm   dust storm)?

D FAHRENHEIT AND CELSIUS

1. "It's a hot day today!"   a. 90° F   b. 19° F
2. "It's very cold outside!"   a. 80° F   b. 28° F
3. "It's a nice warm day!"   a. 26° C   b. 5° C
4. "Look! It's snowing outside!"   a. -5° C   b. 5° C
5. "It's a very hot day!"   a. 40° F   b. 40° C
6. "We're having a big snowstorm!"   a. 10° F   b. 10° C
7. "It's freezing today!"   a. 32° F   b. 32° C

A WRITE THE NUMBERS

1. fourteen	14		6. 17	seventeen
2. twenty-five	_____		7. 33	_____
3. sixty-eight	_____		8. 46	_____
4. ninety-nine	_____		9. 51	_____
5. one hundred and ten	_____		10. 80	_____

B MATCHING: *Cardinal and Ordinal Numbers*

__d__ 1. three	a. eighth
_____ 2. eleven	b. fourth
_____ 3. seven	c. first
_____ 4. eight	d. third
_____ 5. two	e. seventh
_____ 6. one	f. second
_____ 7. sixteen	g. eleventh
_____ 8. four	h. sixteenth

C WHICH NUMBER?

1. Today is my daughter's (five   (fifth)) birthday.
2. Please read page (ten   tenth).
3. We live on the (six   sixth) floor.
4. Mabel is (eighty-ninth   eighty-nine) years old.
5. This is the (two   second) time I've seen this movie.
6. Dr. Martino's office is on the (fourteen   fourteenth) floor.
7. My father is going to be (fiftieth   fifty) years old soon.
8. There were (eighteen   eighteenth) people at our party last night.
9. There are (twenty-first   twenty-one) students in our English class.
10. We're very happy today. It's our (thirty   thirtieth) wedding anniversary.

D LISTENING

Listen and circle the correct number.

1. (five)	nine		5. seventeen	seventy
2. fifth	first		6. second	seventh
3. thirty	forty		7. ninety	nine
4. fifty-two	sixty-two		8. forty	fourteen

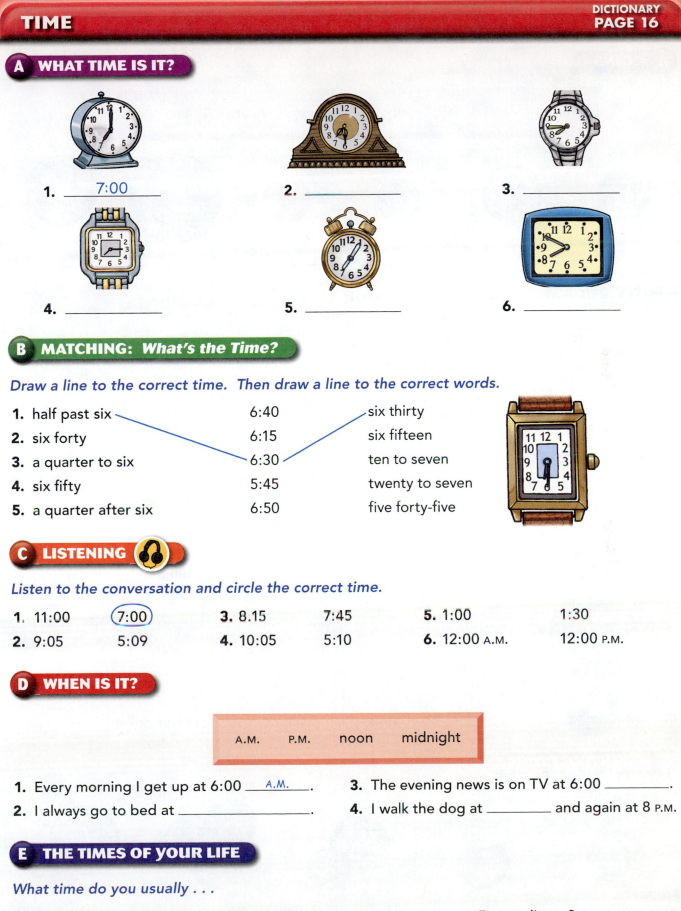

A **WHAT TIME IS IT?**

1. _____7:00_____

2. _____

3. _____

4. _____

5. _____

6. _____

B **MATCHING:** *What's the Time?*

Draw a line to the correct time. Then draw a line to the correct words.

1. half past six   6:40   six thirty

2. six forty   6:15   six fifteen

3. a quarter to six   6:30   ten to seven

4. six fifty   5:45   twenty to seven

5. a quarter after six   6:50   five forty-five

C **LISTENING**

Listen to the conversation and circle the correct time.

1. 11:00   (7:00)   **3.** 8.15   7:45   **5.** 1:00   1:30

2. 9:05   5:09   **4.** 10:05   5:10   **6.** 12:00 A.M.   12:00 P.M.

D **WHEN IS IT?**

A.M.   P.M.   noon   midnight

1. Every morning I get up at 6:00 ___A.M.___.

2. I always go to bed at _____.

3. The evening news is on TV at 6:00 _____.

4. I walk the dog at _____ and again at 8 P.M.

E **THE TIMES OF YOUR LIFE**

What time do you usually . . .

1. get up? ....

2. eat breakfast? ....

3. go to school or work? ....

4. have lunch? ....

5. eat dinner? ....

6. go to sleep? ....

A COINS

| dime | half dollar | nickel | penny | quarter | silver dollar |

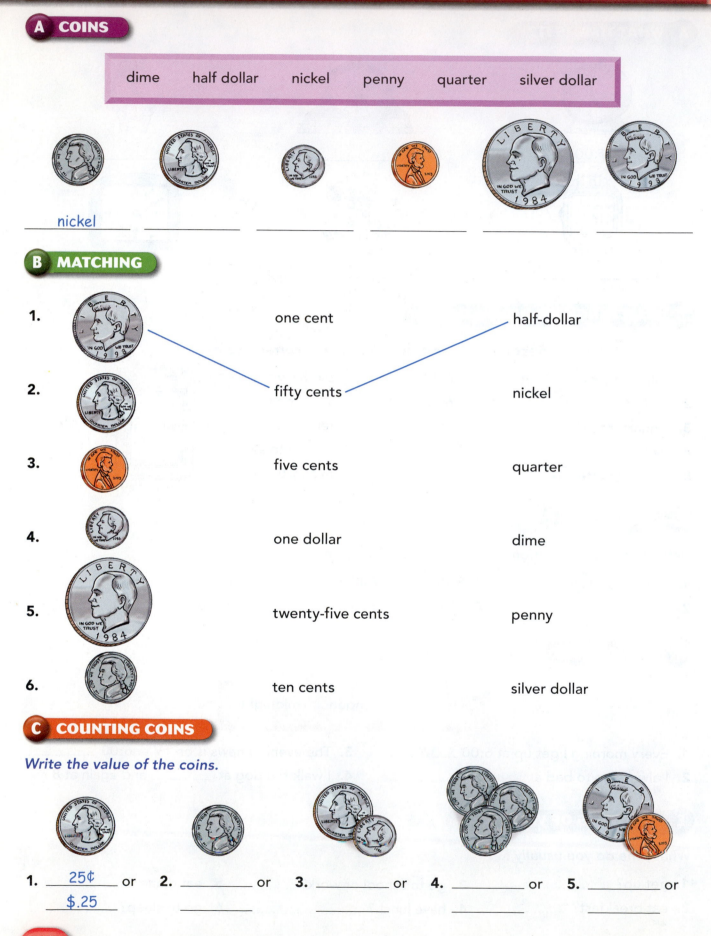

_____nickel_____ _____ _____ _____ _____ _____

B MATCHING

1. one cent   half-dollar

2. fifty cents   nickel

3. five cents   quarter

4. one dollar   dime

5. twenty-five cents penny

6. ten cents   silver dollar

C COUNTING COINS

Write the value of the coins.

1. ___25¢___ or   2. _____ or   3. _____ or   4. _____ or   5. _____ or
   ___$.25___   _____   _____   _____   _____

D COUNTING BILLS

Write the value of the bills.

1. <u> $5.00 </u> 2. _____ 3. _____ 4. _____ 5. _____

E MAKING CHANGE

1. A. That comes to eight dollars.
   B. Okay. Here's ten dollars.
   A. And your change is <u> two dollars </u>.

2. A. That's seventy-five cents.
   B. I have one dollar.
   A. And your change is _____.

3. A. That comes to forty-five dollars.
   B. Here's fifty dollars.
   A. And your change is _____.

4. A. Your total is fifteen dollars.
   B. I can give you _____.
   A. And your change is five dollars.

5. A. That will be forty-five cents.
   B. I have fifty cents.
   A. And your change is _____.

6. A. That comes to ninety-nine dollars.
   B. Here's _____.
   A. And here's a dollar back.

F LISTENING

Listen to the conversation and circle the correct amount.

1. ($1.00) $10.00
2. $.25 $25.00
3. $7.50 $75.00
4. $4.00 $40.00

5. $15.35 $3.55
6. $47.16 $47.60
7. $.55 $1.05
8. $99.99 $9.99

A TODAY

1. What year is it? ....
2. What month is it? ....
3. What day is it? ....
4. What's today's date? ....

B USING THE CALENDAR

Look at the calendar on page 18 of the Picture Dictionary. Write your answers.

What day of the week is . . .

1. January 18? _____Wednesday_____
2. January 27? _____
3. January 17? _____
4. January 8? _____
5. January 19? _____
6. January 30? _____

C DATES: *Words to Numbers*

Write the dates using numbers.

1. July 15, 2005 = _7_/_15_/_05_
2. November 10, 2000 = ____/____/____
3. February 8, 1999 = ____/____/____
4. May 2, 2008 = ____/____/____
5. January 19, 2011 = ____/____/____
6. October 31, 2003 = ____/____/____

D DATES: *Numbers to Words*

Write the dates using words.

1. 3/3/03 = _____March 3, 2003_____
2. 6/11/95 = _____
3. 9/20/06 = _____
4. 4/14/04 = _____
5. 8/29/66 = _____
6. 12/16/12 = _____

E WHAT'S THE SEQUENCE?

	May		July	1	January		October
	September		November		June		August
	February		April		December		March

F CROSSWORD

Across

2. 365 days
3. Saturday and Sunday
5. The day you were born

Down

1. 7 days
4. 24 hours

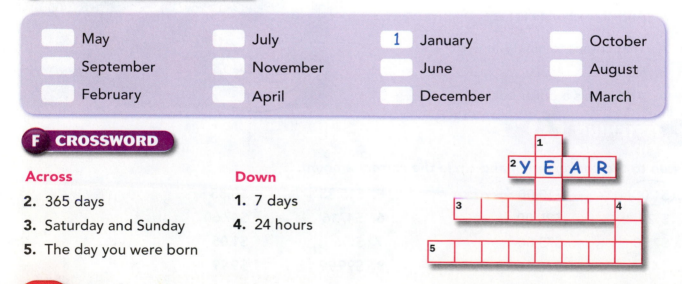

A MATCHING

_b_	1. twice	a.	afternoon
___	2. last	b.	a week
___	3. yesterday	c.	week
___	4. this	d.	night
___	5. last	e.	a day
___	6. three times	f.	evening
___	7. next	g.	a week
___	8. once	h.	morning
___	9. tomorrow	i.	week

B WHAT'S THE ORDER?

Put the times in order from the past (1) to the future (7).

☐	this morning
☐	yesterday morning
1	last week
☐	tonight
☐	next week
☐	tomorrow afternoon
☐	last night

C LISTENING

Listen and circle the correct words to complete the sentences.

1. (evening)   night
2. last night   tomorrow
3. yesterday   this week
4. week   morning
5. afternoon   night
6. next week   last week

D WHICH WORD?

1. I played basketball ((yesterday)   tomorrow) afternoon.
2. I'm going to see a play (last   this) Friday evening.
3. (Afternoon   Winter) is my favorite season.
4. I'm going to go to work early (tomorrow   yesterday) morning.
5. I play tennis (once a   twice) week.
6. I watched a very funny movie on TV (yesterday   last) night.
7. Are you going to be home this (night   evening)?

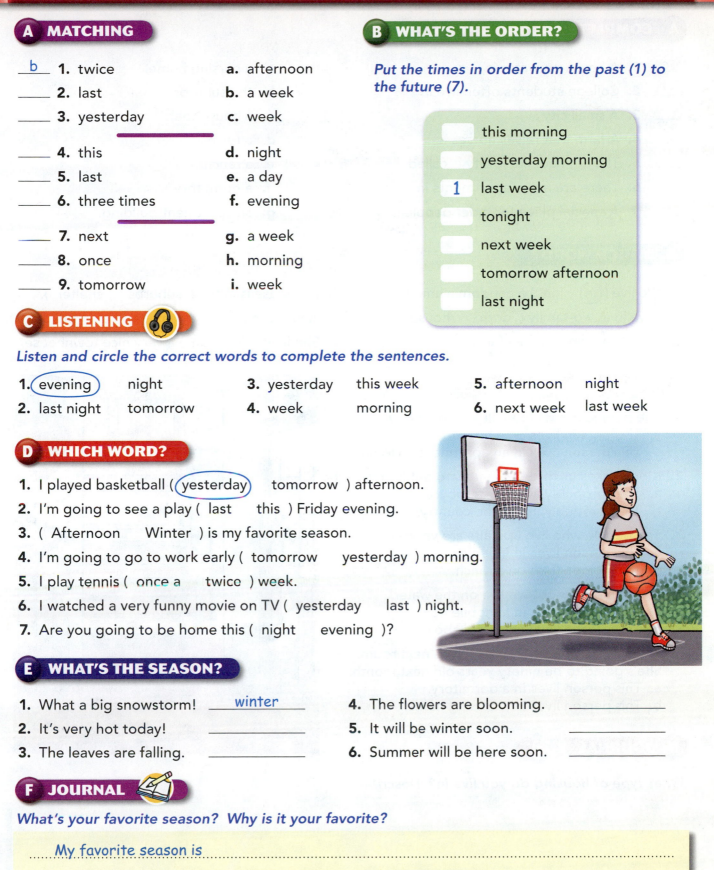

E WHAT'S THE SEASON?

1. What a big snowstorm! ___winter___
2. It's very hot today! _____
3. The leaves are falling. _____
4. The flowers are blooming. _____
5. It will be winter soon. _____
6. Summer will be here soon. _____

F JOURNAL

What's your favorite season? Why is it your favorite?

My favorite season is ....
....
....

A COMPLETE THE SENTENCES

_c_ 1. A house on water is

____ 2. College students often live in

____ 3. A small city is

____ 4. A farm that raises horses is

____ 5. The area outside a city is called

____ 6. There are many apartments in

____ 7. A special place for older people is

a. a nursing home.

b. the suburbs.

c. a houseboat.

d. a town.

e. a ranch.

f. a dormitory.

g. an apartment building.

B WHICH WORD?

1. We live (**in**   on) a condominium.

2. I live in a two-family (dorm   house).

3. They live (on   in) a farm.

4. My house is in the (suburbs   shelter).

5. He lives in an apartment (home   building).

6. She lives (in   on) a very nice townhouse.

C WHERE DO THEY LIVE?

1. The people across the hall are very noisy.
   a. This person lives on a houseboat.
   b. This person lives in an apartment building.

2. It only takes us fifteen minutes to get into the city.
   a. They probably live in the suburbs.
   b. They probably live in the country.

3. The people who live upstairs are very nice.
   a. This person lives in a duplex.
   b. This person lives on a ranch.

4. Sometimes I forget we live on the water!
   a. This person lives in a mobile home.
   b. This person lives on a houseboat.

5. Mrs. Martinez just moved into the next room. She's going to be ninety years old next month.
   a. This person lives in a dormitory.
   b. This person lives in a nursing home.

D JOURNAL

What type of housing do you live in? Describe it.

....

....

....

A CATEGORIES

Look at page 21 of the Pictionary Dictionary and find the following:

3 Things You Can Sit on	6 Things You Plug in	2 Things You Hang on the Wall
loveseat	_____	_____
_____	_____	_____
_____	_____	
	_____	
	_____	
	_____	

B ANALOGIES

drapes	end table	floor	magazine holder	speaker

1. painting : wall *as* rug : _____ floor _____
2. lamp : lampshade *as* window : _____
3. book : bookcase *as* magazine : _____
4. sofa : armchair *as* coffee table : _____
5. TV : DVD player *as* stereo system : _____

C WHAT'S IN THE LIVING ROOM?

Look at page 21 of the Picture Dictionary. Write the correct word.

1. There's a __l__ __a__ __m__ __p__ on the end table.
2. There's a ___ ___ ___ on top of the TV.
3. There's a ___ ___ ___ ___ ___ behind the couch.
4. There's a ___ ___ ___ ___ ___ on the table.
5. There's a ___ ___ ___ ___ ___ ___ under the painting.
6. There's a ___ ___ ___ ___ ___ ___ system in the wall unit.
7. There's a ___ ___ ___ ___ ___ ___ ___ ___ ___ next to the armchair.
8. There's a ___ ___ ___ ___ ___ ___ ___ ___ behind the fireplace screen.

D JOURNAL

What things do you have in your living room? Where are they?

....

....

A MATCHING

_d_ **1.** sugar   **a.** shaker

____ **2.** coffee   **b.** cabinet

____ **3.** serving   **c.** stick

____ **4.** salt   **d.** bowl

____ **5.** candle   **e.** dish

____ **6.** china   **f.** pot

B WHICH WORD DOESN'T BELONG?

1. tray   plate   (pitcher)   saucer
2. table   buffet   napkin   chair
3. fork   candle   knife   spoon
4. china   lamp   candle   chandelier
5. salad bowl   coffee pot   vase   candlestick
6. pitcher   teapot   knife   creamer
7. chandelier   centerpiece   butter dish   salt shaker

C WHICH WORD?

1. These flowers look beautiful in our new (platter   (vase)).
2. You need to use a (spoon   pitcher) when you have soup.
3. Please put the tray on the (coffee pot   buffet).
4. The napkin goes under the (plate   fork).
5. Oh, no! I just spilled coffee on your (tablecloth   chandelier)!
6. Put the candle in the (table   candlestick).
7. This (tablecloth   dining room chair) looks very nice on your table.

D WORD SEARCH

Find nine things that hold liquids.

```
D  J  O  G  H  U  X  I  R  P  T  T  C  S
S  C  M  J  R  Q  C  T  Z  I  E  E  L  Y
F  U  V  N  G  L  A  S  S  T  E  A  B  C
G  P  K  B  O  W  L  O  J  C  P  P  M  R
H  F  M  C  T  L  B  L  I  H  S  O  J  E
Y  E  M  U  G  Q  J  J  M  E  N  T  C  A
T  W  B  W  Y  S  L  Y  D  R  U  A  V  M
Q  I  R  A  B  F  N  E  B  W  V  A  S  E
C  O  F  F  E  E  P  O  T  V  B  Z  X  R
```

A MATCHING

<u>b</u> **1.** alarm   **a.** ruffle
____ **2.** flat   **b.** clock
____ **3.** dust   **c.** frame
____ **4.** bed   **d.** sheet

____ **5.** box   **e.** blanket
____ **6.** electric   **f.** stand
____ **7.** pillow   **g.** spring
____ **8.** night   **h.** case

B WHICH WORD DOESN'T BELONG?

1. blanket	quilt	(mirror)	bedspread
2. pillowcase	clock radio	fitted sheet	flat sheet
3. curtains	box spring	headboard	bed frame
4. chest	bureau	bedspread	bed
5. jewelry box	clock radio	lamp	electric blanket
6. quilt	carpet	blanket	comforter

C MAKE THE BED!

Number these items as they appear on a bed, from top (1) to bottom (6).

____ fitted sheet
____ bed frame
____ flat sheet
____ box spring
_1_ bedspread
____ blanket

D WHAT'S IN THE BEDROOM?

Look at page 23 of the Picture Dictionary. Write the correct word.

1. There's a _p_ _i_ _l_ _l_ _o_ _w_ on the bed.

2. There's a __ __ __ __ __ __ on the floor.

3. There's a __ __ __ __ __ __ __ __ __ __ on the bureau.

4. There's a __ __ __ __ __ __ __ __ __ __ __ on the night table.

5. There are __ __ __ __ __ __ __ __ __ and blinds on the window.

6. There's a __ __ __ __ __ __ __ __ __ __ __ __ to the right of the bed.

7. There's a __ __ __ __ __ __ __ __ __ __ under the mattress and box spring.

8. There's an __ __ __ __ __ __ __ __ blanket between the flat sheet and the bedspread.

A COMPLETE THE SENTENCES

_d_ **1.** I keep my plates, cups, and glasses in a   **a.** refrigerator.

____ **2.** I make toast in a   **b.** cookbook.

____ **3.** I keep food cold in my   **c.** garbage pail.

____ **4.** I put trash and garbage in the   **d.** cabinet.

____ **5.** After I wash dishes, I put them in the   **e.** toaster.

____ **6.** I dry dishes by hand with a   **f.** dish rack.

____ **7.** I look for new recipes in a   **g.** cutting board.

____ **8.** I cut food on a   **h.** dish towel.

B MATCH AND WRITE

Draw a line to complete the word.   Then write the word on the line.

1. dish   mat   _____dishwasher_____

2. place   book   _____

3. cook   maker   _____

4. pot   washer   _____

5. coffee   holder   _____

C WHAT'S IN THE KITCHEN?

Look at page 24 of the Picture Dictionary.   Write the correct word.

1. The __c o f f e e m a k e r__ is to the right of the toaster.

2. There's a __ __ __ __ __ __ __ between the electric can opener and the toaster oven.

3. There are two __ __ __ __ __ __ __ __ __ next to the refrigerator.

4. The __ __ __ __ __ __ __ __ __ is above the electric can opener.

5. There's an __ __ __ __ __ __ __ __ __ __ __ __ __ in the
__ __ __ __ __ __ __ above the refrigerator.

6. There's a __ __ __ __ __ __ __ __ above the stove.

7. There's a __ __ __ __ __ __ __ __ __ on the stove.

D CROSSWORD

Across

2. kitchen ____

4. trash ____

6. spice ____

Down

1. garbage ____

3. paper towel ____

5. can ____

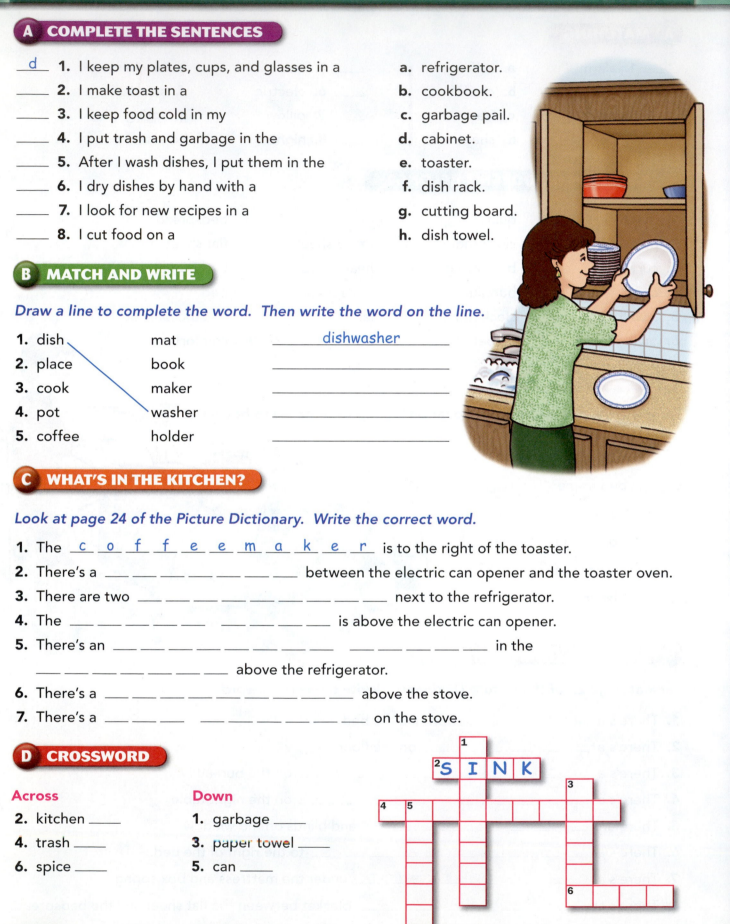

A MATCHING

<u>d</u> **1.** teddy   **a.** seat
_____ **2.** baby   **b.** light
_____ **3.** toy   **c.** suit
_____ **4.** stretch   **d.** bear
_____ **5.** night   **e.** chest

_____ **6.** bumper   **f.** animal
_____ **7.** food   **g.** pad
_____ **8.** changing   **h.** chair
_____ **9.** high   **i.** table
_____ **10.** stuffed   **j.** warmer

B WHICH WORD DOESN'T BELONG?

1. teddy bear   (playpen)   doll   stuffed animal
2. stroller   baby carriage   cradle   walker
3. rattle   booster seat   potty   baby carrier
4. chest   changing table   crib   crib bumper
5. swing   car seat   mobile   booster seat
6. intercom   potty   baby seat   high chair

C LISTENING

Listen and circle the word you hear.

1. potty   (doll)   **3.** walker   stroller   **5.** baby frontpack   baby backpack
2. baby seat   safety seat   **4.** high chairs   night lights   **6.** changing table   changing pad

D ASSOCIATIONS

<u>c</u> **1.** playing   **a.** baby monitor
_____ **2.** sleeping   **b.** high chair
_____ **3.** riding   **c.** stuffed animal
_____ **4.** eating   **d.** stroller
_____ **5.** listening   **e.** crib

E WHICH WORD?

1. The baby is sleeping in her ((cradle)   chest).
2. Put the diaper in the (playpen   diaper pail).
3. The baby's (playpen   rattle) makes a lot of noise.
4. Our baby's favorite toy is her (doll   baby carriage).
5. Put the stuffed animals in the (toy chest   baby seat).
6. The baby's stretch suit is in the (changing pad   chest).
7. We always put on a (swing   night light) when the baby sleeps.
8. Our baby loves to lie in her crib and look at the (mobile   stroller).
9. When we take a walk with our baby, we carry him in a (booster seat   backpack).

A WHICH WORD?

1. Check your weight on the ((scale)   bathtub).
2. Put the (bath mat   rubber mat) in the tub when you take a shower.
3. Please throw away your tissues in the (hamper   wastebasket).
4. Clean the tub with this (sponge   drain).
5. Clean your teeth with your (toothbrush holder   toothbrush).
6. How do I turn on the (fan   vanity)?
7. If the toilet won't flush, use the (drain   plunger).
8. Here's a clean (washcloth   faucet) to wash your face.
9. Please put the toilet (towel   seat) down.
10. Wash your face with (soap   soap dish) and water.

B WHERE ARE THEY?

Look at page 26 of the Picture Dictionary. Write the correct word.

1. There's a plant on the __s__ __h__ __e__ __l__ __f__.
2. The man is standing on the ___ ___ ___ ___ ___.
3. The soap is on the ___ ___ ___ ___ ___ ___.
4. The ___ ___ ___ ___ ___ ___ is over the sink.
5. There are some dirty clothes in the ___ ___ ___ ___ ___ ___.
6. The ___ ___ ___   ___ ___ ___ ___ ___ ___ ___ ___ is on the toilet.
7. There's a ___ ___ ___ ___ ___ ___ ___ ___ ___ ___ ___ next to the vanity.

C MATCHING

__e__ 1. shower	**a.** holder		___ 6. medicine	**f.** rack
___ 2. toothbrush	**b.** mat		___ 7. towel	**g.** cabinet
___ 3. hand	**c.** dish		___ 8. toilet	**h.** freshener
___ 4. soap	**d.** towel		___ 9. air	**i.** dryer
___ 5. rubber	**e.** head		___10. hair	**j.** paper

D WHAT'S IN THE BATHROOM?

Change one letter to write something you find in the bathroom.

1. cut   __c__ __u__ __p__
2. cat   ___ ___ ___
3. pink   ___ ___ ___ ___
4. shell   ___ ___ ___ ___ ___
5. van   ___ ___ ___
6. soup   ___ ___ ___ ___
7. train   ___ ___ ___ ___ ___
8. tower   ___ ___ ___ ___ ___

A HOME REPAIRS

antenna	doorknob	garage	lawn chair	patio	satellite
back	driveway	lamppost	lawnmower	roof	screens

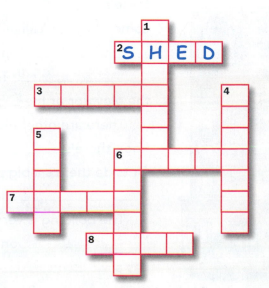

I had a busy weekend. Our television didn't work so I went
on the _____roof_____ [1] to fix the TV _____ [2] and the
_____ [3] dish. There was no light on the front walk, so I
repaired the _____ [4]. The _____ [5] door didn't
open, so I repaired the _____ [6]. I put _____ [7]
in all the windows. I repaired the _____ [8] door so my
car didn't have to stay in the _____ [9]. I fixed the
_____ [10] and then cut the grass with it. After all that work,
I wanted to relax, so I repaired the _____ [11] and fell
asleep in it on the _____ [12].

B ASSOCIATIONS

__b__ 1. lawnmower   **a.** rain   _____ 5. lamppost   **e.** car
_____ 2. mailbox   **b.** grass   _____ 6. garage   **f.** backyard
_____ 3. drainpipe   **c.** fireplace   _____ 7. satellite dish   **g.** light
_____ 4. chimney   **d.** letters   _____ 8. lawn chair   **h.** television

C CROSSWORD

Across

2. I keep my tools in a _____.

3. Turn on the front _____ so we can see.

6. We cook outside on a _____.

7. Be careful when you walk on the _____ steps.

8. We have a beautiful wooden _____ in our
backyard.

Down

1. During a heavy storm, we close every _____.

4. There are three letters in the _____.

5. Close the front door and the _____ door.

6. There's always water in the _____ after it rains.

[Crossword grid: 2 Across = S H E D]

A MATCHING

_b_ **1.** land **a.** way ____ **5.** hall **e.** man
____ **2.** peep **b.** lord ____ **6.** court **f.** pool
____ **3.** stair **c.** box ____ **7.** whirl **g.** yard
____ **4.** mail **d.** hole ____ **8.** door **h.** way

B WHICH WORD?

1. Oh, no! I think I lost the ((key)   lock) to my apartment!
2. Take the (elevator   fire escape) to the fourth floor.
3. Put this garbage in the (storage room   trash chute).
4. If there's a fire, pull the (sprinkler system   fire alarm).
5. I paid a (security deposit   lease) for my new apartment.
6. We park our car outside in the parking (garage   lot).
7. Make sure you always lock the (security gate   fire exit).
8. The (superintendent   tenant) repaired our smoke detector.
9. I found my apartment in the (vacancy sign   classified ads).
10. We keep our extra clothes in the (storage locker   laundry room).

C OUR APARTMENT BUILDING

| buzzer | fire | laundry | lock | sprinkler | swimming |
| doorman | intercom | lobby | parking | stairway | trash |

  Our new apartment building is wonderful. In the lobby, there's a _____doorman_____ [1] who opens the door. When our friends come, they can call us on the _____ [2] and we ring the _____ [3] and let them in. The mailboxes are also in the _____ [4]. To come upstairs to our apartment, you can take the elevator or the _____ [5].

  There are other nice things about our apartment building. On every floor, there's a _____ [6] chute and a _____ [7] room. Outside there's a big _____ [8] pool, and we have our own _____ [9] space.

  The building is very safe, too. There's a dead-bolt _____ [10] on every door, and in case of fire, every apartment has a _____ [11] system, and there's a _____ [12] escape on every floor.

A SERVICE PEOPLE

appliance repairperson	carpenter	exterminator	locksmith	painter	plumber

1. _____painter_____
- walls
- houses
- ceilings

2. _____
- hot water heaters
- toilets
- sinks

3. _____
- stoves
- refrigerators
- dishwashers

4. _____
- wooden steps
- doors
- bookcases

5. _____
- termites
- fleas
- mice

6. _____
- doors
- car doors
- garage doors

B HELP!

1. My kitchen sink is clogged. I need to call the _____plumber_____.

2. I have mice in my basement! Do you know a good _____?

3. The power is out in our house! We need to call the _____.

4. The roof is leaking! Call the _____!

5. Our chimney is dirty. We need to call the _____.

6. We have to use the stove. When is the _____ coming?

7. When is the _____ going to come? The walls in our bedroom are cracked!

8. My mother fixed our front door and broken steps. She's a very good _____.

C LOTS OF PROBLEMS!

I'm very upset about all the problems we're having in our house. Our front steps are clogged **broken** [1], the front doorbell doesn't ring open [2], the paint in our hallway is out peeling [3], our bathtub is leaking working [4], the tiles in the bathroom are closed loose [5], the light in our bedroom won't go on away [6], and there are aunts and cats ants and rats [7] in our basement!

D LISTENING 🎧

Listen and choose the best word to complete each sentence.

1. a. sink
   b. door

2. a. chimney
   b. TV

3. a. termites
   b. tiles

4. a. walls
   b. lights

5. a. bathtub
   b. refrigerator

6. a. front door
   b. heating system

A WHICH WORD?

1. If you're going to sweep the floor, you'll need this ((broom)   sponge).
2. I want to mop the kitchen floor, but I can't find the mop and (vacuum   bucket).
3. Use this (scrub brush   dust cloth) to clean the toilet.
4. This carpet is very dirty! How often do you use the (dry mop   vacuum cleaner)?
5. I need to clean my bathroom, but I don't have any (recycling bins   cleanser).
6. If you're going to dust, you'll need this (feather duster   dustpan).
7. I want to polish my furniture, but I can't find the (ammonia   furniture polish).
8. Do you think this (pail   floor wax) will clean the floor?

B WHICH WORD DOESN'T BELONG?

1. broom   dustpan   dust cloth   carpet sweeper
2. paper towels   hand vacuum   ammonia   window cleaner
3. cleanser   scrub brush   vacuum   sponge
4. whisk broom   bucket   trash can   recycling bin
5. dust cloth   recycling bin   sponge   paper towels
6. dust   dry   feather   sponge

C CROSSWORD: Complete the Words

Across

3. _____ wax
6. carpet _____

Down

1. window _____
2. sponge _____
4. _____ cloth
5. _____ mop

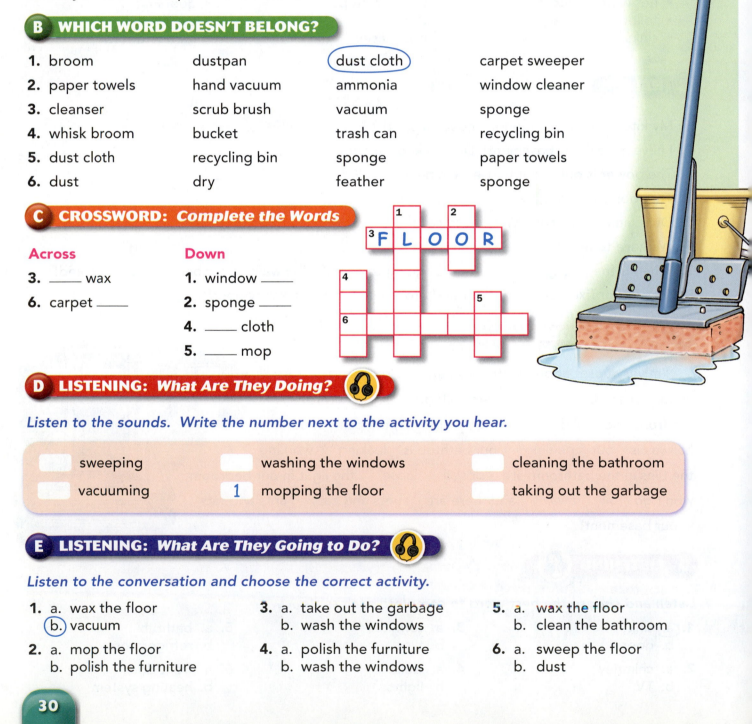

D LISTENING: What Are They Doing?

Listen to the sounds. Write the number next to the activity you hear.

| | sweeping | | washing the windows | | cleaning the bathroom |
| | vacuuming | 1 | mopping the floor | | taking out the garbage |

E LISTENING: What Are They Going to Do?

Listen to the conversation and choose the correct activity.

1. a. wax the floor
   b. vacuum
2. a. mop the floor
   b. polish the furniture
3. a. take out the garbage
   b. wash the windows
4. a. polish the furniture
   b. wash the windows
5. a. wax the floor
   b. clean the bathroom
6. a. sweep the floor
   b. dust

A WHICH WORD?

1. Do you have (electrical tape (a flashlight))? It's dark in here.
2. We have mice! We need (a mousetrap   roach killer) right away!
3. You can measure your height with this (step ladder   yardstick).
4. Hand me that (sandpaper   fly swatter). I'll get that pest!
5. I can fix that piece of wood with this (glue   oil).
6. Don't forget to wear (work gloves   duct tape)!
7. This lamp needs (fuses   an extension cord).
8. He's painting his bicycle with a (paint roller   spray gun).
9. They're all over the kitchen floor! Get the (roach killer   paint thinner) now!
10. There's a problem with the toilet! Where's the (extension cord   plunger)?

B WHAT'S THE NEXT LINE?

_c_ 1. Where's the glue?
____ 2. Can I borrow your paintbrush?
____ 3. I need the flashlight.
____ 4. Do we have any mousetraps?
____ 5. Where's the tape measure?
____ 6. I need some batteries.
____ 7. Could I use your step ladder?
____ 8. Do we have any paint thinner?

a. It's dark in here.
b. This flashlight won't work.
c. I need to fix a chair.
d. I have to fix a light in the ceiling.
e. I have to clean this paintbrush.
f. I saw a mouse in the basement.
g. I want to paint my fence.
h. I need to measure the floor.

C MATCHING

_b_ 1. tape
____ 2. masking
____ 3. insect
____ 4. step
____ 5. work

a. gloves
b. measure
c. ladder
d. spray
e. tape

____ 6. paint
____ 7. fly
____ 8. spray
____ 9. extension
____ 10. duct

f. swatter
g. tape
h. cord
i. roller
j. gun

D LISTENING

Listen and circle the word you hear.

1. (glue)   fuse
2. paint roller   paint pan
3. plunger   duct tape

4. sandpaper   paint thinner
5. insect spray   spray gun
6. fly swatter   lightbulbs

7. spray gun   paintbrush
8. step ladder   fly swatter
9. masking tape   duct tape

A MATCHING

_c_	1. machine	a. stripper
___	2. hand	b. saw
___	3. wire	c. screw
___	4. power	d. drill

___	5. circular	e. wrench
___	6. wood	f. drill
___	7. electric	g. saw
___	8. pipe	h. screw

B HOW ARE THEY USED?

ax	hacksaw	power sander	saw	wrench
electric drill	hammer	screwdriver	router	

Tools that Cut	Power Tools	Tools that Fasten Things
hacksaw		

C WHICH WORD?

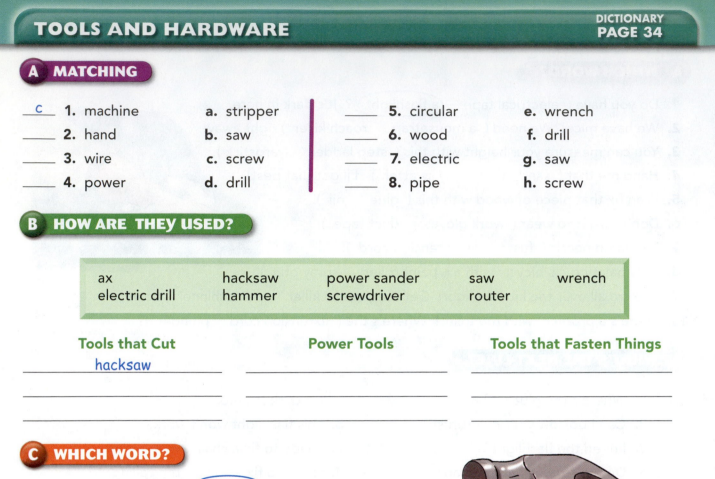

1. Where's the (chisel   (hammer))? I have to bang in this nail.
2. Give me that (bit   wire), please. I have to drill a hole.
3. You can cut this with a (hacksaw   wire stripper).
4. I'm cutting wood for the fireplace with this (scraper   ax).
5. Do we have (pliers   a washer) for this nut and bolt?
6. Be careful! That (power saw   plane) cuts quickly!

D WHICH WORD DOESN'T BELONG?

1. hammer	wrench	(toolbox)	Phillips screwdriver
2. saw	nut	bolt	screw
3. ax	saw	scraper	hacksaw
4. nail	bolt	wood screw	mallet
5. hacksaw	router	power sander	electric drill
6. wrench	wire	pliers	monkey wrench

E LISTENING

Listen to the sounds. Write the number next to the tool you hear.

	saw		hammer		power sander		ax	1	electric drill	

A MATCHING

_c_ **1.** line	**a.** seeds	____ **5.** leaf	**e.** clipper
____ **2.** vegetable	**b.** can	____ **6.** yard waste	**f.** shears
____ **3.** garden	**c.** trimmer	____ **7.** hedge	**g.** blower
____ **4.** watering	**d.** hose	____ **8.** pruning	**h.** bag

B WHAT'S THE NEXT LINE?

_f_ **1.** I need the rake.

____ **2.** Do we have hedge clippers?

____ **3.** Where's the hose?

____ **4.** Could I borrow your lawnmower?

____ **5.** Where are the pruning shears?

____ **6.** Are there any vegetable seeds?

____ **7.** Can you buy some fertilizer?

____ **8.** Turn on the sprinkler.

a. I have to cut back those bushes.

b. The lawn needs water.

c. I want to trim the hedges.

d. I'm going to plant some flowers.

e. I want to plant them in the garden.

f. I have to rake those leaves.

g. I need to cut the grass.

h. I have to water the flowers.

C CROSSWORD: *Complete the Actions*

Across

2. ____ vegetables

4. ____ the lawn

5. ____ the flowers

Down

1. ____ the leaves

2. ____ the bushes

3. ____ the hedge

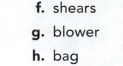

D LIKELY OR UNLIKELY?

Put a check in the best column.

	Likely	Unlikely
1. The lawnmower wasn't working, so I got the watering can.	____	✔
2. I made a hole in the yard with my new shovel.	____	____
3. It was easy to clean up the leaves with the leaf blower.	____	____
4. I always weed my garden with a hedge trimmer.	____	____
5. I filled up three yard waste bags with leaves.	____	____
6. I didn't have a hoe, so I couldn't water the lawn.	____	____
7. I have to put the nozzle on the weeder.	____	____
8. I use fertilizer whenever I plant vegetables.	____	____

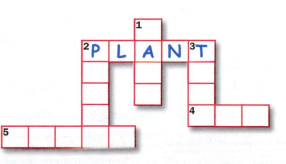

A MAKE A LIST!

Look at pages 36–37 of the Picture Dictionary and make a list of 8 places to buy food.

bakery

_____   _____

_____   _____

_____   _____

B MATCHING

__d__ 1. barber   a. store
____ 2. book   b. restaurant
____ 3. child-care   c. station
____ 4. gas   d. shop
____ 5. fast-food   e. center

____ 6. department   f. center
____ 7. donut   g. station
____ 8. service   h. store
____ 9. copy   i. dealership
____ 10. car   j. shop

C WHICH PLACE?

1. I bought some beautiful roses at the (coffee   (flower)) shop.
2. I'm getting a haircut today at the (barber shop   clinic).
3. I'm going to buy bread at the (bank   bakery).
4. Please pick up my shirts and suit at the (dry cleaners   service station).
5. I'm going to the (copy center   clinic) for a medical checkup.
6. I'm going to the (bus   service) station to get gas and check the oil.
7. Let's get breakfast at the (donut shop   candy store)!
8. Look! There's a sale on sofas and chairs at the (furniture   convenience) store.
9. You can get a hamburger and soda at the (discount store   fast-food restaurant).

D WHAT'S THE PLACE?

| child-care center | drug store | eye-care center |
| furniture store | florist | grocery store |

1. I'm going to the _____ drug store _____ to get some aspirin.
2. I bought new glasses at the _____.
3. We buy our food at the _____ on Central Street.
4. The flowers aren't expensive at the new _____ on Main Street.
5. We leave our daughter at the _____ when we go to work.
6. We bought a beautiful couch at the _____ in the mall.

A GOING TO THE MALL

We like to shop at the __m__ __a__ __l__ __l__ [1]. We buy CDs at the ___ ___ ___ [2] store. Our children look at the puppies and kittens in the ___ ___ ___ [3] shop. They also like to go to the ___ ___ ___ [4] store to see all the things to play with. We buy film for our camera at the ___ ___ ___ ___ ___ [5] shop. When we get hungry, we eat at the ___ ___ ___ ___ ___ [6] shop or go to a ___ ___ ___ ___ ___ ___ ___ ___ ___ [7]. We sometimes go to the movie ___ ___ ___ ___ ___ ___ [8]. We spend a lot of time at the mall!

B ANALOGIES

| health club | jewelry store | library | post office | restaurant | travel agency |

1. eat : restaurant *as* exercise : _____health club_____

2. film : photo shop *as* stamps : _____

3. toy : toy store *as* jewelry : _____

4. shoes : shoe store *as* food : _____

5. video store : movie theater *as* book store : _____

6. mothers : maternity shop *as* travelers : _____

C ASSOCIATIONS

__c__ **1.** park

____ **2.** laundromat

____ **3.** motel

____ **4.** school

____ **5.** video store

____ **6.** hair salon

____ **7.** post office

____ **8.** hardware store

a. wash your clothes

b. buy tools

c. feed the birds

d. send letters

e. get your hair done

f. rent movies

g. sleep away from home

h. go to classes

D LISTENING: *Where Are They?*

Listen to the conversation and circle the correct place.

1. pet shop	(jewelry store)	**5.** video store	movie theater
2. shoe store	music store	**6.** motel	train station
3. photo shop	hardware store	**7.** hotel	pizza shop
4. restaurant	library	**8.** ice cream shop	post office

A WHERE ARE THEY?

Look at pages 40–41 of the Picture Dictionary and write the answers.

1. The police officer is standing in the _i n t e r s e c t i o n_.
2. There's a taxicab in front of the ___ ___ ___ ___ ___ ___ ___ ___ ___ ___.
3. The subway is under the ___ ___ ___ ___ ___ ___.
4. The trash container is on the ___ ___ ___ ___ ___ ___ ___.
5. The courthouse is next to ___ ___ ___ ___ ___ ___ ___ ___.
6. The office building is next to the ___ ___ ___ ___ ___ ___ ___ ___ ___ ___ ___.
7. The jail is across from the ___ ___ ___ ___ ___ ___ ___ ___ ___ ___ ___ ___ ___.

B WHICH WORD DOESN'T BELONG?

1. taxi | garbage truck | motorcycle | (bus driver)
2. cab driver | meter maid | sewer | street vendor
3. street sign | curb | sidewalk | street
4. jail | city hall | office building | parking lot
5. intersection | drive-through window | crosswalk | manhole

C IN THE CITY

bus stop	fire hydrant	meter maid	public telephone	street vendor
crosswalk	intersection	parking lot	street sign	traffic light

1. The _street sign_ tells the name of a street.
2. It costs fifty cents to use a _____.
3. A _____ sells things on the street.
4. You should never park in front of a _____.
5. An _____ is two streets that cross each other.
6. You should wait for the bus at the _____.
7. You can go now. The _____ just turned green.
8. Pedestrians wait for the green light and then walk in the _____.
9. When you drive to the courthouse, leave your car in the _____.
10. When you don't put enough money in a parking meter, a _____ gives you a ticket.

A WHICH WORD DOESN'T BELONG?

1. hair:	long	straight	(young)
2. man:	short	curly	heavy
3. beard:	tall	long	black
4. teenager:	tall	thin	elderly
5. woman:	middle-aged	wavy	pregnant
6. hair:	shoulder length	red	bald
7. man:	hearing impaired	pregnant	elderly

B WHICH WORD?

1. My daughter has long straight ((blond) curly) hair.

2. My brother is short and (wavy   thin).

3. I'm not tall, and I'm not short. I'm average (height   weight).

4. My neighbor is bald and has a (gray   shoulder length) mustache.

5. My niece is (hearing   vision) impaired. She needs special glasses.

6. My son is growing up fast. Soon he'll be a (senior citizen   teenager).

7. This is a big infant! I'm sure she's going to be (tall   long) when she grows up.

8. My granddaughter is pregnant. She's going to have her (toddler   baby) in a few weeks.

C CROSSWORD

```
¹M U S ²T A C ³H E
      4
          5
  6
```

Across

1. He has a brown ____.

4. Uncle Fred is ____.

5. She isn't young. She's ____.

6. Grandma is a ____ citizen.

Down

2. Soon my baby will be a ____.

3. My sons are average ____.

4. She has long ____ hair.

D TRUE OR FALSE?

	True	False
1. Another word for "baby" is "infant."	✔	
2. A tall person is average height.		
3. A middle-aged person is older than a senior citizen.		
4. Toddlers aren't adults.		
5. A slim person isn't heavy.		
6. Shoulder-length hair is shorter than long hair.		

A WHAT'S THE ANSWER?

1. Is the water hot?

No. It's ___cold___.

2. Are the pants tight?

No. They're _____.

3. Is she single?

No. She's _____.

4. Is the window clean?

No. It's _____.

5. Is the tie narrow?

No. It's _____.

6. Are the clothes dry?

No. They're _____.

7. Is he rich?

No. He's _____.

8. Is your neighbor quiet?

No. He's _____.

9. Is the bridge low?

No. It's _____.

10. Is the chair comfortable?

No. It's _____.

11. Is your desk neat?

No. It's _____.

12. Is his skin smooth?

No. It's _____.

B ANTONYMS

Write the opposite word.

1. straight hair _____curly_____ hair

2. a straight road a _____ road

3. a light box a _____ box

4. a light room a _____ room

5. a short woman a _____ woman

6. a short dress a _____ dress

7. an old man a _____ man

8. an old car a _____ car

9. a hard test an _____ test

10. a hard mattress a _____ mattress

11. a dull floor a _____ floor

12. a dull knife a _____ knife

I bought a house recently. It isn't   open   (new) [1].
As a matter of fact, it's very   soft   old [2], but it's clean and
messy   neat [3]. It's a   small   thick [4] house, and it isn't
very   curly   fancy [5]. Still, it's very   heavy   comfortable [6],
and it's in a very   crooked   quiet [7] neighborhood. Best of all,
the price was   low   high [8]. It was very   inexpensive   wealthy [9],
and I like it a lot!

D CROSSWORD: *Opposites*

Across

4. expensive
6. dry
8. hard
10. crooked
11. cold
12. fancy
13. dull
15. smooth
17. married
18. wealthy

Down

1. loud
2. ugly
3. slow
5. difficult
7. ugly
9. thick
14. wide
16. bad
17. fat

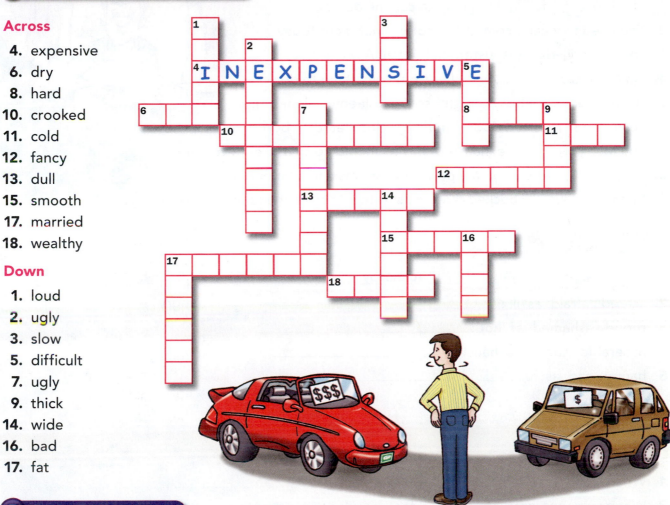

Crossword grid with 4 Across spelling: I N E X P E N S I V E

E DESCRIBE THEM!

Write words that describe . . .

1. your best friend ....
2. your family ....
3. your hair ....
4. your furniture ....

5. your street ....
6. your neighbors ....
7. your classroom ....
8. yourself ....

A HAPPY OR SAD?

Happy Emotions	Sad Emotions
excited	

disappointed
excited
frustrated
happy
homesick
lonely
miserable
proud

B WHICH WORD?

1. I feel ((sick)   full). I'm going to call the doctor.
2. You need to wear a coat. It's (cold   hot) out today.
3. I'm (surprised   disgusted). I got an A on my test!
4. I'm (confused   thirsty). Let's get something to drink.
5. All my friends are busy tonight, so I'm (sleepy   lonely).
6. I can't open my front door. I'm really (frustrated   bored)!
7. You look (pretty   exhausted). You should go to bed early tonight.
8. I'm (angry   proud). My neighbors are making a lot of noise!
9. I was (jealous   shocked) when I saw the bill from the telephone company!

C ANALOGIES

1. angry : mad *as* sad : _____unhappy_____
2. scared : afraid *as* ill : _____
3. proud : ashamed *as* hot : _____
4. miserable : sad *as* exhausted : _____
5. happy : sad *as* full : _____

cold
hungry
sick
tired
unhappy

D FEELINGS

Complete the sentences.

1. When someone interrupts me, I feel ....
2. When someone gets mad at me, I feel ....
3. When I have something important to do, I feel ....
4. When someone bangs into my car, I feel ....
5. When I'm away from home for a long time, I feel ....
6. When I see ...., I feel ....
7. When ...., I feel ....

A   WHICH FRUIT DOESN'T BELONG?

Which fruit . . .

1. isn't a berry?   (lime)   strawberry   blueberry   raspberry
2. isn't a citrus fruit?   grapefruit   coconut   tangerine   lemon
3. isn't a melon?   watermelon   apricot   honeydew   cantaloupe
4. doesn't have a pit?   peach   pineapple   plum   avocado
5. doesn't grow on a tree?   apple   orange   nectarine   strawberry
6. do people cook?   grapes   cantaloupe   plantain   kiwi

B   WHAT'S THE WORD?

1. We always peel the skin off of a __b__ __a__ __n__ __a__ __n__ __a__ before we eat it.
2. ___ ___ ___ ___ ___ ___ are dried plums.
3. It's difficult to remove the shells of ___ ___ ___ ___ because they're so hard.
4. A ___ ___ ___ ___ ___ ___ ___ has delicious milk inside of it.
5. When you dry ___ ___ ___ ___ ___ ___ you get raisins.

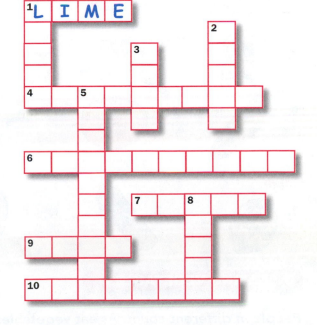

C   CROSSWORD: *Pictures to Words*

Across

1.    4.   6.

7.   9.   10.

Down

1.   2.   3.

5.   8.

¹L	I	M	E

D   LISTENING

Listen to the conversation and circle the word you hear.

1. (cherries)   raspberries   3. tangerines   nectarines   5. banana   papaya
2. apricots   apples   4. prune   plum   6. grapes   dates

41

A WHICH GROUP?

1. chili pepper   red pepper   _jalapeño_

2. acorn squash   butternut squash   _____

3. potato   sweet potato   _____

4. string bean   black bean   _____

5. lettuce   cabbage   _____

bok choy
jalapeño
lima bean
yam
zucchini

B MATCHING

_c_ **1.** sweet   **a.** squash

____ **2.** kidney   **b.** sprout

____ **3.** brussels   **c.** potato

____ **4.** green   **d.** pepper

____ **5.** acorn   **e.** bean

C CROSSWORD: *Pictures to Words*

Across

2.   5.

6.   7.

9.   10.

Crossword grid:
2 across: C A U L I F L O W E R
5, 6, 7, 9, 10 across and 1, 3, 4, 8 down

Down

1.   3.   4.   8.

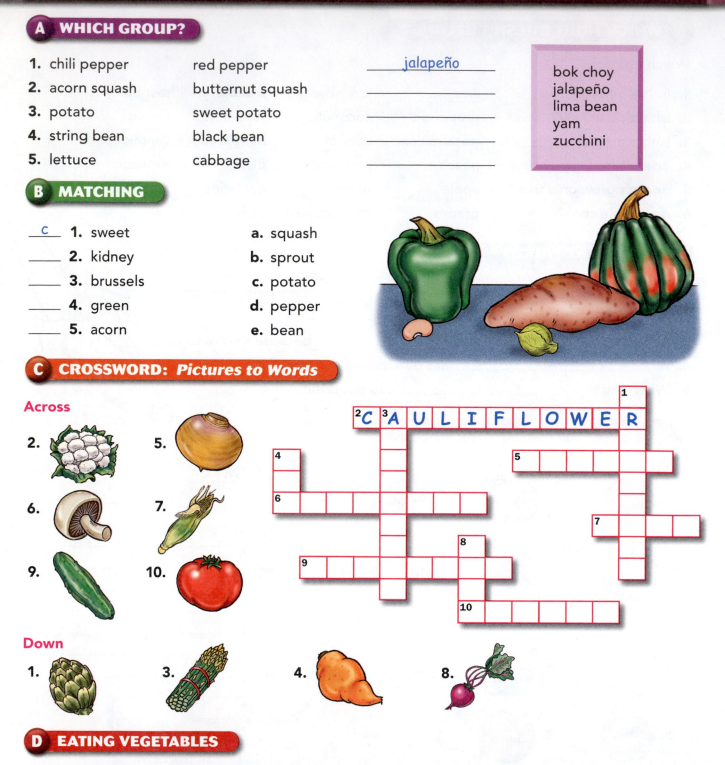

D EATING VEGETABLES

People in different countries eat vegetables in different ways. In your country, which vegetables do people eat raw (uncooked)? Which vegetables do people cook before they eat them?

Raw	Cooked
....	....
....	....
....	....
....	....

A WHICH GROUP?

| bacon | clams | flounder | mussels | stewing beef | turkey |
| chicken thighs | drumsticks | lobster | sausages | tripe | |

Meat	Poultry	Seafood
bacon		

B WHAT'S THE WORD?

| drumsticks | ham | lamb | ribs | scallops | trout |

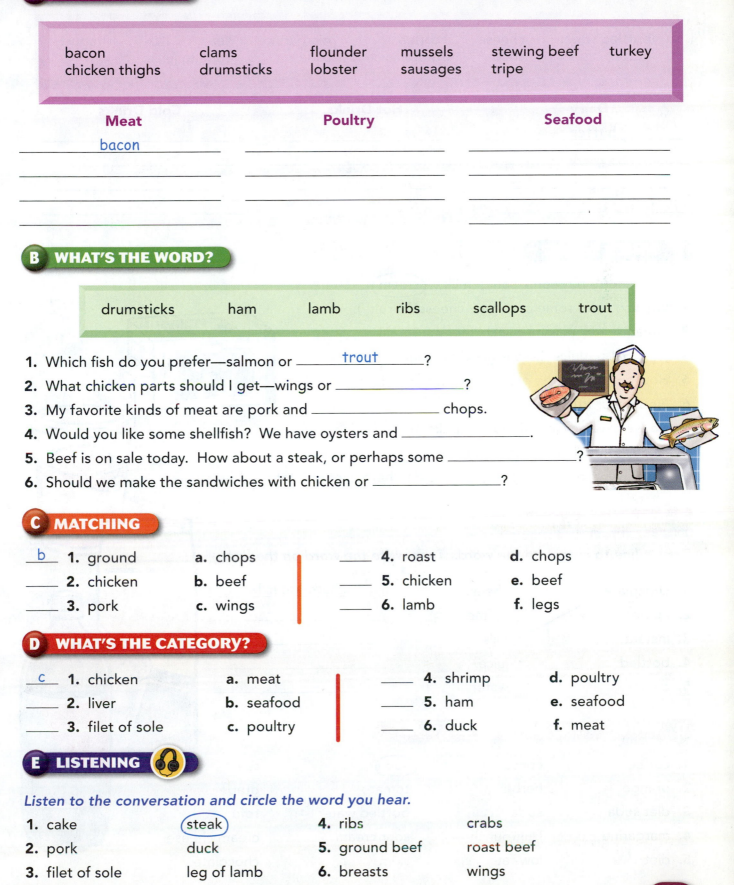

1. Which fish do you prefer—salmon or _____trout_____?
2. What chicken parts should I get—wings or _____?
3. My favorite kinds of meat are pork and _____ chops.
4. Would you like some shellfish? We have oysters and _____.
5. Beef is on sale today. How about a steak, or perhaps some _____?
6. Should we make the sandwiches with chicken or _____?

C MATCHING

_b_ 1. ground   **a.** chops   ____ 4. roast   **d.** chops
____ 2. chicken   **b.** beef   ____ 5. chicken   **e.** beef
____ 3. pork   **c.** wings   ____ 6. lamb   **f.** legs

D WHAT'S THE CATEGORY?

_c_ 1. chicken   **a.** meat   ____ 4. shrimp   **d.** poultry
____ 2. liver   **b.** seafood   ____ 5. ham   **e.** seafood
____ 3. filet of sole   **c.** poultry   ____ 6. duck   **f.** meat

E LISTENING

Listen to the conversation and circle the word you hear.

1. cake   (steak)   **4.** ribs   crabs
2. pork   duck   **5.** ground beef   roast beef
3. filet of sole   leg of lamb   **6.** breasts   wings

A WHICH GROUP?

| bottled water | cheese | coffee | margarine | tea | yogurt |
| butter | cocoa | grape juice | soda | tomato juice | |

Dairy	Hot Drinks	Cold Drinks
butter		

B WHICH WORD?

1. We need to buy some sour (milk   (cream)).
2. We also need some cottage (cheese   fruit).
3. I need skim (milk   punch) for my cereal.
4. (Herbal   Juice) tea is good for you.
5. How do you like the grapefruit (water   juice)?
6. Finish your fruit (mix   punch).
7. Do we have any juice (fruit   paks)?
8. I'll get some diet (soda   cream) at the supermarket.
9. If you want to lose weight, you shouldn't have a lot of (tofu   butter).

C MATCH AND WRITE

Draw a line to complete the word. Then write the word on the line.

1. chocolate   cheese   _chocolate milk_
2. apple   coffee   _____
3. instant   milk   _____
4. bottled   juice   _____
5. cream   water   _____

D WHICH WORD DOESN'T BELONG?

1. coffee   cocoa   (soda)   tea
2. orange   herbal   tomato   grape
3. diet soda   soda   bottled water   tofu
4. margarine   fruit punch sour cream   cream cheese
5. diet   low-fat   skim   chocolate

A WHICH GROUP?

| ice cream | mozzarella | pastrami | potato chips | potato salad |

1. nuts   popcorn   _potato chips_
2. frozen lemonade   frozen dinners   _____
3. corned beef   salami   _____
4. cole slaw   macaroni salad   _____
5. American cheese   provolone   _____

B MATCHING

_c_ 1. ice   **a.** slaw | ___ 5. seafood   **e.** chips
___ 2. cole   **b.** beef | ___ 6. frozen   **f.** salad
___ 3. cheddar   **c.** cream | ___ 7. potato   **g.** juice
___ 4. corned   **d.** cheese | ___ 8. frozen orange   **h.** lemonade

C WHICH WORD?

1. Do you want a ((ham)   popcorn) sandwich for lunch?
2. This potato (chips   salad) is delicious.
3. My favorite snack food is (pretzels   bologna).
4. Do you want cheddar or (pastrami   Swiss) cheese?
5. I'm getting thirsty. Do we have any frozen (orange juice   dinners)?

D CROSSWORD: *Pictures to Words*

Across

3.
4. _____ chips
6.
7.

Down

1.
2. frozen _____
5. _____ beef

³ B O L O G N A

45

A WHICH GROUP?

bread	English muffins	mayonnaise	soup
cake	fruit	relish	tuna fish
cereal	ketchup	rice	vegetables
crackers	macaroni	rolls	vinegar

Packaged Goods	Canned Goods	Condiments	Baked Goods
cereal			

B WHICH WORD?

1. Should we make our sandwiches on pita bread or (cake   (rolls))?
2. To make cookies at home, you need flour and (pickles   sugar).
3. Let's put some (olives   jam) in the salad.
4. Tuna (butter   fish) is good for you.
5. There isn't any (cereal   mayonnaise) for our sandwiches.
6. This soup needs some (vinegar   spices).
7. I'm making some (noodles   cooking oil) for lunch.

C MATCHING

_e_	**1.** tuna		**a.** sauce
___	**2.** peanut		**b.** mix
___	**3.** soy		**c.** dressing
___	**4.** olive		**d.** bread
___	**5.** pita		**e.** fish
___	**6.** cake		**f.** butter
___	**7.** salad		**g.** oil

D ASSOCIATIONS

_b_	**1.** salt		**a.** cheese
___	**2.** ketchup		**b.** pepper
___	**3.** peanut butter		**c.** milk
___	**4.** chips		**d.** bread
___	**5.** jam		**e.** jelly
___	**6.** cookies		**f.** mustard
___	**7.** macaroni		**g.** salsa

E JOURNAL

What condiments and packaged foods are popular in your country?

....
....
....

A WHICH WORD?

1. Use paper ((towels)   plates) to clean up this mess.
2. I forgot to get disposable (diapers   wrap) at the store.
3. Wash your hands with liquid (cups   soap).
4. We need (sandwich   trash) bags for our lunches.
5. The baby is hungry. Give her some (wipes   formula).
6. They forgot to get (toilet   waxed) paper for the bathroom.
7. Please buy some aluminum (paper   foil) when you go to the store.
8. When we go on a picnic, we always take paper (straws   plates) with us.

B WHICH WORD DOESN'T BELONG?

1. cat food   baby food   dog food
2. paper plates   paper cups   paper towels
3. plastic wrap   trash bags   aluminum foil
4. diapers   straws   napkins
5. formula   sandwich bags   wipes

C ASSOCIATIONS

<u>b</u> **1.** cat food   **a.** washing
___ **2.** straws   **b.** pet
___ **3.** trash bags   **c.** eating
___ **4.** diapers   **d.** babies
___ **5.** soap   **e.** drinking
___ **6.** paper plates   **f.** garbage

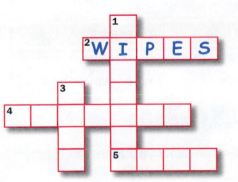

D CROSSWORD

Across

2. We clean the baby with these ____.
4. We feed the baby with ____.
5. We wash our hands with liquid ____.

Down

1. We wipe our nose with ____.
3. We save leftovers with plastic ____.

A MATCHING

__b__ 1. shopping   **a.** machine   ____ 5. cash   **e.** bag

____ 2. checkout   **b.** basket   ____ 6. plastic   **f.** newspaper

____ 3. can-return   **c.** belt   ____ 7. shopping   **g.** register

____ 4. conveyor   **d.** counter   ____ 8. tabloid   **h.** cart

B WHICH WORD?

1. I only need a few things. I'll get a shopping ((basket)   cart).
2. Household items are in the next (counter   aisle).
3. Do you want a paper or plastic (bag   bagger)?
4. The (manager   customer) can help you find something.
5. All the cash registers use electronic (packers   scanners).
6. You can find fruits and vegetables in the (deli   produce) section.
7. I always read the (magazines   candy) when I'm in the checkout line.
8. Shoppers can save money when they use (the cash register   coupons).

C TRUE OR FALSE?

Answer the following questions about the scene on page 55 of the Picture Dictionary. Write T if the statement is true and F if the statement is false.

__T__ 1. The manager is talking to a clerk.

____ 2. There are two shoppers in the express checkout line.

____ 3. Someone is in front of the bottle-return machine.

____ 4. The cashiers at this supermarket wear green vests.

____ 5. The customer in Aisle 1 has a shopping basket.

____ 6. You can find gum and candy in the Produce Section.

D ASSOCIATIONS

__b__ 1. paper bag   **a.** scale   ____ 4. tabloid   **d.** express checkout

____ 2. cash register   **b.** bagger   ____ 5. candy   **e.** magazine

____ 3. produce   **c.** conveyor belt   ____ 6. six items   **f.** gum

E LISTENING

Listen and circle the word you hear.

1. (checkout lines)   checkout counters   4. cash register   cashier
2. shoppers   shopping carts   5. plastic   paper
3. coupon   candy   6. can-return   bottle-return

A WHAT'S THE CONTAINER?

bag	box	bunch	can	jar	roll

1. _____box_____
- cereal
- crackers
- raisins

2. _____
- bananas
- grapes
- carrots

3. _____
- toilet paper
- paper towels
- aluminum foil

4. _____
- soup
- tuna fish
- soda

5. _____
- potato chips
- flour
- cookies

6. _____
- baby food
- mayonnaise
- olives

B WHAT'S THE WORD?

bottle	dozen	head	pack	six-pack
box	gallon	loaf	pound	tube

1. a _____pound_____ of cheese

2. a _____ of lettuce

3. a _____ of toothpaste

4. a _____ of milk

5. a _____ of salad dressing

6. a _____ of bread

7. a _____ eggs

8. a _____ of crackers

9. a _____ of soda

10. a _____ of gum

C WHICH WORD?

1. We need a ((container)   carton) of yogurt.
2. Let's buy a few (cans   packs) of soup.
3. We need a (six-pack   pound) of butter.
4. Please get a (roll   stick) of aluminum foil.
5. Don't forget to buy a (liter   head) of lettuce.
6. Can you get a (half-gallon   bunch) of ice cream?

D LISTENING

Listen and circle the words you hear.

1. a six-pack   (two six-packs)
2. a loaf   two loaves
3. a gallon   a half-gallon
4. pack   package

5. box   bottle
6. pint   a few pints
7. quart   carton
8. bunches   boxes

A ABBREVIATIONS

_b_ **1.** teaspoon
2. tablespoon
3. fluid ounce
4. pint
5. quart

a. Tbsp.
b. tsp.
c. qt.
d. fl. oz.
e. pt.

____ **6.** gallon
____ **7.** ounce
____ **8.** pound
____ **9.** ounces
____ **10.** pounds

f. lbs.
g. ozs.
h. gal.
i. lb.
j. oz.

B WHICH IS EQUAL?

_c_ **1.** 32 fl. ozs.
____ **2.** 2 cups
____ **3.** 3 tsps.
____ **4.** 128 fl. ozs.
____ **5.** 16 ozs.

a. 1 tablespoon
b. 1 gallon
c. 1 quart
d. 1 pound
e. 1 pint

C TRUE OR FALSE?

Write T if the statement is true and F if the statement is false.

_T_ **1.** There are eight ounces in half a pound.
____ **2.** There are three tablespoons in a teaspoon.
____ **3.** One fluid ounce is equal to six teaspoons.
____ **4.** There are three pints in a quart.
____ **5.** There are more than three quarts in a gallon.

D WHAT'S THE NUMBER?

1. 8 fl. ozs. = _1_ cup
2. 1 pt. = ____ cups
3. 32 fl. ozs. = ____ pints
4. 2 qts. = ____ fl. ozs.

5. 1 gal. = ____ fl. ozs.
6. 16 ozs. = ____ lb.
7. 2 lbs. = ____ ozs.
8. 6 tsps. = ____ Tbsps.

E WHICH WORD?

1. I need (3/4 lb.   128 fl. ozs.) of ground beef, please.
2. Add a (teaspoon   pound) of salt to the chili.
3. The recipe says to add 8 (tablespoons   quarts) of butter.
4. There are two (pounds   cups) of pineapple juice in this punch.
5. I bought (an ounce   a gallon) of milk at the supermarket today.
6. The recipe says to put half a (pound   cup) of cream into the mixture.

50

A MATCHING

_c_ **1.** Chop up

2. Grate

3. Beat

a. the cheese.

b. the eggs.

c. the vegetables.

____ **4.** Peel

____ **5.** Pour

____ **6.** Roast

d. the chicken.

e. the orange.

f. the lemonade.

B HELP IN THE KITCHEN

> bake   beat

1. How long should I __bake__ the cookies?

2. How long should I _____ the eggs?

> pour   slice

5. First _____ the milk.

6. Then _____ the tomato.

> breaking   simmering

3. I'm _____ the eggs.

4. The onions are _____.

> boil   grill

7. Let's _____ some hamburgers.

8. Let's _____ some water for tea.

C SPELLING RULE

> To add –*ing*: When a verb ends in *e*, drop the *e* and add *ing*:
> slic~~e~~ + ing = slicing

1. She's (*slice*) ____slicing____ bread.

2. He's (*bake*) _____ potatoes.

3. She's (*grate*) _____ cheese.

4. He's (*combine*) _____ eggs and milk.

D CROSSWORD

Across

4. ____ the leftovers to reheat them.

5. ____ the flour and eggs.

6. I'm ____ some salt to the soup.

Down

1. ____ the chili every few minutes.

2. He's stir- ____ some vegetables.

3. ____ the garlic for a few minutes.

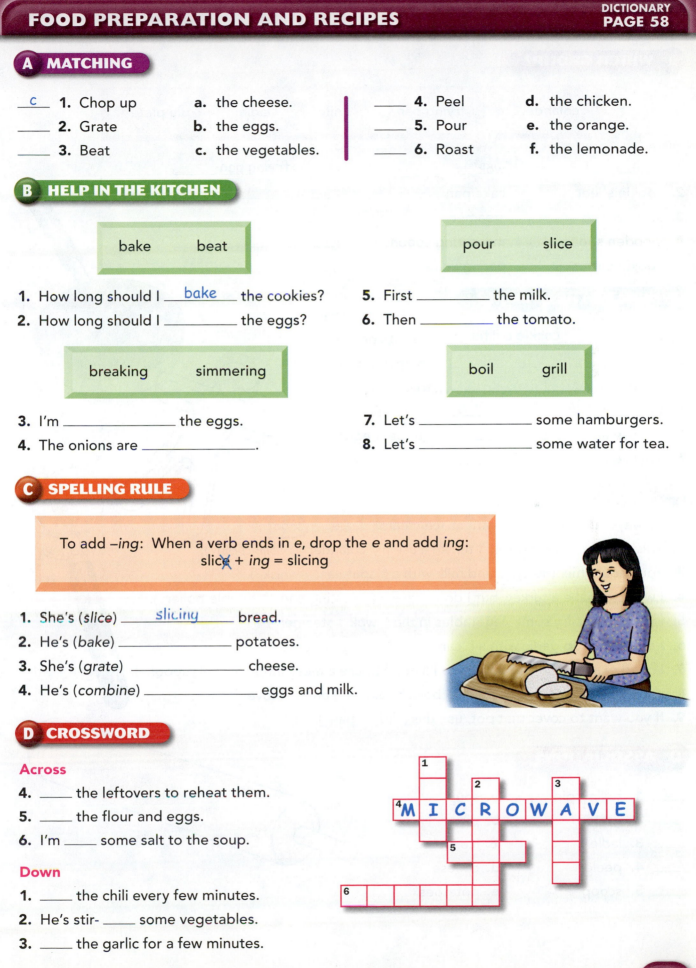

Crossword:
4 across: M I C R O W A V E

51

A WHICH GROUP?

colander	frying pan	knife	ladle	pie plate

1. double boiler   wok   _frying pan_
2. cookie sheet   cake pan   _____
3. strainer   steamer   _____
4. wooden spoon   measuring spoon   _____
5. cookie cutter   paring knife   _____

B WHAT'S THE UTENSIL?

1. We use a ___cookie cutter___ to cut cookies.
2. We use a _____ to open bottles.
3. We use a _____ to open cans.
4. We use a _____ to grate cheese.
5. We use an _____ to beat eggs.
6. We use a _____ to peel vegetables.

C WHICH WORD?

1. I always serve ice cream with an ice cream (ladle   (scoop)).
2. This strainer is very small. I think I'll use a (colander   rolling pin).
3. You should mix the eggs and milk with a (spatula   whisk).
4. I want to make a turkey, but I don't have a (roasting pan   double boiler).
5. I think I'll stir-fry some vegetables in the (wok   steamer).
6. I always cut up garlic with a (carving knife   garlic press).
7. I need exactly one cup of milk so I'll need to use a measuring (cup   spoon).
8. The meatballs are cooking in a (bowl   skillet) on the stove.
9. If you want to cover that pot, use this (lid   pan).

D ASSOCIATIONS

_b_ 1. rolling pin   a. soup
____ 2. grater   b. pies
____ 3. ladle   c. ice cream
____ 4. peeler   d. cheese
____ 5. scoop   e. potatoes

A ORDERING FAST FOOD

<u> f </u> 1. I'd like a fish   a. chicken.
_____ 2. I'll have a bowl of   b. cheeseburger.
_____ 3. I'll have some fried   c. fries.
_____ 4. I'll have a slice of   d. yogurt.
_____ 5. I'll have some french   e. chili.
_____ 6. I'll have a frozen   f. sandwich.
_____ 7. I'd like a   g. pizza.

B WHICH GROUP?

| burrito | hamburger | ice cream | ketchup | plastic utensils |

1. cheeseburger   chicken sandwich   _hamburger_
2. frozen yogurt   milkshake   _____
3. straws   napkins   _____
4. taco   nachos   _____
5. mayonnaise   mustard   _____

C CROSSWORD: *Pictures to Words*

Across

2.   4.   7.

8.   9.   10.

Down

1.   3.   5.

6.   8.

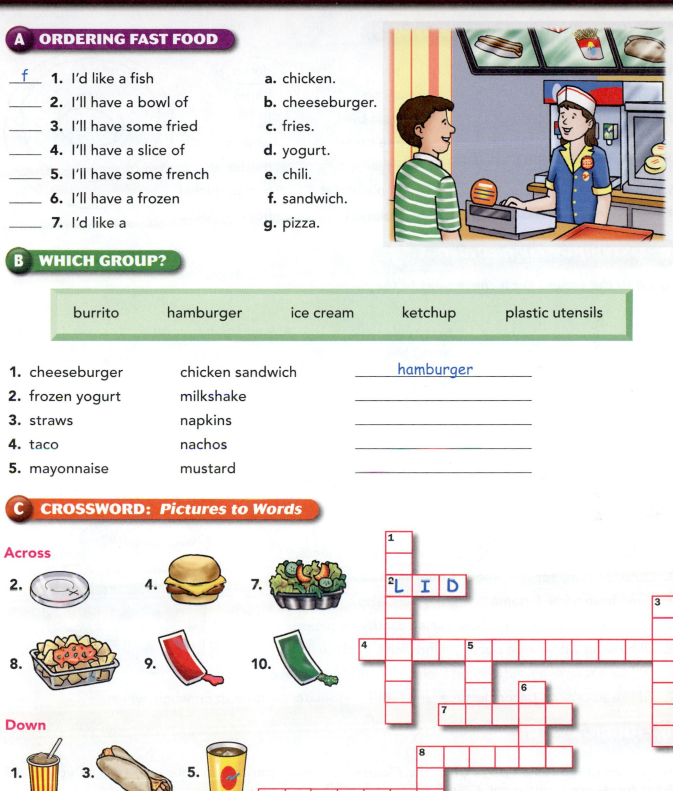

A WHICH WORD DOESN'T BELONG?

1. tea   lemonade   milk   (donut)
2. roll   bun   bacon   bagel
3. tuna fish   iced tea   roast beef   BLT
4. danish   submarine roll   pita bread   white bread
5. donut   pastry   eggs   muffin
6. rye   biscuit   whole wheat   pumpernickel
7. coffee   iced tea   croissant   hot chocolate

B LISTENING: *Taking Orders*

Listen to the order. Put a check next to the correct item.

1. ✓ roast beef   4. ☐ danish
   ☐ corned beef   ☐ tuna fish

2. ☐ croissant   5. ☐ BLT
   ☐ biscuit   ☐ tea

3. ☐ rye bread   6. ☐ bacon
   ☐ white bread   ☐ bagel

C WHICH WORD?

1. I'll have a ((hot chocolate) pastry) to drink, please.
2. Do you have (toast roast) beef sandwiches?
3. Can I have some (home ham) fries, also?
4. I'd like a (chicken kitchen) salad sandwich, please.
5. I'll have an extra-large decaf (sandwich coffee).
6. I'd like a tuna fish sandwich on (pita pancakes) bread, please.
7. I'd like to order a bacon, lettuce, and (BLT tomato) sandwich on whole wheat.

D JOURNAL

Are any of the foods on page 61 of the Picture Dictionary popular in your country? Which ones? What foods are popular for a quick meal or snack?

....
....
....
....

A MATCHING

__c__ **1.** salad   **a.** chair   _____ **4.** dining   **d.** seat

_____ **2.** high   **b.** tray   _____ **5.** bread   **e.** room

_____ **3.** dessert   **c.** bar   _____ **6.** booster   **f.** basket

B WHAT ARE THEY DOING?

Look at the restaurant scenes on pages 62 and 63 of the Picture Dictionary and complete the sentences.

clear	leave	seat	serve	take

1. The waiter who is holding the tray is _____serving_____ the meal.

2. The hostess is _____ the customers.

3. The busperson near the dessert tray is _____ the table.

4. The waitress near the salad bar is _____ the orders.

5. The female customer with blond hair is _____ a tip.

C WHICH WORD?

1. I'll get you another (salad bar   (spoon)) from the kitchen.

2. My name is Barbara, and I'll be your (waitress   customer) this evening.

3. I'd like a (table   high chair) for three, please.

4. You need to (seat   set) the table.

5. When we go to a restaurant, we like to sit in a (booth   booster seat).

6. There's a job opening at this restaurant for a (dishroom   dishwasher).

D THE PLACE SETTING

Look at the place setting on page 63 of the Picture Dictionary and complete the sentences.

1. The _____teaspoon_____ is between the knife and the soup spoon.

2. The _____ is to the left of the teaspoon.

3. The _____ is under the salad fork and the dinner fork.

4. The _____ is on the bread-and-butter plate.

5. The _____ is to the right of the teaspoon.

6. The _____ is between the salad fork and the dinner plate.

7. The _____ is on the dinner plate.

E YOUR PLACE SETTING

How do you set a table at home? On a separate piece of paper, draw your place setting.

A ORDERING DINNER

Complete the conversation and then practice it with a friend.

| antipasto | meatloaf | mixed vegetables | pudding | shrimp cocktail |

A. May I take your order?

B. Yes, please. For the appetizer, I'd like the ___shrimp cocktail___. [1]

A. And what kind of salad would you like?

B. I'll have the _____. [2]

A. And for the main course?

B. I'd like the _____ [3], please.

A. What side dish would you like with that?

B. Hmm. I think I'll have the _____. [4]

A. Would you care for some dessert?

B. Yes. I'll have _____ [5], please.

B LISTENING: Ordering at a Restaurant

Listen to the order. Put a check next to the correct items.

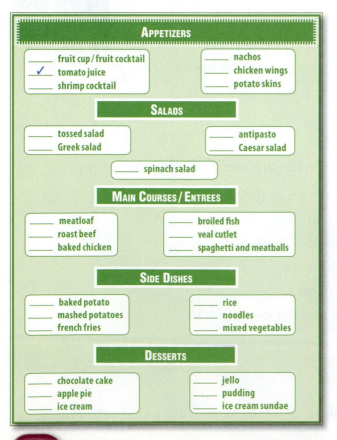

APPETIZERS

_____ fruit cup / fruit cocktail
✓ tomato juice
_____ shrimp cocktail
_____ nachos
_____ chicken wings
_____ potato skins

SALADS

_____ tossed salad
_____ Greek salad
_____ antipasto
_____ Caesar salad
_____ spinach salad

MAIN COURSES / ENTREES

_____ meatloaf
_____ roast beef
_____ baked chicken
_____ broiled fish
_____ veal cutlet
_____ spaghetti and meatballs

SIDE DISHES

_____ baked potato
_____ mashed potatoes
_____ french fries
_____ rice
_____ noodles
_____ mixed vegetables

DESSERTS

_____ chocolate cake
_____ apple pie
_____ ice cream
_____ jello
_____ pudding
_____ ice cream sundae

C YOUR RESTAURANT

You are the owner of a popular restaurant in your country. Create a menu for your restaurant.

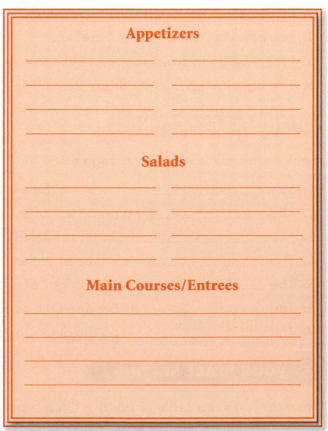

Appetizers

_____ _____
_____ _____
_____ _____
_____ _____

Salads

_____ _____
_____ _____

Main Courses/Entrees

_____
_____
_____
_____
_____

A ASSOCIATIONS

<u>b</u> **1.** strawberries
____ **2.** lemons
____ **3.** carrots
____ **4.** blueberries
____ **5.** snow
____ **6.** lettuce
____ **7.** eggplant

a. orange
b. red
c. green
d. purple
e. blue
f. yellow
g. white

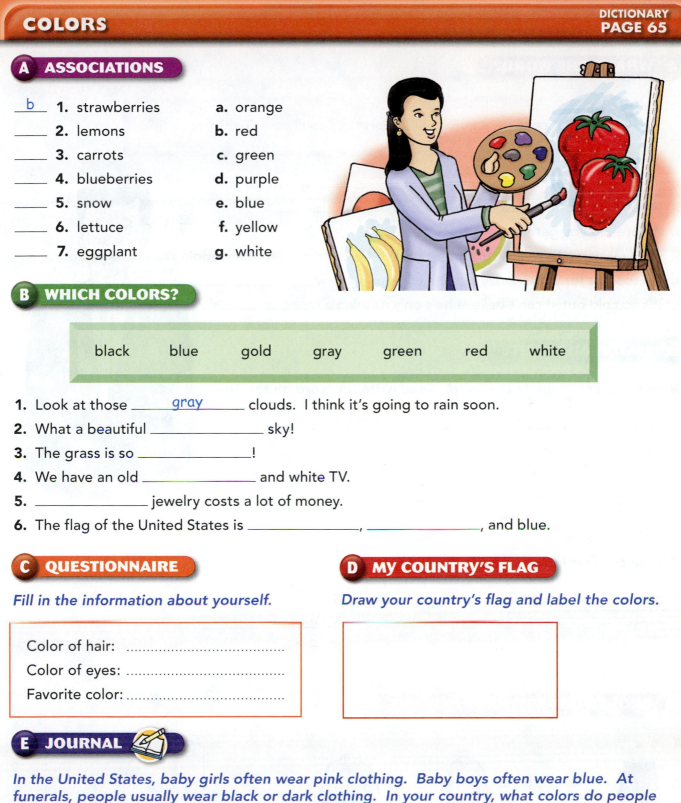

B WHICH COLORS?

| black | blue | gold | gray | green | red | white |

1. Look at those _____gray_____ clouds. I think it's going to rain soon.

2. What a beautiful _____ sky!

3. The grass is so _____!

4. We have an old _____ and white TV.

5. _____ jewelry costs a lot of money.

6. The flag of the United States is _____, _____, and blue.

C QUESTIONNAIRE

Fill in the information about yourself.

Color of hair: ....
Color of eyes: ....
Favorite color: ....

D MY COUNTRY'S FLAG

Draw your country's flag and label the colors.

E JOURNAL

In the United States, baby girls often wear pink clothing. Baby boys often wear blue. At funerals, people usually wear black or dark clothing. In your country, what colors do people wear in different situations?

57

A WHAT'S THE WORD?

| coat | gown | shorts | suit | T-shirt | tie |

1. I'm going to wear a red bow _____tie_____ with my new tuxedo.
2. What a shame! She just ripped her evening _____.
3. Where did you get your new sport _____?
4. Are you going to wear your three-piece _____ to the wedding?
5. It's too hot for pants today. I think I'll wear my new _____.
6. It's so cold out. I can't believe he's only wearing a _____!

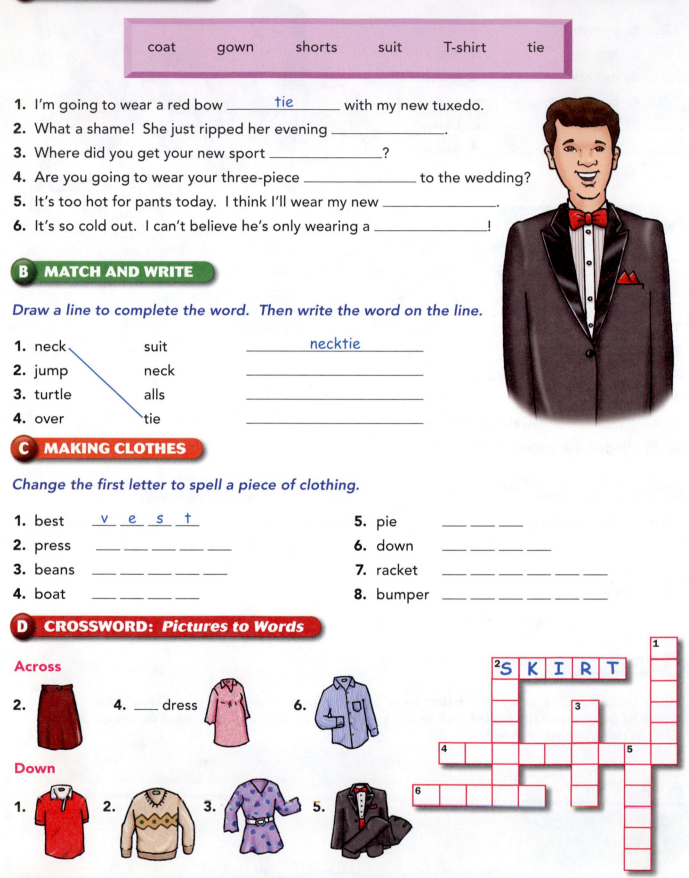

B MATCH AND WRITE

Draw a line to complete the word. Then write the word on the line.

1. neck ⟶ suit   _____necktie_____
2. jump   neck   _____
3. turtle   alls   _____
4. over   tie   _____

C MAKING CLOTHES

Change the first letter to spell a piece of clothing.

1. best   __v__ __e__ __s__ __t__   5. pie   __ __ __
2. press   __ __ __ __ __   6. down   __ __ __ __
3. beans   __ __ __ __ __   7. racket __ __ __ __ __ __
4. boat   __ __ __ __   8. bumper __ __ __ __ __ __

D CROSSWORD: *Pictures to Words*

Across

2.   4. ___ dress   6.

Down

1.   2.   3.   5.

A MATCHING

_c_ **1.** rain	**a.** muffs	_____ **5.** sweater	**e.** coat
_____ **2.** ear	**b.** mask	_____ **6.** baseball	**f.** jacket
_____ **3.** down	**c.** boots	_____ **7.** trench	**g.** breaker
_____ **4.** ski	**d.** vest	_____ **8.** wind	**h.** cap

B WHICH GROUP?

cap	gloves	poncho	ski hat	windbreaker
earmuffs	leather jacket	rain hat	sunglasses	

Jackets	**Hats**	**Accessories**
leather jacket	_____	_____
_____	_____	_____
_____	_____	_____

C WHAT DO WE USE?

down jacket	rain boots	scarf	trench coat
mittens	raincoat	ski mask	umbrella

. . . when it's raining   **. . . when it's snowing**

rain boots	_____	_____	_____
_____	_____	_____	_____

D MATCHING: *Which Part of the Body?*

_b_ **1.** ear muffs	**a.** legs	_____ **4.** muffler	**d.** eyes
_____ **2.** tights	**b.** ears	_____ **5.** sunglasses	**e.** feet
_____ **3.** gloves	**c.** hands	_____ **6.** rain boots	**f.** neck

E WHICH WORD?

1. It might rain later. Do you think I need ((an umbrella)   ear muffs)?

2. It isn't very cold, but you might want to wear a light (ski mask   jacket).

3. Winter is coming soon. I need to buy a new (overcoat   baseball cap).

4. This (sweater   ski) jacket is perfect for snowy days.

5. Can I borrow a pair of (sunglasses   mittens)? It's cold tonight.

6. This (parka   trench coat) will keep you warm.

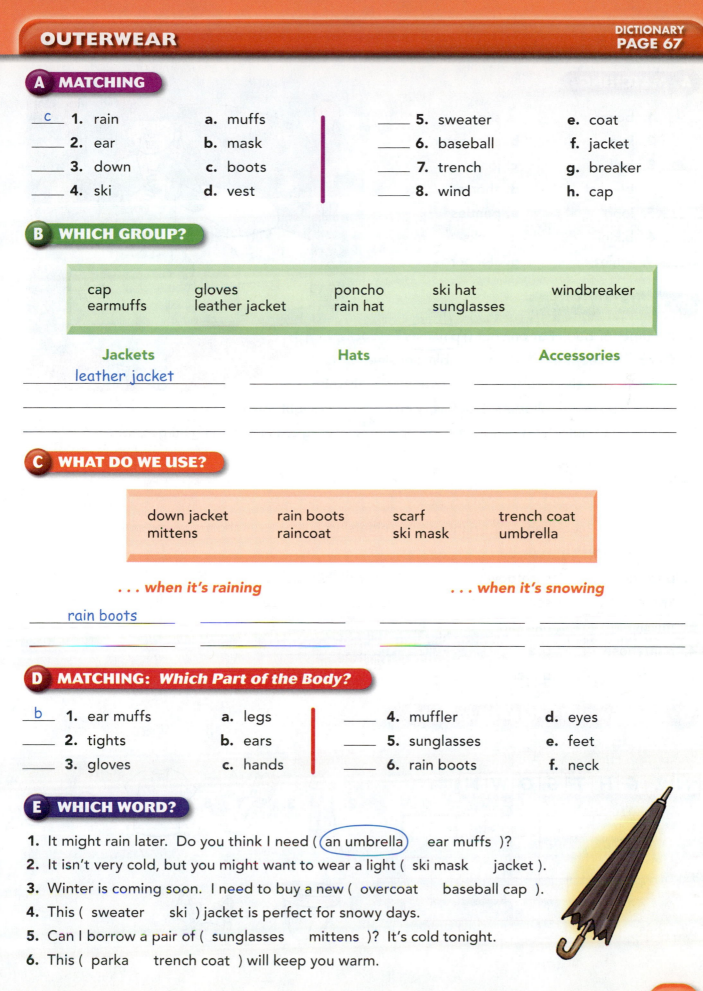

59

A MATCHING

_d_	**1.** boxer	**a.**	slip
___	**2.** knee	**b.**	supporter
___	**3.** half	**c.**	johns
___	**4.** blanket	**d.**	shorts
___	**5.** long	**e.**	panties
___	**6.** bikini	**f.**	socks
___	**7.** athletic	**g.**	sleeper

B WHICH WORD?

1. It's time for bed. Put on your ((pajamas)   socks).
2. Our baby sleeps in a (slipper   blanket sleeper).
3. You can wear this (robe   bra) over your nightshirt.
4. Those (boxers   slippers) look very nice with your nightgown.
5. It's snowing outside! Wear your (boxer shorts   long underwear) if you go out.

C WHICH GROUP?

knee-highs	panties	nightshirt	boxer shorts	camisole

1. pajamas	nightgown	_nightshirt_
2. knee socks	socks	_____
3. full slip	half slip	_____
4. pantyhose	bra	_____
5. briefs	underpants	_____

D CROSSWORD: *Pictures to Words*

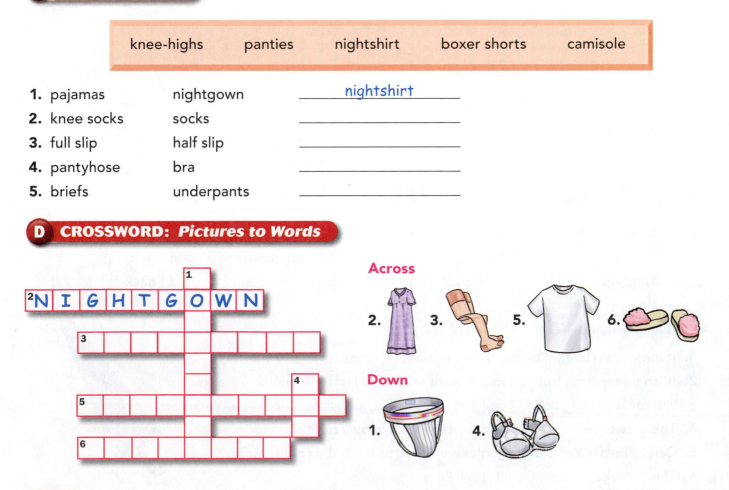

Across

2.   3.   5.   6.

Down

1.   4.

² N I G H T G O W N

A WHICH WORD?

1. If you go running, you should wear ((sweatpants)   a tank top). It's a very cool day.
2. It's very hot outside! I think I'll wear my (cowboy boots   sandals).
3. It's too warm for a sweatshirt. I think I'll wear a (T-shirt   sweatband).
4. I'm going to wear (shoes   boots) today. It might snow.
5. Summer is almost here. I should buy a new (bathing   warm-up) suit.
6. I can't play basketball because I don't have my (high-tops   moccasins).

B WHICH WORD DOESN'T BELONG?

1. work boots   hiking boots   cowboy boots   (high-tops)
2. pumps   tennis shoes   leotard   sandals
3. T-shirt   bike shorts   tank top   sweatshirt
4. swimming trunks   lyrca shorts   sweatshirt   sweatpants
5. hiking   cowboy   work   tennis

C WHAT DO WE WEAR?

We wear these . . .

_e_ **1.** jogging through the park.   **a.** thongs

___ **2.** at the beach.   **b.** sneakers

___ **3.** climbing a mountain.   **c.** high heels

___ **4.** with a fancy dress.   **d.** work boots

___ **5.** at a ballgame.   **e.** running shoes

___ **6.** at a construction site.   **f.** hiking boots

D WHAT'S THE SYNONYM?

athletic shoes	bathing suit	bike shorts	flip-flops	high-top sneakers	running suit

1. high-tops   _high-top sneakers_   **4.** thongs   _____

2. swimming trunks _____   **5.** jogging suit _____

3. lycra shorts   _____   **6.** sneakers   _____

E LISTENING 🎧

Listen to the conversation and circle the word you hear.

1. shorts   (shoes)   **3.** leotards   lycra shorts   **5.** jogging suit   swimsuit

2. tank top   T-shirt   **4.** sweatshirt   sweatband   **6.** pumps   flip-flops

A WHERE DO WE WEAR THEM?

| belt | chain | necklace | watch |
| bracelet | locket | ring | wedding band |

Neck	Finger	Wrist	Waist
chain			

B WHAT DO WE USE?

<u>d</u> **1.** We use this to keep a very small picture in.

_____ **2.** We use these to keep pants up.

_____ **3.** We use this to keep makeup in.

_____ **4.** We keep credit cards and money in this.

_____ **5.** We carry books in this.

_____ **6.** We use this to keep keys together.

_____ **7.** We use these to connect the cuffs of fancy shirts.

_____ **8.** We keep coins in this.

_____ **9.** We use this to keep our hair in place.

a. barrette

b. cuff links

c. book bag

d. locket

e. change purse

f. suspenders

g. key chain

h. wallet

i. makeup bag

C MATCH AND WRITE

Draw a line to complete the word. Then write the word on the line.

1. pocket   lace   _____pocketbook_____

2. hand   ring   _____

3. neck   case   _____

4. back   book   _____

5. brief   pack   _____

6. ear   kerchief   _____

D WHICH WORD DOESN'T BELONG?

1. necklace   (key chain)   pearls   beads

2. ring   earrings   bracelet   tote bag

3. wallet   book bag   backpack   briefcase

4. handbag   purse   bracelet   pocketbook

5. ring   key ring   wedding band engagement ring

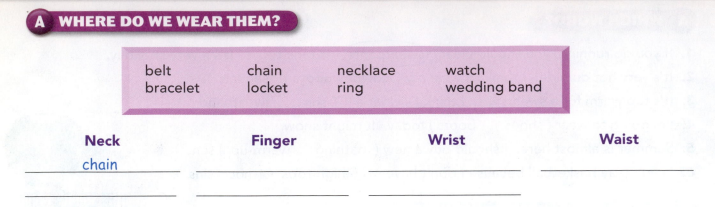

A MATCHING

<u> c </u> **1.** flannel   **a.** pants

_____ **2.** nylon   **b.** hat

_____ **3.** corduroy   **c.** shirt

_____ **4.** straw   **d.** socks

_____ **5.** V-neck   **e.** stockings

_____ **6.** ankle   **f.** sweater

B WHICH WORD?

1. I prefer the (turtleneck   knee-high) sweater.

2. Do you have any crew (sweaters   socks)?

3. This (low   striped) shirt is half-price.

4. That coat is too (large   paisley).

5. I'm looking for an (ankle   extra-small) jersey.

6. My husband likes (polka-dotted   flannel) ties.

7. What do you think of these (silk   leather) boots?

8. I'm looking for a (straw   clip-on) hat.

C LISTENING: *What Are They Describing?*

Listen and write the number next to the correct description.

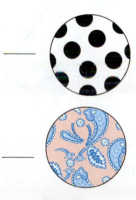

1

D WHICH WORD DOESN'T BELONG?

1. silk	large	linen	wool
2. crewneck	cardigan	denim	V-neck
3. flowered	sleeveless	long-sleeved	short-sleeved
4. knee-high	ankle	V-neck	crew
5. solid	medium	extra-small	large
6. cotton	polyester	denim	clip-on

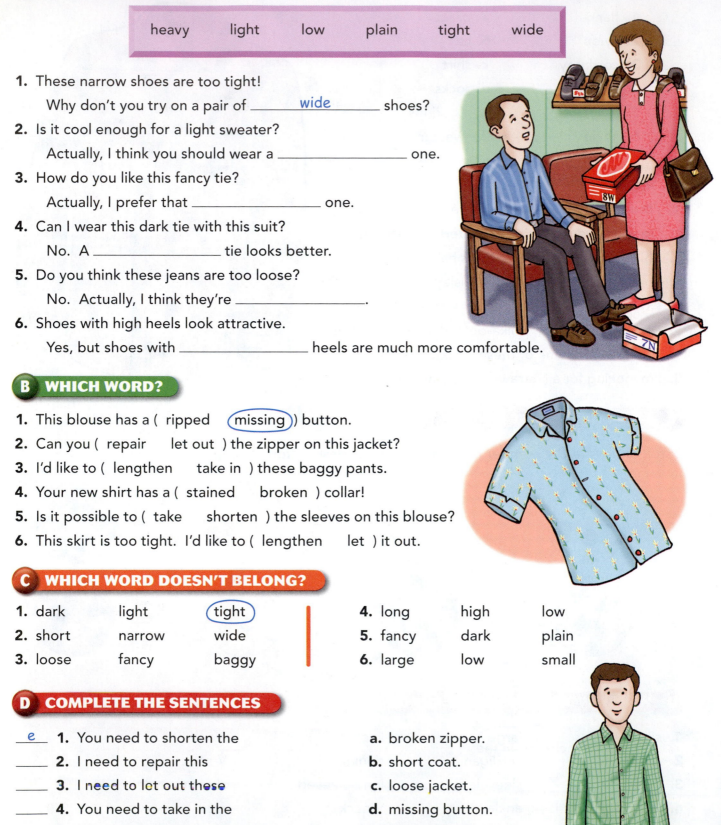

A WHAT'S THE WORD?

heavy	light	low	plain	tight	wide

1. These narrow shoes are too tight!

   Why don't you try on a pair of _____wide_____ shoes?

2. Is it cool enough for a light sweater?

   Actually, I think you should wear a _____ one.

3. How do you like this fancy tie?

   Actually, I prefer that _____ one.

4. Can I wear this dark tie with this suit?

   No. A _____ tie looks better.

5. Do you think these jeans are too loose?

   No. Actually, I think they're _____.

6. Shoes with high heels look attractive.

   Yes, but shoes with _____ heels are much more comfortable.

B WHICH WORD?

1. This blouse has a (ripped   (missing)) button.
2. Can you (repair   let out) the zipper on this jacket?
3. I'd like to (lengthen   take in) these baggy pants.
4. Your new shirt has a (stained   broken) collar!
5. Is it possible to (take   shorten) the sleeves on this blouse?
6. This skirt is too tight. I'd like to (lengthen   let) it out.

C WHICH WORD DOESN'T BELONG?

1. dark	light	(tight)		4. long	high	low
2. short	narrow	wide		5. fancy	dark	plain
3. loose	fancy	baggy		6. large	low	small

D COMPLETE THE SENTENCES

_e_ 1. You need to shorten the	a. broken zipper.
___ 2. I need to repair this	b. short coat.
___ 3. I need to let out these	c. loose jacket.
___ 4. You need to take in the	d. missing button.
___ 5. I can replace that	e. long sleeves.
___ 6. You need to lengthen that	f. tight pants.

A DOING MY LAUNDRY

dryer	fold	hang	iron	load	put	sort	unload

I'm going to do my laundry now. First, I'm going to _____sort_____ [1] the laundry into dark and light colors. Then I'll _____ [2] the washer, let the clothes wash, and then _____ [3] the washer. I don't have a _____ [4], so after the clothes are washed, I have to _____ [5] the clothes on the clothesline. When the clothes are dry, I have to _____ [6] them and then _____ [7] them. Finally, I'll _____ [8] them in my bureau or in the closet.

B MATCH AND WRITE

Draw a line to complete the word. Then write the word on the line.

1. laundry   trap   _____laundry basket_____
2. fabric   board   _____
3. ironing   clothing   _____
4. spray   basket   _____
5. lint   remover   _____
6. wet   softener   _____
7. static cling   machine   _____
8. washing   starch   _____

C CROSSWORD

Across

1. You dry your clothes in this.
5. You hang wet clothing on this.
7. You hang your shirt on this.

Down

1. You put your clothes in the bureau in this.
2. You use this to hang clothes on the clothesline.
3. You use this to clean difficult stains.
4. You hang your clothes here.
6. You use this on wrinkled clothing.

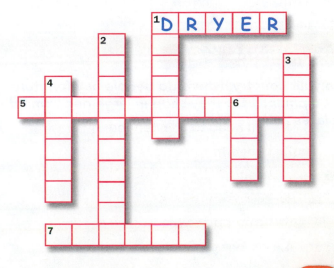

A WHICH DEPARTMENT?

_f_ 1. a bracelet
____ 2. a sofa
____ 3. a blouse
____ 4. a tie
____ 5. a refrigerator
____ 6. a DVD player
____ 7. pajamas for a young girl
____ 8. an iron

a. Women's Clothing
b. Household Appliances
c. Housewares
d. Children's Clothing
e. Men's Clothing
f. Jewelry Counter
g. Electronics
h. Furniture

B WHICH WORD?

1. Let's take the (water fountain   (escalator)) up to the third floor.
2. The (elevator   ladies' room) is the fastest way to the second floor.
3. I'm thirsty. Is there a (Customer Service Counter   water fountain) nearby?
4. I'm hungry. Let's go to the (snack bar   Customer Assistance Counter).
5. Where's the perfume counter? Let's look at the (water fountain   directory).
6. You can pick up the television at the (Gift Wrap Counter   customer pickup area).

C LISTENING

Listen to the conversation. Write the number next to the correct place.

____	Furniture Department	____	snack bar
____	Electronics Department	____	Perfume Counter
1	Jewelry Counter	____	elevator
____	Children's Clothing Department	____	escalator

D JOURNAL

In your country, where do people buy furniture, clothing, household appliances, and electronic equipment? Do they shop in large department stores or in smaller stores? Describe these places and the items they sell.

....

....

....

A WHAT'S THE WORD?

discount	exchange	label	receipt	sale price	size

1. This is where you see the size.   _label_
2. This is how big an item is (S, M, L, XL).   _____
3. This paper shows how much you paid.   _____
4. This shows how much you save.   _____
5. This is the price after the discount.   _____
6. You change one item for another when you do this.   _____

B WHAT'S THE ANSWER?

_f_ 1. What size is the jacket?   a. Dry clean only.
___ 2. What's the material?   b. $74.20.
___ 3. What are the care instructions?   c. $100.
___ 4. Where are the care instructions?   d. On the label.
___ 5. What's the regular price?   e. $4.20.
___ 6. What's the discount?   f. Small.
___ 7. What's the sale price?   g. 30%.
___ 8. What's the sales tax?   h. Cotton.
___ 9. What's the total price?   i. $70.

C WHICH WORD?

1. This jersey is too small. I need to (pay for   (return)) it.
2. This shirt is on sale. What's the (receipt   regular price)?
3. I want to (buy   get) some information about this hat.
4. Before you buy this coat, you should (exchange   try) it on.
5. There's a big (discount   price) on these jackets. I think I'll buy one.
6. This item doesn't have a (receipt   price tag). I wonder how much it costs.

D JOURNAL

How do you shop for clothes in your country? Can you negotiate prices? Is it easy to return items?

....
....
....

A ANOTHER WAY TO SAY IT

Look at page 76 of the Picture Dictionary. Find another way to say the same thing.

1. video camera = _camcorder_
2. CD = _____
3. TV = _____
4. VCR = _____

5. personal CD player = _____
6. tape deck = _____
7. stereo system = _____
8. video = _____

B ASSOCIATIONS

_c_ 1. VCR
___ 2. CD player
___ 3. tape recorder
___ 4. radio
___ 5. turntable
___ 6. camcorder

a. record
b. tuner
c. videotape
d. battery pack
e. audiocassette
f. compact disc

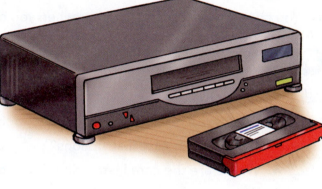

C ANALOGIES

| audiocassette | DVD | headphones | turntable | video game system | videotape |

1. music : CD *as* movie : _____DVD_____
2. CD : record *as* CD player : _____
3. video : VCR *as* video game : _____
4. tape recorder : audiotape *as* camcorder : _____
5. boombox : portable stereo system *as* audiotape : _____
6. sound system : speaker *as* portable digital audio player : _____

D WHAT DO WE USE?

We use this . . .

_e_ 1. to listen to music by ourselves.
___ 2. to change the channel on TV.
___ 3. to play movies.
___ 4. to listen to different stations for news or music.
___ 5. to wake up to music in the morning.
___ 6. to charge batteries.

a. radio
b. DVD player
c. remote
d. battery charger
e. headphones
f. clock radio

A TELEPHONE OR CAMERA?

film	answering machine	fax machine	memory disk
cordless	slide projector	cellular	lens

Telephone

cordless

_____

_____

_____

Camera

_____

_____

_____

_____

B WHAT DO WE USE?

We use this . . .

___d___ **1.** to take a picture.

_____ **2.** to show slides.

_____ **3.** to add, subtract, multiply, and divide.

_____ **4.** to show a movie.

_____ **5.** to organize appointments.

_____ **6.** to store a camera.

_____ **7.** to take digital pictures.

_____ **8.** to store digital photos.

a. a slide projector

b. a movie screen

c. a memory disk

d. a camera

e. a digital camera

f. a calculator

g. a camera case

h. a PDA

C MATCHING

___g___ **1.** cordless

_____ **2.** fax

_____ **3.** voltage

_____ **4.** zoom

_____ **5.** flash

_____ **6.** battery

_____ **7.** memory

_____ **8.** digital

a. machine

b. lens

c. camera

d. charger

e. regulator

f. disk

g. phone

h. attachment

D WHICH WORD?

1. I need to add a lot of numbers. Do you sell ((adding)   answering) machines?

2. I make a lot of calls when I travel. Which (cordless   cell) phone do you recommend?

3. You can hold your camera up on this (tripod   film) when you take a group photo.

4. I need to buy (a memory disk   film) for my 35 millimeter camera.

5. I won't be home, so leave a message on my (fax   answering) machine.

A MATCHING

_e_ **1.** flat panel   **a.** disk
___ **2.** CD-ROM   **b.** program
___ **3.** floppy   **c.** drive
___ **4.** desktop   **d.** protector
___ **5.** surge   **e.** screen
___ **6.** spreadsheet   **f.** computer

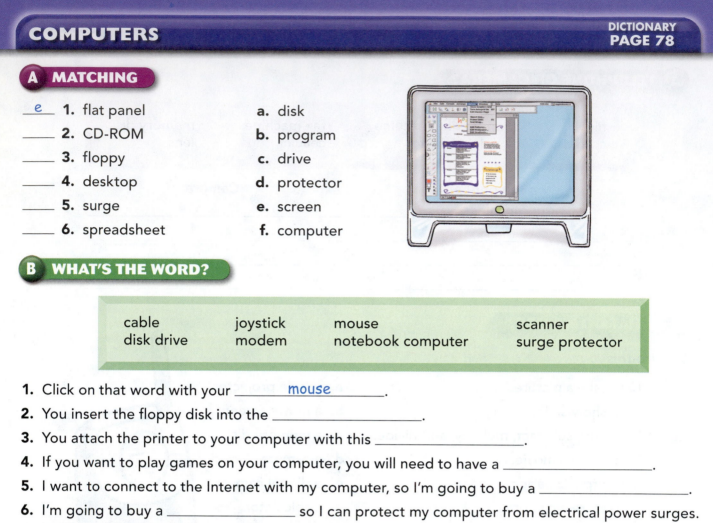

B WHAT'S THE WORD?

cable   joystick   mouse   scanner
disk drive   modem   notebook computer   surge protector

1. Click on that word with your _____ _mouse_ _____.
2. You insert the floppy disk into the _____.
3. You attach the printer to your computer with this _____.
4. If you want to play games on your computer, you will need to have a _____.
5. I want to connect to the Internet with my computer, so I'm going to buy a _____.
6. I'm going to buy a _____ so I can protect my computer from electrical power surges.
7. I copy pictures from newspapers and magazines onto my computer with my _____.
8. I'm going to buy a _____ because I like to do my work when I travel.

C CROSSWORD: *Pictures to Words*

Across

1.   3.

6.   7. ____ ball

Down

2.   4.   5.

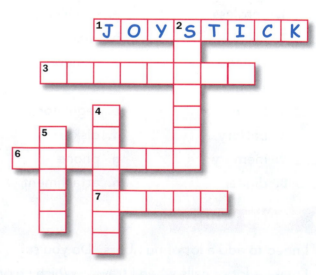

A TOYS

construction set	pail and shovel	tricycle
doll house	skateboard	train set

Toys We Use Inside

construction set

_____

_____

Toys We Use Outside

_____

_____

_____

B MATCHING

_d_ **1.** jump   **a.** ball

____ **2.** rubber   **b.** animal

____ **3.** doll   **c.** hoop

____ **4.** hula   **d.** rope

____ **5.** stuffed   **e.** house

____ **6.** action   **f.** kit

____ **7.** jigsaw   **g.** figure

____ **8.** model   **h.** set

____ **9.** modeling   **i.** puzzle

____ **10.** swing   **j.** clay

C WHAT'S THE WORD?

bicycle	construction set	inflatable pool	rubber ball
coloring book	doll house	paint set	stuffed animal

1. It's hot! Let's cool off in the _____inflatable pool_____!

2. My daughter always sleeps with her _____.

3. You can use your new crayons in your _____.

4. My son Timmy likes to ride his _____.

5. Let's play catch! Throw me that _____.

6. My daughter paints beautiful pictures with her _____.

7. We bought small tables, chairs, rugs, and beds for Susie's _____.

8. My children built a city with bridges and parks with their _____.

D JOURNAL

Write about a special toy you had when you were very young. Why was it special?

....

....

....

A MATCHING

_c_ **1.** security   **a.** machine

____ **2.** safe deposit   **b.** card

____ **3.** cash   **c.** guard

____ **4.** credit   **d.** vault

____ **5.** deposit   **e.** check

____ **6.** traveler's   **f.** box

____ **7.** bank   **g.** slip

B WHICH WORD?

1. Ask the ((teller)   ATM) for change for $100.

2. I don't have any cash. Can I write you a (check   deposit slip)?

3. To put money in your bank account, fill out this (withdrawal   deposit) slip.

4. To take money out of your account, fill out a (deposit   withdrawal) slip.

5. I don't use cash when I shop. I use my (credit card   passbook).

6. My wife works at the First City Bank. She's a bank (book   officer).

7. When you travel to a foreign country, you need to exchange (slips   currency).

8. Don't carry a lot of cash when you go on vacation. It's a good idea to get
(bankbooks   traveler's checks).

C WHAT DO WE DO AT THE BANK?

_e_ **1.** make   **a.** currency

____ **2.** cash   **b.** a loan

____ **3.** open   **c.** a check

____ **4.** exchange   **d.** traveler's checks

____ **5.** apply for   **e.** a deposit

____ **6.** get   **f.** an account

D WHICH WORD DOESN'T BELONG?

1. teller	bank officer	(cash machine)	security guard
2. check	safe deposit box	traveler's check	deposit slip
3. cash machine	vault	safe deposit box	teller
4. deposit slip	withdrawal slip	bankbook	currency
5. bank vault	check	traveler's check	credit card

A WHAT'S THE WORD?

bill	checkbook	monthly statement
cash	money order	payment

1. I can't write a check. I don't have my _____ checkbook _____ with me.
2. The bank will send your _____ in the mail.
3. I need a _____ for $98.79, please.
4. My house wasn't very expensive, but my mortgage _____ is very high.
5. Some stores don't accept credit cards, so you have to pay with _____.
6. My credit card _____ is very high because I did a lot of shopping last month.

B WHICH ONE DOESN'T BELONG?

1. check   credit card   (gas bill)   money order
2. heating bill   checkbook   water bill   rent
3. write a check   remove your card   enter your PIN   insert the ATM card
4. telephone bill   car payment   electric bill   oil bill
5. check register   account number   check number   PIN number

C WHICH WORD?

1. What's your credit card ((number)   order)?
2. Don't forget to pay your (money   heating) bill!
3. I'm too busy to go to a bank. I prefer to bank (payment   online).
4. When you use an ATM machine, you need to enter your (PIN   check) number.
5. I'm trying to balance my (bill   checkbook), but I'm having a lot of trouble.
6. I don't have very much money in my bank account. I need to make a (withdrawal   deposit).

D WHAT'S THE ORDER?

Number the following in the correct order.

	remove your card
	withdraw cash
1	insert the ATM card
	select a transaction
	take your receipt
	enter your PIN number

E LISTENING

Listen and put a check next to the actions you hear.

☐	pay bills	☐	make deposits
☐	use checkbooks	☐	take transaction slips
✓	write checks	☐	select transactions
☐	use credit cards	☐	transfer funds
☐	make withdrawals	☐	remove my card
☐	balance my checkbook		

A MATCHING

_c_ 1. stamp
____ 2. mailing
____ 3. mail
____ 4. postal

a. address
b. clerk
c. machine
d. slot

____ 5. first
____ 6. priority
____ 7. parcel
____ 8. money

e. mail
f. order
g. class
h. post

B SENDING MAIL

1. I want to send this package ((parcel post)   postal clerk), please.
2. Write the mailing address on the (zip code   envelope).
3. I'm going to the post office to mail a (letter carrier   letter).
4. How do you want to send this (parcel   postmark)?
5. I'd like a book of (postage   stamps), please.
6. Please mail this (postcard   mailbox) at the post office.
7. I have to send this letter by (parcel   certified) mail.
8. How much is the (postmark   postage)?
9. I have to send this parcel (post   mail).
10. The letter carrier is sitting in the mail (truck   box).
11. You can buy stamps from the postal clerk or the stamp (slot   machine).
12. Moving? Don't forget a (selective service registration   change-of-address) form!

C WHICH WORD DOESN'T BELONG?

1. postmark — (scale) — address — stamp
2. mail carrier — postal worker — mail truck — postal clerk
3. envelope — postcard — aerogramme — mail slot
4. priority mail — mail bag — certified mail — overnight mail
5. postcard — roll of stamps — letter — parcel
6. money order — first class — parcel post — express mail
7. return address — zip code — postage — letter carrier

D ADDRESSING AN ENVELOPE

Write a friend's mailing address and your return address on the envelope.

A WHERE WILL YOU FIND THESE?

| an atlas | a CD | a DVD | a magazine | a newspaper |
| an audiotape | a dictionary | a journal | microfilm | |

Periodical Section   **Reference Section**   **Media Section**

a journal _____   _____   _____

_____   _____   _____

_____   _____   _____

B AT THE LIBRARY

author	clerk	microfilm reader	reference librarian
CDs	library card	online catalog	shelves
checkout desk	magazines	periodical	title

To find a book at the library, ask the ____reference librarian___ 1,
or look in the _____ 2. You can search for the
name of the _____ 3 or the _____ 4 of the book.
Many books are on the _____ 5. There are also many
newspapers and _____ 6 in the _____ 7
section. You can use a _____ 8 to find
old newspapers on microfilm. You can also find audiotapes or
_____ 9 in most libraries. To take a book out, give your
_____ 10 to the library _____ 11
at the _____ 12.

C LIBRARY ADVICE

_e_ **1.** I don't know the title or the author.

____ **2.** I don't know the meaning of this word.

____ **3.** Is there a DVD about my subject?

____ **4.** I need to look at a map.

____ **5.** I'd like to read a book in Spanish.

____ **6.** I want to make a copy of this article.

____ **7.** I want to take this book out.

____ **8.** I'd like to find a book for my grandson.

____ **9.** Where can I find general information
about this person?

a. There's an atlas in the reference section.

b. The children's section is over there.

c. The copy machine is on the second floor.

d. Check in the foreign language section.

e. Look in the card catalog under the subject.

f. Look it up in the dictionary.

g. Look in the encyclopedia.

h. Go to the checkout desk.

i. Go to the media section.

A MATCH AND WRITE

Draw a line to complete the word. Then write the word on the line.

1. police   hall   ___police officer___
2. activities   pool   _____
3. emergency   engine   _____
4. recycling   officer   _____
5. swimming   director   _____
6. town   operator   _____
7. sanitation   center   _____
8. fire   worker   _____

B WHICH WORD?

1. There are three emergency operators at the ((police station)   dump).
2. I'm going to visit my grandmother at the (senior   recycling) center.
3. We leave our children at the child-care (worker   center) every Tuesday.
4. Our children like to play in the (emergency   game) room.
5. Take your bottles and cans to the (recreation   recycling) center.
6. There's a large (playroom   meeting room) in city hall.
7. I went to the (game   emergency) room when I cut myself.
8. I'm a (sanitation   child-care) worker at the city dump.
9. My brother is an (activities director   eldercare worker) at the recreation center.

C CROSSWORD

Across

5. A ____ works in an ambulance.
6. Another word for paramedic is ____.
7. This person is the leader of a city.

Down

1. Many people go to ____ on Sunday mornings.
2. When you're very sick, you sometimes go to a ____.
3. This person fights fires.
4. Babies at the child-care center sleep in a ____.

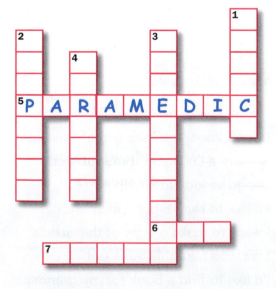

A MATCH AND WRITE

Draw a line to complete the word. Then write the word on the line.

1. car — accident   __car accident__
2. lost   derailment   _____
3. bank   power line   _____
4. train   accident   _____
5. chemical   violence   _____
6. downed   child   _____
7. power   spill   _____
8. gang   robbery   _____
9. drug   outage   _____

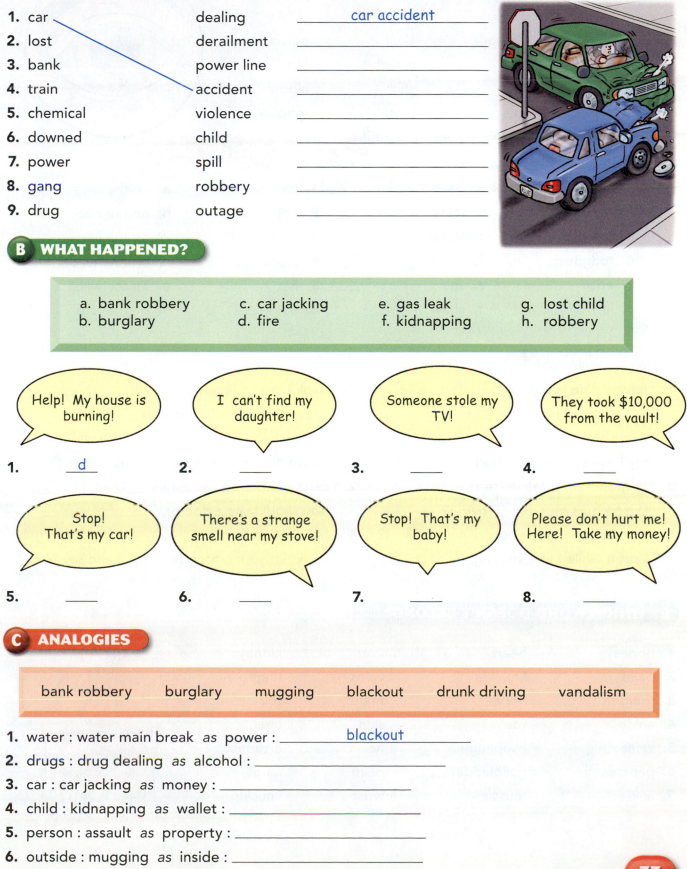

B WHAT HAPPENED?

| a. bank robbery | c. car jacking | e. gas leak | g. lost child |
| b. burglary | d. fire | f. kidnapping | h. robbery |

Help! My house is burning!

I can't find my daughter!

Someone stole my TV!

They took $10,000 from the vault!

1. ___d___   2. _____   3. _____   4. _____

Stop! That's my car!

There's a strange smell near my stove!

Stop! That's my baby!

Please don't hurt me! Here! Take my money!

5. _____   6. _____   7. _____   8. _____

C ANALOGIES

bank robbery   burglary   mugging   blackout   drunk driving   vandalism

1. water : water main break *as* power : _____blackout_____
2. drugs : drug dealing *as* alcohol : _____
3. car : car jacking *as* money : _____
4. child : kidnapping *as* wallet : _____
5. person : assault *as* property : _____
6. outside : mugging *as* inside : _____

A WHICH WORD DOESN'T BELONG?

1. iris	(nose)	cornea	pupil
2. knee	gums	calf	shin
3. tongue	ribcage	skull	pelvis
4. forehead	nose	mouth	hip
5. calf	knee	shin	elbow
6. armpit	lip	teeth	tongue

B ASSOCIATIONS

__e__ **1.** eyes	**a.** hear
____ **2.** ears	**b.** taste
____ **3.** teeth	**c.** stand
____ **4.** tongue	**d.** smell
____ **5.** nose	**e.** see
____ **6.** leg	**f.** chew

C WHERE DO THEY GO?

__b__ **1.** tie	**a.** on the ears
____ **2.** belt	**b.** on the neck
____ **3.** lipstick	**c.** on the lips
____ **4.** stockings	**d.** on the head
____ **5.** hat	**e.** on the waist
____ **6.** earrings	**f.** on the legs

D WHICH WORD?

1. I have a pain in my leg.
Is it your (skin (shin))?

2. What's the matter with your hand?
My (waist   wrist) hurts.

3. My grandfather fell yesterday.
Did he hurt his (hip   hair)?

4. What happened to your (liver   chin)?
I cut it while I was shaving.

5. I think I have a fever.
Let me feel your (forehead   jaw).

6. Can you help me? I can't walk very well.
When did you break your (arm   leg)?

7. I can't bend my (eyelashes   knee).
You should see a doctor.

8. I have a sore throat.
Stick out your (tongue   lip) and say "Ahh."

E WHICH WORD DOESN'T BELONG?

1. (bones)	heart	liver	kidneys
2. palm	knuckle	veins	fingernail
3. thumb	nerve	finger	toe
4. ankle	toe	skin	heel
5. veins	esophagus	heart	arteries
6. pancreas	gallbladder	palm	lungs
7. ankle	muscle	wrist	knuckle

F ASSOCIATIONS

_f_ 1. brain   **a.** digest food

____ 2. finger   **b.** swallow

____ 3. hand   **c.** breathe

____ 4. stomach   **d.** hold

____ 5. heart   **e.** point

____ 6. lungs   **f.** think

____ 7. throat   **g.** pump blood

G WHERE DO THEY GO?

_d_ 1. gloves   **a.** on the wrist

____ 2. scarf   **b.** on the finger

____ 3. shoes   **c.** on the neck

____ 4. ring   **d.** on the hands

____ 5. watch   **e.** on the feet

H WHICH WORD?

1. My son can't breathe very well.

   Did the doctor check his ((lungs) lips)?

2. Why do you think I'm nervous?

   You're biting your (muscles   fingernails).

3. My sister had a car accident!

   Did she break any (gums   bones)?

4. My father is having chest pains.

   The doctor should check his (skin   heart).

5. I think I ate too much!

   Does your (stomach   thigh) hurt?

6. It hurts when I talk.

   You must have a sore (throat   thumb).

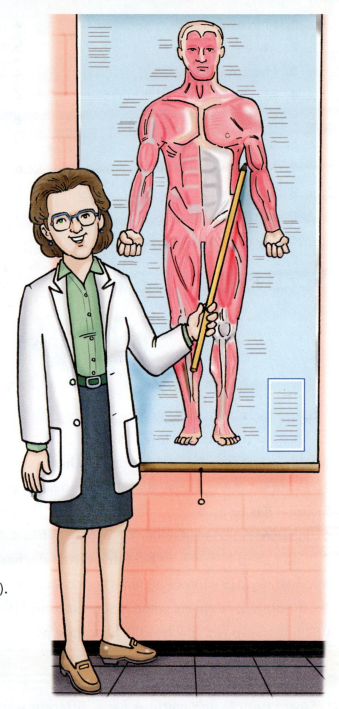

I LISTENING

Listen to the conversation and circle the word you hear.

1. (back)   bladder   5. pupil   tooth

2. bones   nose   6. hip   lip

3. thumb   stomach   7. shin   chin

4. throat   nose   8. gums   thumb

A MATCH THE AILMENTS

_d_	**1.** I have a fever.	**a.**	I have laryngitis.
____	**2.** My ear hurts.	**b.**	I have a backache.
____	**3.** I hurt my back.	**c.**	I have a headache.
____	**4.** My skin is red and it hurts.	**d.**	I have a temperature.
____	**5.** My head hurts.	**e.**	I have a runny nose.
____	**6.** It's hard to talk.	**f.**	I have an earache.
____	**7.** My nose is bleeding.	**g.**	I have a bloody nose.
____	**8.** My stomach feels bad.	**h.**	I have a sore throat.
____	**9.** My throat hurts.	**i.**	I have a sunburn.
____	**10.** My nose is running.	**j.**	I have a stomachache.

B WHAT'S THE MATTER?

backache	chills	fever	sore throat	stomachache
cavity	diarrhea	rash	stiff neck	sunburn

1. Jane feels cold. She has the _____ _chills_ _____.
2. I ate candy all day. Now I have a _____.
3. When Sally swallows, it hurts. She has a _____.
4. Linda sat in the sun all day. Now she has a _____.
5. John has to go to the bathroom often. He has _____.
6. Howard is scratching his skin a lot. He has a _____.
7. Sue pulled a muscle in her back. Now she has a _____.
8. My daughter's forehead feels very warm. She has a _____.
9. Arnold's tooth hurts when he chews food. He has a _____.
10. I fell asleep with my head in a strange position. Now I have a _____.

C JOURNAL

Different people and cultures have different ways to stop the hiccups. How do you stop the hiccups? How did you learn this way?

D FEELING TERRIBLE!

1. My grandmother fell down.
   Did she (sprain   burp) her ankle?

2. I twisted my knee.
   Did you (burn   dislocate) it?

3. I think I have a rash.
   Is it (itchy   bloated)?

4. My wife is sneezing and wheezing.
   She sounds (swollen   congested).

5. I feel nauseous.
   Are you going to (vomit   bruise)?

6. My shoes don't fit!
   Are your feet (dizzy   swollen)?

7. I didn't sleep last night.
   You look (exhausted   itchy).

8. I feel bloated.
   Try to (scrape   burp).

9. Jane fell down and hurt her knee.
   Is she (bleeding   cutting)?

10. I have a cold. I'm congested.
    Are you (twisting   coughing)?

E CROSSWORD: *Pictures to Words*

Across

1.

6.

8.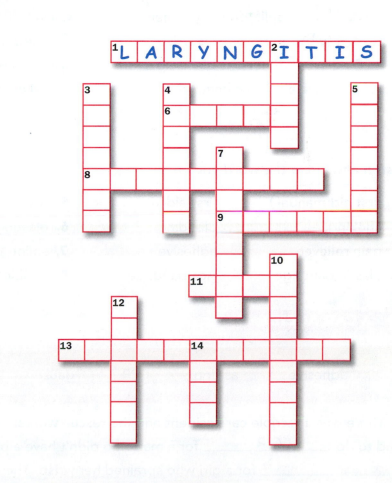

9.

11.

13.

Down

2.

3.

4.

5.

7.

10.

12.

14.

| ¹L | A | R | Y | N | G | ²I | T | I | S |

A MATCHING

_e_ 1. first-aid
____ 2. elastic
____ 3. hydrogen
____ 4. sterile
____ 5. adhesive
____ 6. antihistamine
____ 7. pain
____ 8. antiseptic cleansing

a. peroxide
b. tape
c. cream
d. wipe
e. kit
f. pad
g. bandage
h. reliever

B WHAT'S THE TREATMENT?

_c_ 1. My friend has no pulse!
____ 2. That man is choking!
____ 3. I have a splinter in my finger!
____ 4. My brother broke his wrist!
____ 5. My friend's arm is bleeding a lot!
____ 6. I have a terrible headache!

a. Do the Heimlich Maneuver!
b. Make a splint!
c. Do CPR!
d. Take some aspirin!
e. Use these tweezers!
f. Make a tourniquet!

C LISTENING

Listen and circle the word you hear.

1. (first-aid manual)   first-aid kit
2. choking   bleeding
3. pain reliever   adhesive
4. elastic bandage   Ace bandage

5. tourniquet   tweezers
6. elastic   Heimlich
7. splint   sterile
8. antibiotic   antiseptic

D A CAR ACCIDENT

| adhesive | aspirin | CPR | gauze | rescue | splint |

There was a terrible car accident and the rescue workers were very busy. First, they had to do _____CPR_____ [1] for a man who didn't have a pulse. Then, they had to make a _____ [2] for a girl who sprained her wrist. They also had to use a lot of _____ [3] and _____ [4] tape for all the people with scrapes and cuts. Many people had to take _____ [5] for their pain. And for a few people who weren't breathing, they had to perform_____ [6] breathing. It was a terrible accident.

A MATCH AND WRITE

Draw a line to complete the word. Then write the word on the line.

1. chicken — infection
2. ear — shock
3. strep — reaction
4. electric — pox
5. allergic — disease
6. heart — throat

<u>chicken pox</u>

_____

_____

_____

_____

_____

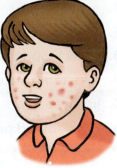

B ILLNESS OR EMERGENCY?

allergic reaction	diabetes	heart attack	measles
asthma	fall	heart disease	mumps
chicken pox	frostbite	heatstroke	unconscious

Illnesses	Emergencies
asthma	allergic reaction

C ASSOCIATIONS

<u>c</u> 1. earache   **a.** strep throat | ____ 4. shortness of breath   **d.** chicken pox

____ 2. laryngitis   **b.** heart attack | ____ 5. fever and runny nose   **e.** asthma

____ 3. chest pain   **c.** ear infection | ____ 6. itchy skin   **f.** influenza

D WHICH WORD?

1. I think my husband is having a heart ((attack) disease).
2. My uncle was (electric in) shock after he fell.
3. My grandmother fell and was (injured depression).
4. It hurts when I swallow. I might have (frostbite strep throat).
5. Help! My son is having an (allergic reaction ear infection)!
6. If you have (hypertension TB), you might have a heart attack.
7. I have trouble breathing when I run because I have (the mumps asthma).
8. I have to be careful about my diet because I have (diabetes depression).

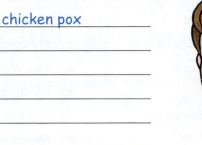

A ASSOCIATIONS

_d_ 1. examine eyes
___ 2. measure weight
___ 3. draw blood
___ 4. take temperature
___ 5. listen to heart
___ 6. check blood pressure
___ 7. take pictures

a. scale
b. X-ray machine
c. stethoscope
d. eye chart
e. blood pressure gauge
f. needle
g. thermometer

B WHAT WILL THEY USE?

eye chart	room	stethoscope	table	X-ray machine
gauge	scale	syringe	thermometer	

1. I'd like to weigh you. Please step on the _____ scale _____.
2. Put this _____ under your tongue.
3. Please sit down on the examination _____.
4. Look at the _____, and I'll check your vision.
5. We need to take some blood with this _____.
6. A doctor uses a _____ to listen to your heart.
7. Let's take a picture. Please step over here to the _____.
8. The doctor walked into the examination _____ and greeted the patient.
9. I'm going to use this blood pressure _____ to take your blood pressure.

C THE MEDICAL EXAM

asked	drew	listen to	took
checked	examined	measured	

I had a medical appointment yesterday, and the doctor did many things. At the beginning of the appointment, the doctor _____ examined _____ [1] my eyes, nose, and throat. She also _____ [2] my height and weight. Then, she used a stethoscope to _____ [3] my heart. Then I told her I wasn't feeling well so she _____ [4] my temperature and _____ [5] my blood pressure, and then she _____ [6] some blood. Finally, the doctor _____ [7] me some questions about my health and gave me some advice.

MEDICAL AND DENTAL PROCEDURES

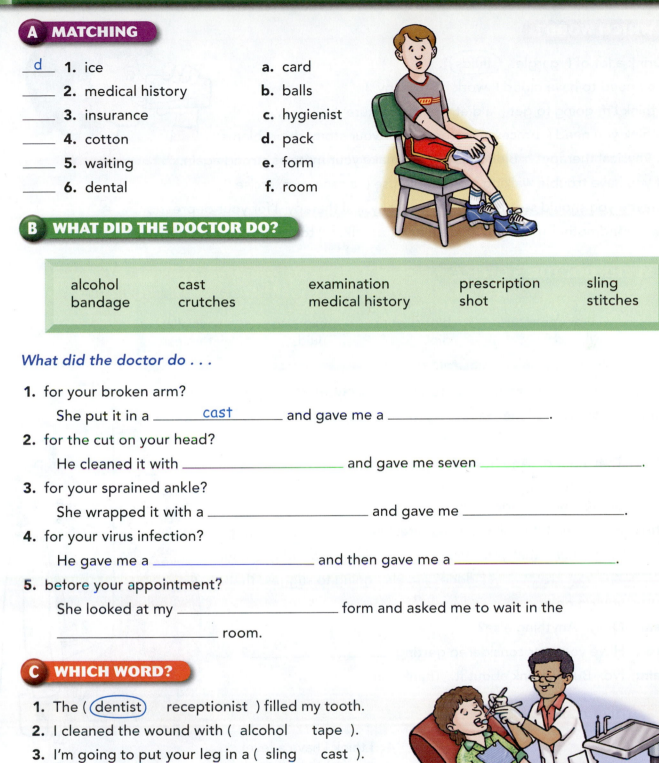

A MATCHING

__d__ **1.** ice

_____ **2.** medical history

_____ **3.** insurance

_____ **4.** cotton

_____ **5.** waiting

_____ **6.** dental

a. card

b. balls

c. hygienist

d. pack

e. form

f. room

B WHAT DID THE DOCTOR DO?

alcohol	cast	examination	prescription	sling
bandage	crutches	medical history	shot	stitches

What did the doctor do . . .

1. for your broken arm?

She put it in a _____cast_____ and gave me a _____.

2. for the cut on your head?

He cleaned it with _____ and gave me seven _____.

3. for your sprained ankle?

She wrapped it with a _____ and gave me _____.

4. for your virus infection?

He gave me a _____ and then gave me a _____.

5. before your appointment?

She looked at my _____ form and asked me to wait in the _____ room.

C WHICH WORD?

1. The ((dentist)   receptionist) filled my tooth.

2. I cleaned the wound with (alcohol   tape).

3. I'm going to put your leg in a (sling   cast).

4. The dental (drill   hygienist) cleaned my teeth.

5. I got three (fillings   bandages) in my teeth yesterday.

6. The doctor used stitches to (dress   close) my wound.

7. Use this (insurance card   ice pack) to reduce swelling.

8. The doctor will see you in the (examination   waiting) room.

9. The nurse wore (gloves   a brace) when he cleaned a wound.

10. The physician wore (crutches   a mask) to protect herself from infection.

A WHICH WORD?

1. Drink a lot of (gargle (fluids)).
2. You need to have blood (work therapy).
3. I think I'm going to get (a diet acupuncture).
4. I think you need (braces surgery) for your stomach problems.
5. (Physical therapy Blood tests) will make your muscles strong again.
6. If you have trouble walking, you should use (a cane exercise).
7. Maybe you should see a (counselor physical therapy) for your depression.
8. My grandmother uses (an air purifier a walker) to help her get around her apartment.

B AT THE DOCTOR'S OFFICE

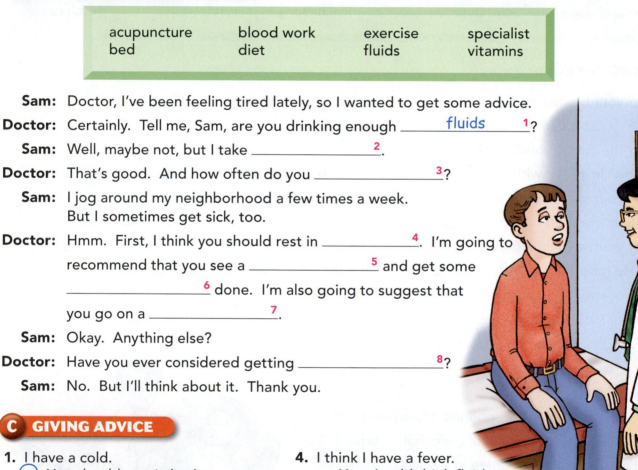

| acupuncture | blood work | exercise | specialist |
| bed | diet | fluids | vitamins |

Sam: Doctor, I've been feeling tired lately, so I wanted to get some advice.

Doctor: Certainly. Tell me, Sam, are you drinking enough ____fluids____ 1?

Sam: Well, maybe not, but I take _____ 2.

Doctor: That's good. And how often do you _____ 3?

Sam: I jog around my neighborhood a few times a week.
But I sometimes get sick, too.

Doctor: Hmm. First, I think you should rest in _____ 4. I'm going to
recommend that you see a _____ 5 and get some
_____ 6 done. I'm also going to suggest that
you go on a _____ 7.

Sam: Okay. Anything else?

Doctor: Have you ever considered getting _____ 8?

Sam: No. But I'll think about it. Thank you.

C GIVING ADVICE

1. I have a cold.
   a. You should rest in bed.
   b. You should get braces.

2. My back is aching.
   a. You need blood tests.
   b. You should use a heating pad.

3. My pants feel too tight!
   a. Why don't you go on a diet?
   b. Here! Use a wheelchair.

4. I think I have a fever.
   a. You should drink fluids.
   b. You need to exercise.

5. I have a sore throat!
   a. Try this cane.
   b. Gargle with this medicine.

6. My allergies are really bothering me.
   a. You need to get an air purifier.
   b. I think you should take vitamins.

A SOLUTIONS

1. My throat hurts.
   Use a throat ((lozenge)   syrup).

2. I'm coughing a lot.
   Use some (cough   eye) drops.

3. I'm tired. I don't have any energy.
   Take some (vitamins   teaspoons).

4. I have a headache.
   Take some (antacid tablets   aspirin).

5. I have a rash on my back.
   Use this (tablespoon   ointment).

6. I have an upset stomach.
   Take (antacid   cold) tablets.

7. I have a stuffy nose.
   Use (decongestant spray   eye drops).

8. My muscles are sore.
   Use this (reliever   ointment).

9. I have a rash. It itches a lot.
   Put this (cream   syrup) on it.

10. I'm allergic to aspirin.
    Use non-aspirin (pain reliever   spray).

B WHAT'S THE MEDICINE?

Choose the correct medicine.

1. Rx   Take one teaspoon every four hours.
   a. aspirin   (**b.**) cough syrup

2. Rx   Use three times a day.
   a. vitamins   **b.** nasal spray

3. Rx   Use every night before you go to bed.
   a. eye drops   **b.** tablespoon

4. Rx   Put two tablets in a glass of water.
   a. antacid   **b.** cough drops

5. Rx   Use instead of soap.
   a. tablet   **b.** cream

6. Rx   Take two caplets and rest in bed.
   a. decongestant spray   **b.** aspirin

7. Rx   Take one every day.
   a. vitamin   **b.** cough syrup

C LISTENING: What's the Dosage?

Listen to the directions. Circle the correct answer.

1. (3 tablespoons)   3 teaspoons
2. 2 caplets   2 tablets
3. 4 capsules   4 caplets
4. 1 teaspoon   1 tablespoon

5. 1 tablet   1 pill
6. 5 capsules   5 caplets
7. 4 teaspoons   4 capsules
8. 7 caplets   11 tablets

A WHO ARE THEY?

a. allergist	d. gastroenterologist	g. ophthalmologist	j. therapist
b. audiologist	e. gerontologist	h. orthodontist	
c. cardiologist	f. gynecologist	i. pediatrician	

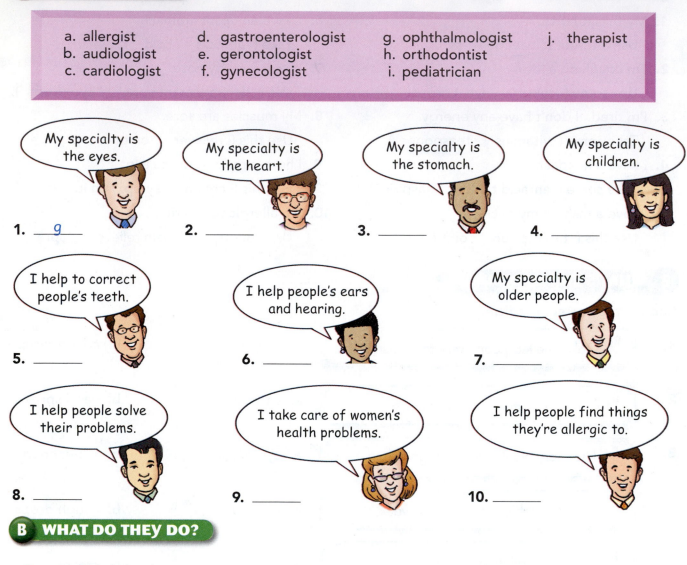

My specialty is the eyes.

1. ___g___

My specialty is the heart.

2. _____

My specialty is the stomach.

3. _____

My specialty is children.

4. _____

I help to correct people's teeth.

5. _____

I help people's ears and hearing.

6. _____

My specialty is older people.

7. _____

I help people solve their problems.

8. _____

I take care of women's health problems.

9. _____

I help people find things they're allergic to.

10. _____

B WHAT DO THEY DO?

__e__ 1. Ophthalmologists   a. give counseling.

____ 2. Physical therapists   b. work with the ear, nose, and throat.

____ 3. ENT specialists   c. use needles to heal.

____ 4. Psychiatrists   d. fix the spinal cord and nerves.

____ 5. Chiropractors   e. work with people's vision.

____ 6. Acupuncturists   f. help people recover from injuries.

C LISTENING: *What Kind of Doctor?*

Listen to the sentence and circle the correct answer.

1. (cardiologist) counselor

2. acupuncturist orthodontist

3. allergist chiropractor

4. gynecologist audiologist

5. pediatrician gerontologist

6. gastroenterologist physical therapist

7. allergist psychiatrist

8. ophthalmologist ENT specialist

A WHICH WORD?

1. Put on this hospital (bed   (gown)).
2. The lab technician put the (I.V.   gurney) in my arm.
3. If you can't walk to the bathroom, use the bed (pan   table).
4. Women usually have babies in the (waiting   delivery) room.
5. The (X-ray   lab) technician will take a picture of your ribcage.
6. I'm only (a volunteer   an obstetrician). I can't deliver babies.
7. The nurse will write the information on the (cast   medical chart).
8. You can change the position of the bed. Push the bed (control   pan).
9. The (surgeon   patient) did Mrs. Martino's operation early this morning.

B WHAT DO THEY DO?

__d__ **1.** A surgeon
____ **2.** A midwife
____ **3.** An EMT
____ **4.** An orderly
____ **5.** A physician
____ **6.** A dietitian
____ **7.** An anesthesiologist
____ **8.** A patient

a. does CPR.
b. receives medical treatment.
c. reads your medical chart.
d. does surgery.
e. helps you sleep before surgery.
f. delivers babies.
g. cleans the operating room.
h. tells you what to eat.

C CROSSWORD

Across

2. The ____ put the patient in the wheelchair.
5. A lab ____ does blood tests.
7. You can see the patient's heart rate on the vital signs ____.
8. A ____ helps deliver babies.

Down

1. A ____ nurse helps the surgeon in the operating room.
3. This person works with X-rays.
4. Press the call ____ if you need a nurse.
6. They brought the patient into the emergency room on a ____.

²O ³R D E R L Y

A ASSOCIATIONS

__b__ 1. toothbrush   a. hair

____ 2. blush   b. teeth

____ 3. emery board   c. cheeks

____ 4. mascara   d. eyelashes

____ 5. comb   e. skin

____ 6. body lotion   f. fingernails

B WHAT DO I USE?

__b__ 1. I use a razor   a. to wash my hair.

____ 2. I use shampoo   b. to shave.

____ 3. I use shoe polish   c. to tie my shoes.

____ 4. I use dental floss   d. to shine my shoes.

____ 5. I use hairspray   e. to clean between my teeth.

____ 6. I use sunscreen   f. to keep my hair neat.

____ 7. I use shoelaces   g. to cut my fingernails and toenails.

____ 8. I use a nail clipper   h. to protect my skin from the sun.

C WHICH WORD DOESN'T BELONG?

1. perfume   cologne   (mascara)   aftershave

2. shampoo   shower cap   rinse   conditioner

3. bobby pins   hair clips   nail polish   barrettes

4. mouthwash   hairspray   toothpaste   dental floss

5. lipstick   blush   eye shadow   styptic pencil

6. emery board   shoe polish   nail polish   nail brush

D WHAT DO THEY NEED?

1. I'm styling my hair. Can I have some ((hair gel)   shampoo)?

2. Do you have a (blow dryer   shower cap)? I need to dry my hair.

3. I just finished shaving. Do you have any (shaving cream   aftershave)?

4. I'd like to (take a bath   whiten my teeth). Where is the soap?

5. My hands are so dry! Can I borrow some (deodorant   hand lotion)?

6. When I put on makeup, I like to use an (eyebrow pencil   electric shaver).

7. Do you have any mouthwash so I can (gargle   bathe)?

8. I want to do my nails, but I can't find the nail (polish   pencil).

9. Do you think I should use (a razor   moisturizer) before I put on makeup?

A MATCH AND WRITE

Draw a line to complete the word. Then write the word on the line.

1. baby   pin
2. diaper   chair
3. child-care   swab
4. rocking   food
5. cotton   diaper
6. training   center
7. disposable   pants

baby food
_____
_____
_____
_____
_____
_____

B WHICH WORD?

1. I have to wash the (formula   (teething ring)).
2. Give the baby his (diaper pins   vitamins).
3. The baby loves to (play   read) with her new toys.
4. Put this bib on the baby before you (feed   bathe) her.
5. We need to buy a new (food   nipple) for this bottle.
6. She doesn't like milk. She drinks (baby lotion   formula).
7. I always clean my baby's ears with (cotton swabs   baby wipes).
8. You can wash the baby's hair with this baby (shampoo   food).
9. The child-care worker likes to (bathe   rock) the baby in her arms.
10. Please throw those used (disposable   cloth) diapers in the trash!
11. Uh-oh! It looks like we need to (change   dress) the baby's diaper.
12. I want to wash the baby's hair. Where's the (baby shampoo   teething ring)?

C CROSSWORD: *Pictures to Words*

Across

5.   6.   7.

Down

1.   2.

3.   4.

A WHICH TYPE OF SCHOOL?

1. How old is your son?

He's nine years old. He goes to ((elementary) law) school.

2. I think I want to be a doctor.

You'll have to go to (adult medical) school.

3. My daughter is going to be four years old.

When is she going to begin (nursery trade) school?

4. I want to be an electrician.

You'll need to go to a (vocational graduate) school.

5. Do you want to go to college next year?

I can't. I'm still in (medical high) school.

6. Are you a student?

Yes. I'm studying English at (a junior an adult) school.

7. I want to be a lawyer after I graduate from college.

You'll have to go to (law high) school.

8. Are you a student?

Yes. I'm studying engineering at a (community middle) college.

9. Our little Johnny is growing up so fast!

I know. Now he's in elementary school, and soon he'll be in (junior high graduate) school.

B ASSOCIATIONS

_C_ **1.** lawyer	**a.** medical school
____ **2.** physician	**b.** university
____ **3.** teenager	**c.** law school
____ **4.** plumber	**d.** elementary school
____ **5.** young child	**e.** trade school
____ **6.** professor	**f.** high school

C WHICH WORD DOESN'T BELONG?

1. preschool   (college)   nursery school   elementary school

2. high school   adult school   university   graduate school

3. law school   middle school   elementary school   high school

4. trade school   law school   graduate school   medical school

5. adult   community   trade   medical

A AT SCHOOL

1. Put your books in your (bleachers **locker**).
2. I'm going to the (cafeteria   science lab) for lunch.
3. I'm going to the (library   field) to practice soccer.
4. I'm sick. I'm going to see the (nurse   custodian).
5. We're going to run around the (coach   track).
6. You should change your clothes in the (locker room   hallway).
7. Carla likes biology. She's often in the (auditorium   science lab).
8. I'm going to the principal's office to see the (principal   cafeteria worker).
9. I'm going to get some career advice in the (cafeteria   guidance office).
10. All basketball players should go to the (classroom   gymnasium) for practice.

B ASSOCIATIONS

__c__ 1. science teacher   **a.** gym
____ 2. P.E. teacher   **b.** cleaning
____ 3. teacher   **c.** science lab
____ 4. custodian   **d.** classroom

____ 5. school nurse   **e.** books
____ 6. librarian   **f.** cafeteria
____ 7. security officer   **g.** sickness
____ 8. lunchroom   **h.** safety
      monitor

C MY SCHOOL

auditorium	library	nurse's office	track
guidance office	main office	science lab	

I went to a new school today for the first time. The assistant principal gave me a tour of the school and showed me all the important places. First, she took me to the ___guidance office___ [1] to meet my guidance counselor. Then, she took me to the _____ [2], where I could find all the books in the school. After that, she showed me the _____ [3], where I should go if I feel sick. Then, she took me to the _____ [4], where all the students get together for important events. Next, she took me to meet a few of my teachers. My science teacher was in the _____ [5], and my P.E. teacher was outside at the _____ [6]. At the end of the tour, we went back to the _____ [7] so I could meet the school secretary. I know I'm going to like my new school!

A WHERE DO THESE SUBJECTS BELONG?

| biology | driver's ed | French | industrial arts | Spanish |
| chemistry | English | home economics | physics | |

Sciences	Languages	Lifeskills
biology		

B ASSOCIATIONS

_d_ **1.** sports, exercise
____ **2.** countries, mountains, rivers
____ **3.** flowers, animals
____ **4.** dates, wars, famous people
____ **5.** cooking, sewing
____ **6.** painting, drawing
____ **7.** computers, programs
____ **8.** grammar, literature

a. geography
b. English
c. home economics
d. physical education
e. computer science
f. biology
g. art
h. history

C LISTENING: *What Are They Talking About?*

Listen and circle the correct word.

1. physics   (geography)
2. art   Spanish
3. French   computer science

4. health   physical education
5. history   health
6. government   chemistry

D CROSSWORD: *Which Class?*

Across

2. tools, metal, wood
7. all about our bodies
8. playing and listening to songs
9. important people and events

Down

1. national systems, policies
3. biology, physics, chemistry
4. grammar, novels, poems
5. 4 x 2 = 8
6. the language of Mexico

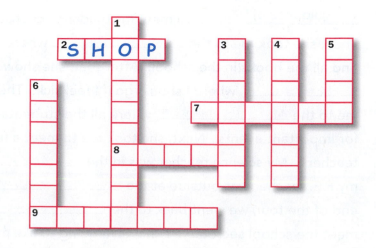

A WHAT ACTIVITIES DO THEY DO?

_c_ **1.** I like to play chess.

____ **2.** I'm acting in a play.

____ **3.** I like to sing.

____ **4.** I like to write poetry.

____ **5.** I'm the president of the class.

____ **6.** I like to cheer for sports.

____ **7.** I like to write about school news.

____ **8.** I use video equipment.

____ **9.** I play the violin.

____ **10.** I play drums when we march.

a. She's in the drama club.

b. She's on the pep squad.

c. He's in the chess club.

d. He works for the school newspaper.

e. He's in the orchestra.

f. She's part of the A.V. crew.

g. She's in the school band.

h. He's in school government.

i. She works for the literary magazine.

j. He's in the choir.

B WHICH ACTIVITY IS THE BEST?

1. I want to meet people from other countries.

The (debate   (international)) club is best for you.

2. I love sports!

You should join the (football team   chess club).

3. I want to play music, especially classical music.

You should be in the (orchestra   band)

4. I'd like to take pictures of the students and the school.

You ought to join the (yearbook   A.V. crew).

5. I want to help my local neighborhood.

You should do some (cheerleading   community service).

C WHICH ACTIVITY DOESN'T BELONG?

1. computer club	debate club	(football)
2. orchestra	student government	band
3. football	drama	cheerleading
4. A.V. crew	school newspaper	drama
5. choir	literary magazine	school newspaper

D LISTENING: *What Are They Talking About?*

Listen and circle the correct word.

1. yearbook	(chorus)	**4.** drama	orchestra
2. computer club	school newspaper	**5.** community service	debate club
3. football	band	**6.** international club	pep squad

A MATH ASSOCIATIONS

__b__ 1. plus
____ 2. times
____ 3. minus
____ 4. divided by

a. multiplication
b. addition
c. division
d. subtraction

B SYMBOLS AND WORDS

__d__ 1. 9 times 2 equals 18.
____ 2. 18 divided by 9 is 2.
____ 3. 18 minus 9 equals 9.
____ 4. 9 plus 9 is 18.

a. $18 \div 9 = 2$
b. $9 + 9 = 18$
c. $18 - 9 = 9$
d. $9 \times 2 = 18$

____ 5. $12 \div 3 = 4$
____ 6. $9 + 4 = 13$
____ 7. $16 - 9 = 7$
____ 8. $6 \times 3 = 18$

e. 9 plus 4 is 13.
f. 6 times 3 equals 18.
g. 12 divided by 3 is 4.
h. 16 minus 9 equals 7.

C MATH SENTENCES

Write the math problems for these sentences.

$5 \times 4 = 20$			

1. Five times four is twenty.
2. Twenty-four minus ten is fourteen.
3. Sixteen divided by four equals four.
4. Seven plus eighteen is twenty-five.

D WORDS AND FRACTIONS

__c__ 1. one half
____ 2. one quarter
____ 3. two thirds
____ 4. one third
____ 5. three fourths

a. 1/4
b. 1/3
c. 1/2
d. 3/4
e. 2/3

E WORDS AND PERCENTS

__d__ 1. fifty percent
____ 2. ten percent
____ 3. one hundred percent
____ 4. seventy-five percent
____ 5. thirty-three percent

a. 10%
b. 75%
c. 33%
d. 50%
e. 100%

F. WHAT FRACTION IS IT?

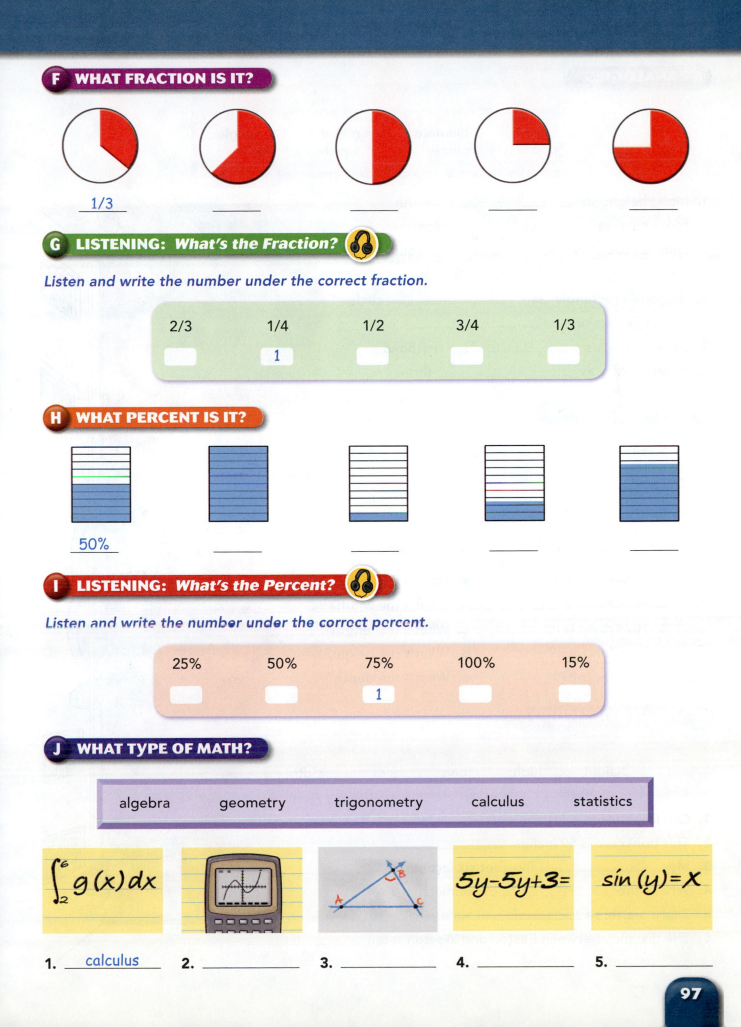

1/3   ___   ___   ___   ___

G. LISTENING: *What's the Fraction?*

Listen and write the number under the correct fraction.

2/3	1/4	1/2	3/4	1/3
	1			

H. WHAT PERCENT IS IT?

50%   ___   ___   ___   ___

I. LISTENING: *What's the Percent?*

Listen and write the number under the correct percent.

25%	50%	75%	100%	15%
		1		

J. WHAT TYPE OF MATH?

algebra   geometry   trigonometry   calculus   statistics

1. _calculus_   2. _____   3. _____   4. _____   5. _____

A ANALOGIES

cube	diameter	meter	triangle
depth	ellipse	square	wide

1. high : height as _____wide_____ : width

2. foot : mile as _____ : kilometer

3. sphere : circle as _____ : square

4. length: long as _____ : deep

5. diagonal : rectangle as _____ : circle

6. rectangle : square as _____ : circle

7. circle : cone as _____ : pyramid

8. square : four as _____ : three

B ABBREVIATIONS

__b__ 1. kilometer   a. mi.

____ 2. inch   b. km.

____ 3. mile   c. "

____ 4. foot   d. cm.

____ 5. centimeter   e. m.

____ 6. meter   f. '

C WHICH HAS THE SAME MEANING?

__b__ 1. How wide is it?   a. What's the distance?

____ 2. How tall is it?   b. What's the width?

____ 3. How deep is it?   c. What's the length?

____ 4. How long is it?   d. What's the height?

____ 5. How far is it?   e. What's the depth?

D WHAT'S THE WORD?

feet	height	high	long	miles	width

1. Our living room is fifteen feet _____long_____.

2. This bookcase is 59 inches _____.

3. My _____ is five feet six inches.

4. What's the _____ of your kitchen?

5. There are three _____ in a yard.

6. The distance between Easton and Weston is ten _____.

A WHICH PART OF SPEECH?

_b_ **1.** sofa
____ **2.** of
____ **3.** bring
____ **4.** we

a. preposition
b. noun
c. pronoun
d. verb

____ **5.** he
____ **6.** the
____ **7.** quickly
____ **8.** beautiful

e. adverb
f. adjective
g. article
h. pronoun

B PUNCTUATION MATCH

Match the symbol with its name.

_c_ **1.**

a. comma

____ **2.**

b. exclamation point

____ **3.**

c. period

____ **4.**

d. question mark

____ **5.**

e. semi-colon

____ **6.**

f. quotation marks

____ **7.**

g. apostrophe

____ **8.**

h. colon

C THE WRITING PROCESS

| brainstorm | feedback | first draft | revise |
| corrections | final copy | organize | title |

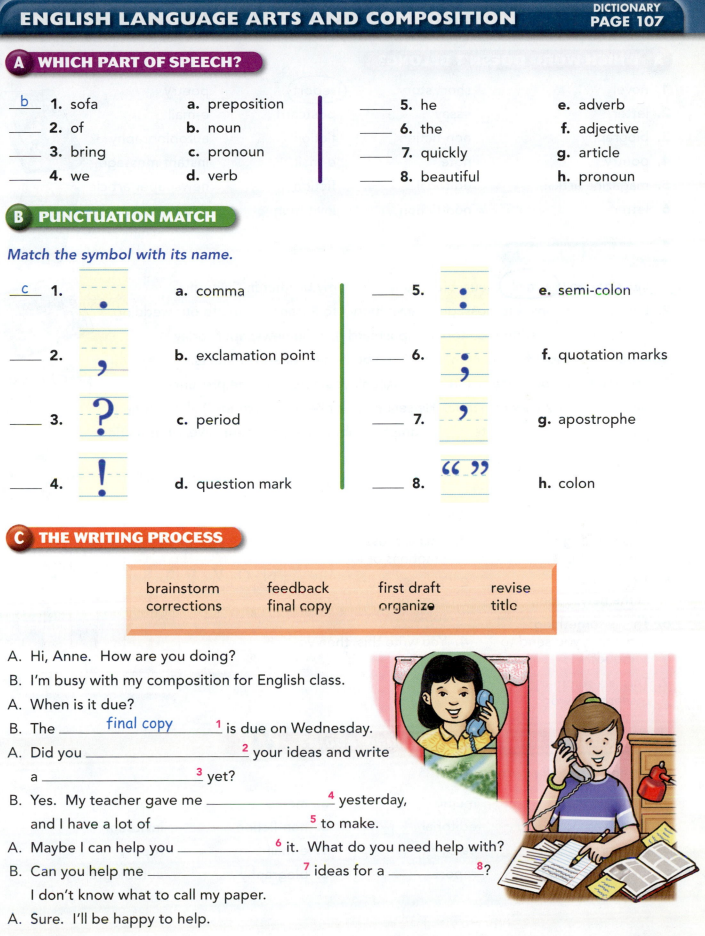

A. Hi, Anne. How are you doing?

B. I'm busy with my composition for English class.

A. When is it due?

B. The _____final copy_____ ¹ is due on Wednesday.

A. Did you _____ ² your ideas and write

a _____ ³ yet?

B. Yes. My teacher gave me _____ ⁴ yesterday,

and I have a lot of _____ ⁵ to make.

A. Maybe I can help you _____ ⁶ it. What do you need help with?

B. Can you help me _____ ⁷ ideas for a _____ ⁸?

I don't know what to call my paper.

A. Sure. I'll be happy to help.

B. Thanks!

A WHICH WORD DOESN'T BELONG?

1. novel	short story	report	poetry
2. letter	essay	postcard	e-mail
3. biography	non-fiction	fiction	autobiography
4. poetry	note	e-mail	instant message
5. magazine article	editorial	fiction	newspaper article
6. letter	non-fiction	invitation	thank-you note

B WHICH WORD?

1. I just got an (e-mail   autobiography) from my brother in California.
2. Let's mail an (instant message   invitation) to Susan to come to our wedding.
3. There's an interesting (editorial   postcard) in the newspaper today.
4. I prefer to read (fiction   non-fiction) because it deals with facts.
5. Did you send your sister a (report   thank-you note) for the present?
6. My boyfriend is very romantic. He sends me (poems   memos) all the time.
7. This new (thank-you note   biography) about the president is very interesting.

C CROSSWORD

Across

3. This is a long story in a book.
5. This is usually in the newspaper.
6. This is something short that you send to somebody.
7. This is a summary of research or work.

Down

1. This expresses emotions or ideas.
2. This is a short composition on one topic.
4. You write this, then you mail it.

³N O V E ⁴L

D LISTENING: What Are They Talking About?

Listen and circle the correct word.

1. novel	memo	5. memo	short story
2. thank-you note	editorial	6. non-fiction	invitation
3. postcard	essay	7. e-mail	report
4. instant message	report	8. biography	autobiography

A WHICH WORD?

1. Let's take a hike in the ((forest)   pond).
2. We're going to take our canoe down the (waterfall   river).
3. They went fishing in the (rainforest   brook).
4. It isn't a mountain. It's just a little (hill   stream).
5. Let's take our boat into the (plateau   bay).
6. The (seashore   canyon) is the best place for surfing.
7. You'll have to take a boat to that (peninsula   island).
8. We took a nice walk through the (meadow   pond).
9. There's a farm in the (valley   desert) between the two mountain ranges.

B WHICH WORD DOESN'T BELONG?

1. stream   brook   river   (forest)
2. meadow   shore   plains   plateau
3. canyon   woods   jungle   rainforest
4. river   ocean   rainforest   lake
5. hill   mountain   sand dune   valley
6. desert   island   peninsula   seashore

C WHAT'S THE PLACE?

__c__ 1. a hot and dry place   a. island
____ 2. the tallest part of a mountain   b. ocean
____ 3. a place with trees and animals   c. desert
____ 4. high and flat land   d. woods
____ 5. water and waves   e. dune
____ 6. a hill of sand   f. rainforest
____ 7. a hot place with lots of trees and rain g. peak
____ 8. land surrounded by water   h. plateau

D JOURNAL

What type of geographical area do you like most? What do you like to do there?

....

....

....

....

A   WHAT'S THE OBJECT?

1. We measure liquids with a graduated c y l i n d e r .
2. We heat things with a __ __ __ __ __ __ __   __ __ __ __ __ __ .
3. We see small things with a __ __ __ __ __ __ __ __ __ __ .
4. We grow bacteria in a __ __ __ __ __   __ __ __ __ .
5. We store data with a __ __ __ __ __ __ __ __ __ .
6. We attract metals with a __ __ __ __ __ __ .
7. We weigh objects with a __ __ __ __ __ .

B   WHICH WORD?

1. Pour this liquid into the (computer   (test tube)).
2. We need a (microscope   prism) to see very small things.
3. Measure some water and pour it into the (Petri dish   beaker).
4. It's very hot! Be careful and use the (crucible tongs   balance)!
5. Put this on a (magnet   slide) and look at it under the microscope.
6. Use a (flask   dropper) to put a few drops of that chemical into the test tube.

C   WHAT DO WE USE IT FOR?

_b_ **1.** prism	**a.** weigh objects
___ **2.** funnel	**b.** bend light
___ **3.** balance	**c.** hold objects
___ **4.** forceps	**d.** drip liquids
___ **5.** flask	**e.** pour liquids
___ **6.** dropper	**f.** keep chemicals

D   THE SCIENTIFIC METHOD

doing	draw	form	make	plan	state

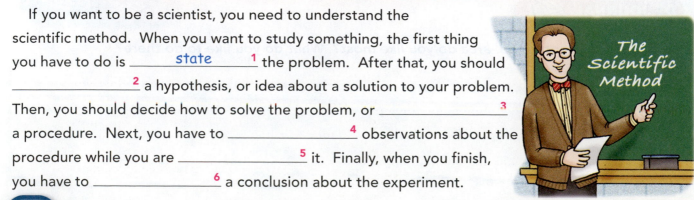

If you want to be a scientist, you need to understand the
scientific method. When you want to study something, the first thing
you have to do is _____state_____ ¹ the problem. After that, you should
_____ ² a hypothesis, or idea about a solution to your problem.
Then, you should decide how to solve the problem, or _____ ³
a procedure. Next, you have to _____ ⁴ observations about the
procedure while you are _____ ⁵ it. Finally, when you finish,
you have to _____ ⁶ a conclusion about the experiment.

The Scientific Method

A DO YOU REMEMBER?

Students in the US sometimes memorize the names of the nine planets by learning:

"**M**y **V**ery **E**nergetic **M**other **J**ust **S**erved **U**s **N**ine **P**izzas."

Without looking at the Picture Dictionary, can you write the names of the nine planets in the correct order?

M: _____Mercury_____   M: _____   U: _____

V: _____   J: _____   N: _____

E: _____   S: _____   P: _____

B WHICH KIND OF MOON?

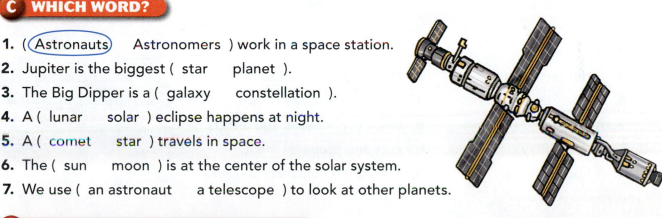

1. _____crescent_____   2. _____   3. _____   4. _____
   moon   moon   moon   moon

C WHICH WORD?

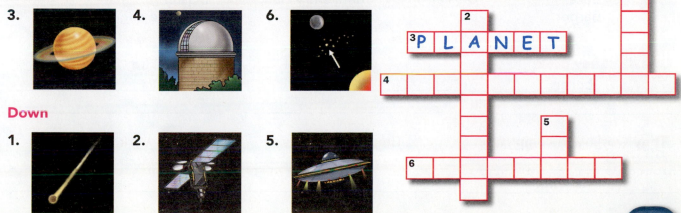

1. ((Astronauts)   Astronomers) work in a space station.
2. Jupiter is the biggest (star   planet).
3. The Big Dipper is a (galaxy   constellation).
4. A (lunar   solar) eclipse happens at night.
5. A (comet   star) travels in space.
6. The (sun   moon) is at the center of the solar system.
7. We use (an astronaut   a telescope) to look at other planets.

D CROSSWORD: *Pictures to Words*

Across

3.    4.    6.

Down

1. 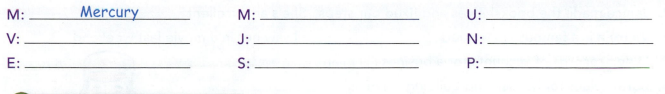   2.   5.

³ P L A N E T

A WHAT'S THE OCCUPATION?

accountant	architect	assembler	bricklayer	cashier
actress	artist	baker	carpenter	chef

1. Albert is a _____bricklayer_____. He works on construction sites and builds walls.

2. Janice made the bookshelves and fixed our steps. She's an excellent _____.

3. Victoria is a famous Hollywood _____. I saw her in a movie last weekend.

4. I keep records of accounts for a business. I'm an _____.

5. I draw plans for houses and buildings. I'm an _____.

6. Stacy puts parts together in a factory. She's an _____.

7. I work with money. I use a cash register. I'm a _____.

8. My uncle cooks food at a restaurant. He's a _____.

9. I draw and paint. I'm studying to be an _____.

10. George is a _____. He makes delicious bread.

B WHAT DO THEY DO?

_d_	1. A firefighter	a.	cleans buildings.
____	2. A farmer	b.	enters information into a computer.
____	3. A janitor	c.	cuts and styles hair.
____	4. A foreman	d.	puts out fires.
____	5. A delivery person	e.	cleans rooms in a hotel.
____	6. A hairdresser	f.	grows vegetables to sell.
____	7. A butcher	g.	delivers packages and letters.
____	8. A data entry clerk	h.	cuts and prepares meat.
____	9. A housekeeper	i.	manages a construction crew.

C WHICH GROUP?

accountant	bricklayer	custodian	housekeeper
baker	cashier	data entry clerk	mason
barber	chef	hairdresser	software engineer

They cook.   **They clean.**   **They cut hair.**

___baker___

_____   _____   _____

They work with computers.   **They build things.**   **They work with money.**

_____   _____   _____

_____   _____   _____

Draw a line to complete the word. Then write the word on the line.

1. fire   sitter   _firefighter_
2. fore   keeper   _____
3. dock   scaper   _____
4. baby   fighter   _____
5. home   man   _____
6. land   worker   _____
7. house   maker   _____

E **LISTENING: What's the Job?**

Listen and circle the correct word.

1. garment worker   (gardener)   5. butcher   home attendant
2. fisher   farmer   6. assembler   food-service worker
3. artist   engineer   7. housekeeper   garment worker
4. carpenter   homemaker   8. health-care aide firefighter

F **CAREER ADVICE**

Look at pages 112–113 of the Picture Dictionary. Recommend one or more jobs for these people.

I like to work outside.

I like to work with children.

1. ....

2. ....

I like to work alone.

I like to build things.

3. ....

4. ....

I like to help people.

I like to work with food.

5. ....

6. ....

I'm very creative.

I'm a "people person."

7. ....

8. ....

A WHAT'S THE OCCUPATION?

mechanic	musician	photographer	police officer	sanitation worker
messenger	pharmacist	pilot	receptionist	travel agent

1. I deliver letters and packages to people. I'm a _____ messenger _____.
2. I answer the telephone and take messages in an office. I'm a _____.
3. I help people plan the perfect vacation. I'm a _____.
4. I collect trash from city neighborhoods. I'm a _____.
5. I give concerts all over the world. I'm a professional _____.
6. I take pictures. I'm a _____ for the city newspaper.
7. I want to fight crime. Someday I want to be a _____.
8. I studied chemistry in college. Now I'm a _____.
9. I work on cars. I'm an excellent _____.
10. I fly airplanes. I'm a _____.

B WHERE DO THEY WORK?

__c__ **1.** A waitress works

_____ **2.** A salesperson works

_____ **3.** A medical assistant works

_____ **4.** A teacher works

_____ **5.** A pharmacist works

_____ **6.** A machine operator works

_____ **7.** A manager works

a. in a factory.

b. in a school.

c. in a restaurant.

d. in a pharmacy.

e. in a department store.

f. in an office.

g. in a doctor's office.

C ASSOCIATIONS

__g__ **1.** veterinarian

_____ **2.** mail carrier

_____ **3.** translator

_____ **4.** seamstress

_____ **5.** secretary

_____ **6.** photographer

_____ **7.** welder

_____ **8.** manicurist

_____ **9.** trash collector

_____ **10.** waiter

a. languages

b. cameras

c. garbage

d. offices and phones

e. food and drinks

f. letters and packages

g. animals

h. machines and metal

i. dresses and suits

j. nail polish and fingernails

D WHAT'S THE WORD?

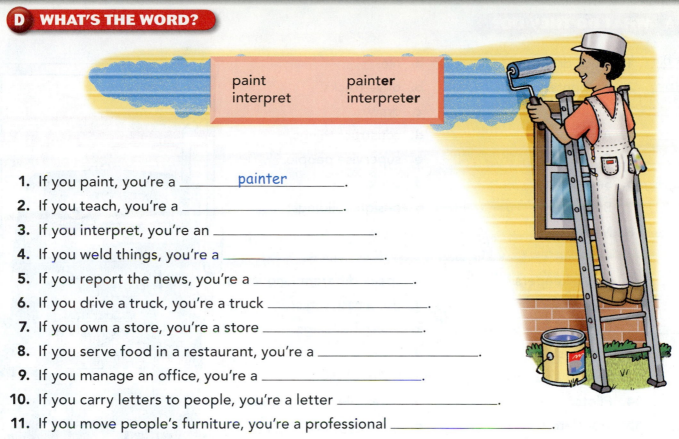

paint	painter
interpret	interpreter

1. If you paint, you're a _____painter_____.
2. If you teach, you're a _____.
3. If you interpret, you're an _____.
4. If you weld things, you're a _____.
5. If you report the news, you're a _____.
6. If you drive a truck, you're a truck _____.
7. If you own a store, you're a store _____.
8. If you serve food in a restaurant, you're a _____.
9. If you manage an office, you're a _____.
10. If you carry letters to people, you're a letter _____.
11. If you move people's furniture, you're a professional _____.
12. If you wait on people at a restaurant (and you're a man), you're a _____.

E CROSSWORD: Pictures to Words

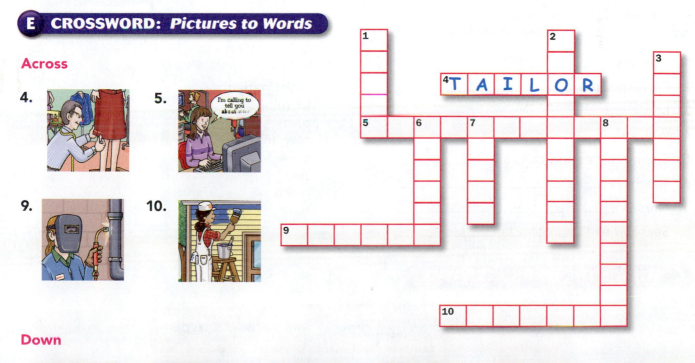

Across

4.
5.
9.
10.

Down

1.
2.
3.
6.
7.
8.

A WHAT DO THEY DO?

_b_ **1.** Truck drivers   **a.** file.

____ **2.** Carpenters   **b.** drive trucks.

____ **3.** Architects   **c.** draw.

____ **4.** Artists   **d.** construct things.

____ **5.** Chefs   **e.** supervise people.

____ **6.** Secretaries   **f.** cook.

____ **7.** Bakers   **g.** design buildings.

____ **8.** Managers   **h.** bake.

____ **9.** Housekeepers   **i.** speak different languages.

____ **10.** Assemblers   **j.** use a cash register.

____ **11.** Construction workers   **k.** guard buildings.

____ **12.** Farmers   **l.** clean.

____ **13.** Security guards   **m.** build things.

____ **14.** Pilots   **n.** assemble components.

____ **15.** Translators   **o.** grow vegetables.

____ **16.** Cashiers   **p.** fly airplanes.

B WHAT ARE THEIR SKILLS?

1. Painters _____ _paint_ _____.

2. Repairpeople _____.

3. Musicians _____.

4. Waiters _____.

5. Seamstresses and tailors _____.

6. Teachers _____.

7. Nurses _____.

8. Secretaries _____.

> assist patients
> fix things
> paint
> play an instrument
> serve food
> sew
> teach
> type

C WHAT'S THE WORK ACTIVITY?

| assemble | draw | grow | manage | type |

_____ _draw_ _____   _____   _____   _____   _____
- designs   - letters   - restaurants   - components   - vegetables
- pictures   - reports   - offices   - parts   - fruits

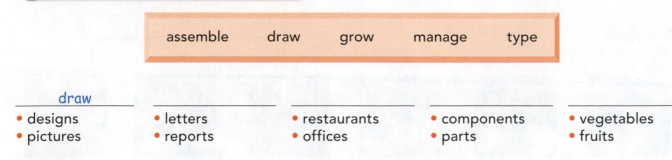

D ASSOCIATIONS

_b_ 1. mow
____ 2. translate
____ 3. sing
____ 4. wash
____ 5. sew
____ 6. serve
____ 7. use

a. equipment and cash registers
b. lawns
c. clothing
d. songs
e. food and drinks
f. dishes and clothes
g. languages

____ 8. operate
____ 9. deliver
____ 10. take
____ 11. prepare
____ 12. take care of
____ 13. write
____ 14. manage

h. packages and letters
i. offices and restaurants
j. patients and elderly people
k. reports and letters
l. inventory
m. equipment and machinery
n. food

E WHAT DOES IT MEAN?

_c_ 1. assemble components
____ 2. mow lawns
____ 3. build
____ 4. repair
____ 5. translate
____ 6. operate equipment

a. cut the grass
b. use machinery
c. put things together
d. speak two languages
e. construct
f. fix things

F LISTENING: *What Do They Do?*

Listen and put a check next to the correct sentence.

1.
___ I deliver food.
✓ I assemble parts.

2.
___ I type.
___ I serve food.

3.
___ I translate.
___ I teach.

4.
___ I construct things.
___ I design buildings.

5.
___ I draw things.
___ I guard buildings.

6.
___ I'm a farmer.
___ I'm a veterinarian.

7.
___ I paint.
___ I play the piano.

8.
___ I sell things.
___ I wash dishes.

9.
___ I assist patients.
___ I act in movies.

A LOOKING FOR A JOB

_f_	**1.** Respond to	**a.** an application form.
____	**2.** Prepare	**b.** a thank-you note.
____	**3.** Fill out	**c.** your skills.
____	**4.** Go to	**d.** an interview.
____	**5.** Talk about	**e.** hired.
____	**6.** Ask about	**f.** an ad.
____	**7.** Write	**g.** the benefits.
____	**8.** Get	**h.** a resume.

B WHICH WORD?

1. I saw a ((help)   job) wanted sign in the window.

2. Do you have previous (evenings   experience)?

3. I saw a want (ad   sign) for this job.

4. Previous experience is (available   required).

5. Did you request an (interview   information)?

6. Did you look in the (announcement   classified) ads?

7. Are there any part-time jobs (available   experience)?

8. You'll like this job. The salary is (required   excellent).

9. I'm looking for a part-(time   position) job.

C ABBREVIATIONS

_b_	**1.** hour	**a.** prev.
____	**2.** required	**b.** hr.
____	**3.** excellent	**c.** exper.
____	**4.** Monday through Friday	**d.** PT
____	**5.** part-time	**e.** FT
____	**6.** previous	**f.** M-F
____	**7.** experience	**g.** excel.
____	**8.** full-time	**h.** req.

D LISTENING: *Requesting Information*

Listen and put a check next to the correct job description.

1. _✓_ PT, eve.
____ FT, M-F, eve.

2. ____ FT, no exper. req.
____ FT, prev. exper. req.

3. ____ PT, eve.
____ FT, M-F, eve.

4. ____ excel. benefits
____ excel. pay

5. ____ PT, 30 hr./wk.
____ FT, 40 hr./wk.

6. ____ PT, eves. $14/hr.
____ FT, days, $13/hr.

A WHICH WORD?

1. Do you know how to use the paper (machine (shredder))?
2. Is there (an adding   a coffee) machine in the employee lounge?
3. I don't understand. I'm going to ask the (copier   boss).
4. Look in the (supply   file) cabinet for more paper and pens.
5. Ms. Norris is the new office (manager   cutter).
6. She's in her (cubicle   mailbox).
7. This new (coat rack   swivel chair) is very comfortable for my back.
8. A visitor in the (supply room   reception area) is waiting to see you.
9. You have a message in your (mailbox   mailroom).

B MATCHING

__c__ **1.** conference   **a.** assistant
____ **2.** administrative **b.** cabinet
____ **3.** message   **c.** room
____ **4.** storage   **d.** board

____ **5.** file   **e.** board
____ **6.** vending   **f.** manager
____ **7.** presentation **g.** machine
____ **8.** office   **h.** cabinet

C ROGER'S DAILY ROUTINE

| coat closet | letters | messages | presentations |
| coffee machine | mailboxes | photocopier | secretary |

Roger is the ___secretary___ [1] in our office. He arrives every day at 8:30 in the morning. First, he puts his jacket in the _____ [2] and checks the message board for any important messages. Then he sorts the mail and puts it in our _____ [3]. He sometimes goes to the _____ [4] to make copies. After that, he goes to the _____ [5] to get something to drink. During the day, he's very busy. He often takes _____ [6] or types _____ [7]. Sometimes, he even gives _____ [8] to us about office equipment.

D WHERE IS THE CONVERSATION TAKING PLACE?

__e__ **1.** "Good morning. May I help you?"   **a.** in the conference room
____ **2.** "We'll have nine people at this meeting." **b.** at the vending machine
____ **3.** "No sugar or cream. I like it black."   **c.** in the storage room
____ **4.** "Does this accept dollar bills?"   **d.** in the mailroom
____ **5.** "I'd like to send it first class."   **e.** in the reception area
____ **6.** "This is where we keep extra equipment."   **f.** at the coffee machine

A WHAT'S THE WORD?

| cellophane tape | letter tray | pencil sharpener |
| glue stick | organizer | rotary card file |

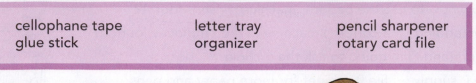

1. My desk is a mess! I need to organize my papers.

You should use a ___<u>letter tray</u>___.

2. I need to attach some mailing labels to these envelopes.

Use this _____.

3. I can never remember phone numbers and addresses.

You should use a _____.

4. My appointment book has a torn page!

Fix it with some _____.

5. I'm always late for meetings!

You need an _____.

6. This pencil isn't sharp enough to write!

Do you have an electric _____?

B WHICH WORD?

1. Don't use a paper clip to attach those papers. Use a (thumbtack   (stapler)).

2. Please put an address on this (appointment book   envelope).

3. This glue stick doesn't work. Use some rubber (cement   stamp).

4. Write the names of all the employees on this (legal   desk) pad.

5. This printer needs a new (ink   typewriter) cartridge.

6. I have the rubber stamp, but I don't have the (desk   ink) pad.

7. Do we have any (thumbtacks   clipboards) for the bulletin board?

8. You can hold those pencils together with a rubber (stamp   band).

9. Write the name and phone number on this small (legal   Post-It note) pad.

10. I made a mistake with the typewriter. Do you have (an eraser   correction fluid)?

C WHAT DO WE USE IT FOR?

_b_	**1.** pushpin		**a.** to organize documents
____	**2.** mailing label		**b.** to attach paper to a message board
____	**3.** memo pad		**c.** to hold papers together
____	**4.** rubber cement		**d.** to write down messages
____	**5.** envelope		**e.** to put an address on an envelope
____	**6.** paper clip		**f.** to send a letter in the mail
____	**7.** file folder		**g.** to glue papers together

A WHICH WORD?

1. These boxes are very heavy!
   Use a (work station   **forklift**).

2. I'm here for an interview.
   Go to the (loading dock   personnel office).

3. I have a problem with my paycheck.
   You should go to the (payroll   personnel) office.

4. Where's the hand truck?
   It's in the (assembly line   freight elevator).

5. I smell smoke!
   Get the (fire extinguisher   time cards)!

6. I have a question about this machine.
   Ask your (line supervisor   worker).

7. Where can I keep my coat and bag?
   In the (shipping   locker) room.

B MATCHING

_b_ **1.** union	**a.** belt	___ **6.** quality	**f.** clerk
___ **2.** work	**b.** notice	___ **7.** loading	**g.** line
___ **3.** suggestion	**c.** truck	___ **8.** assembly	**h.** control
___ **4.** conveyor	**d.** station	___ **9.** time	**i.** dock
___ **5.** hand	**e.** box	___ **10.** shipping	**j.** clock

C WHAT DO THEY DO?

_e_ **1.** A quality control supervisor	**a.** loads containers and boxes.
___ **2.** A packer	**b.** stores shipments and boxes.
___ **3.** The warehouse	**c.** gives paychecks to workers.
___ **4.** The conveyor belt	**d.** records when workers arrive and leave.
___ **5.** The payroll office	**e.** checks products for defects.
___ **6.** A time clock	**f.** transports products to and from machines.

D CROSSWORD

Across

3. Load the boxes into the freight ____.

4. Keep your belongings in the locker ____.

Down

1. We need to hire a new shipping ____.

2. Take this shipment to the loading ____.

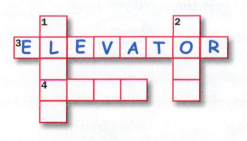

A WHICH GROUP?

| brick | cement | dump truck | jackhammer | pickup truck | shovel |
| bulldozer | crane | lumber | pickax | plywood | sledgehammer |

Building Materials	Tools	Vehicles
brick		

B WHICH WORD?

1. Use that (scaffolding   (wheelbarrow)) to move the bricks.
2. Study the (blueprints   ladder) before you start the job.
3. Please give me that (trowel   trailer).
4. Be careful when you come down the (ladder   shovel).
5. He operates that (front-end loader   tape measure) very well.
6. We don't have enough (blueprints   insulation) to finish the job.
7. Put on your (crane   toolbelt) before you go to the construction site.
8. Are we going to have enough (shingles   sledgehammers) for the roof?
9. We need a (pickup   concrete mixer) truck to make the foundation for this house.

C MATCH AND WRITE

Draw a line to complete the word. Then write the word on the line.

1. back — prints   backhoe
2. blue   wood   _____
3. bull — hoe   _____
4. dry   hammer   _____
5. ply   dozer   _____
6. jack   wall   _____

D LISTENING

Listen and circle the word you hear.

1. brick   (beam)
2. trowel   shovel
3. trailer   crane
4. cement mixer   cherry picker
5. backhoe   wheelbarrow
6. bulldozer   tape measure
7. cherry picker   cement mixer
8. girder   trailer
9. insulation   tape measure
10. pipe   wire

A WHAT DO THEY PROTECT?

Match the word with the part of the body that it protects.

_g_ **1.** goggles   **a.** head

____ **2.** helmet   **b.** face

____ **3.** safety earmuffs   **c.** feet

____ **4.** mask   **d.** hands

____ **5.** latex gloves   **e.** ears

____ **6.** safety boots   **f.** toes

____ **7.** toe guard   **g.** eyes

B MATCH AND WRITE

1. fire   hat

2. hard   exit

3. electrical   hazard

4. emergency   extinguisher

fire extinguisher _____

_____

_____

_____

C WHAT'S THE WORD?

biohazard	electrical hazard	fire extinguisher
defibrillator	emergency exit	first-aid kit

1. Be careful around those unconnected wires and cables. It's an ___ _electrical hazard_ ___.

2. I cut my finger on that machine. Do we have a _____?

3. Chemical waste from factories is a very serious _____.

4. I think his heart stopped! Use the _____.

5. There's a fire! Go out through the _____!

6. There's a fire! Get the _____!

D WHICH WORD?

1. I use a (hard hat   (back support)) when I lift heavy things.

2. Here! This (respirator   safety vest) will help you breathe.

3. Stop! Don't drink that liquid! It's (poisonous   electrical)!

4. If you work with food, you should wear a (respirator   hairnet).

5. This (corrosive   poisonous) material might damage the machine.

6. I use (goggles   earplugs) when I work with loud equipment.

7. Any machine can be (dangerous   radioactive) without proper training.

8. You need special clothing to clean up (flammable   radioactive) materials.

9. We should clean up this (flammable   poisonous) liquid, or there might be a fire.

A JUST IN TIME!

> arrival and departure   conductor   platform   timetable   train
> baggage   information   ticket window   track   train station

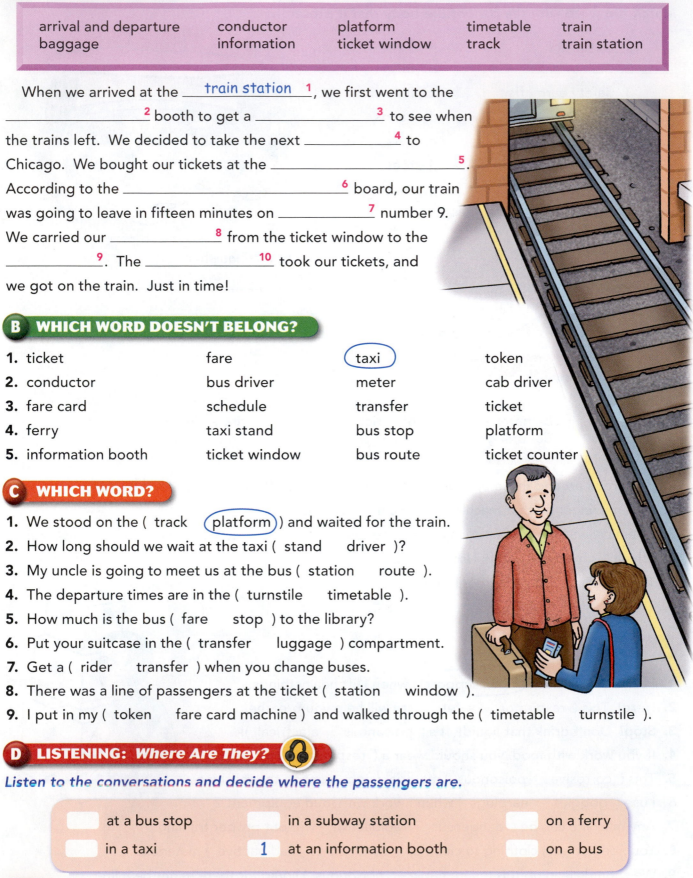

When we arrived at the ____train station____ 1, we first went to the
_____ 2 booth to get a _____ 3 to see when
the trains left. We decided to take the next _____ 4 to
Chicago. We bought our tickets at the _____ 5.
According to the _____ 6 board, our train
was going to leave in fifteen minutes on _____ 7 number 9.
We carried our _____ 8 from the ticket window to the
_____ 9. The _____ 10 took our tickets, and
we got on the train. Just in time!

B WHICH WORD DOESN'T BELONG?

1. ticket   fare   (taxi)   token
2. conductor   bus driver   meter   cab driver
3. fare card   schedule   transfer   ticket
4. ferry   taxi stand   bus stop   platform
5. information booth   ticket window   bus route   ticket counter

C WHICH WORD?

1. We stood on the (track (platform)) and waited for the train.
2. How long should we wait at the taxi (stand   driver)?
3. My uncle is going to meet us at the bus (station   route).
4. The departure times are in the (turnstile   timetable).
5. How much is the bus (fare   stop) to the library?
6. Put your suitcase in the (transfer   luggage) compartment.
7. Get a (rider   transfer) when you change buses.
8. There was a line of passengers at the ticket (station   window).
9. I put in my (token   fare card machine) and walked through the (timetable   turnstile).

D LISTENING: *Where Are They?*

Listen to the conversations and decide where the passengers are.

> [ ] at a bus stop   [ ] in a subway station   [ ] on a ferry
> [ ] in a taxi   [1] at an information booth   [ ] on a bus

A WHAT KIND OF CAR?

1. My car has a flat tire!
   I'll send a (limousine   (tow truck)).

2. I need a car for my family.
   You should get a (moving   mini) van.

3. I carry around a lot of tools and wood.
   Do you drive a (pickup   tow) truck?

4. I'm concerned about the environment.
   You should get (a hybrid   an S.U.V.).

5. I want to get some exercise instead of driving.
   You should get a (jeep   bicycle).

6. I'd love to go on a trip across the country.
   You can borrow my (R.V.   moped).

7. I like to drive small cars.
   You should buy a (van   sports car).

8. Our daughter is getting married.
   Are you going to rent a (camper   limousine)?

B MATCH AND WRITE

Draw a line to complete the word. Then write the word on the line.

1. pickup	van	pickup truck
2. tractor	scooter	_____
3. moving	car	_____
4. station	truck	_____
5. sports	trailer	_____
6. motor	vehicle	_____
7. recreational	wagon	_____

C WHICH VEHICLE DOESN'T BELONG?

1. pickup truck	tow truck	(sports car)	semi
2. motorcycle	minivan	moped	motor scooter
3. van	moving van	limousine	sedan
4. semi	hatchback	convertible	sports car
5. jeep	truck	S.U.V.	R.V.

A WHAT SHOULD THEY USE?

_c_ 1. "It's starting to rain."
____ 2. "Check the oil, please."
____ 3. "I have to change the tire."
____ 4. "Make a right."
____ 5. "Fill it up."
____ 6. "It's getting dark."
____ 7. "My battery is dead."
____ 8. "The back window is foggy!"

a. jumper cables
b. rear defroster
c. windshield wipers
d. turn signal
e. lug wrench
f. gas cap
g. dipstick
h. headlights

B MATCH AND WRITE

Draw a line to complete the word. Then write the word on the line.

1. wind   light   _____windshield_____
2. head   shift   _____
3. gear   shield   _____
4. tail   cap   _____
5. arm   pipe   _____
6. hub   roof   _____
7. sun   rest   _____

C WHICH WORD?

1. Put on your turn (light   (signal)).
2. Your license (rack   plate) is falling off!
3. I have a spare (tire   tank) in my trunk.
4. There's a problem with your fan (filter   belt).
5. Be safe. Always wear a (seat belt   brake light).
6. Look in your side (pump   mirror) before you pass.
7. My (navigation   fuel injection) system helps me find my way.
8. It costs more money, but I just bought a car with (a CD player   tires).

D LISTENING: *Checklist*

Listen to the car dealers. Put a check next to the items each car has.

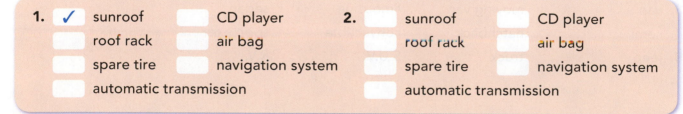

1. ✓ sunroof   ☐ CD player   2. ☐ sunroof   ☐ CD player
   ☐ roof rack   ☐ air bag   ☐ roof rack   ☐ air bag
   ☐ spare tire ☐ navigation system ☐ spare tire ☐ navigation system
   ☐ automatic transmission   ☐ automatic transmission

1. The sun is bright. I'll put the ((visor)   accelerator) down.

2. I can't start the car. I think the (ignition   brake) is broken.

3. It's very hot in this car! Turn on the air (bag   conditioner).

4. The map is in the (glove compartment   shoulder harness).

5. I had a small accident today. My (spark plug   fender) is damaged.

6. We need to stop for gas. The gas (gauge   pump) says we're almost empty.

7. The light is green! Why doesn't that driver go? You should honk your (vent   horn).

8. This car doesn't have automatic transmission. It has a (stickshift   headrest).

F ASSOCIATIONS

_c_	**1.** speedometer	**a.**	how much gas
____	**2.** odometer	**b.**	how hot or cold
____	**3.** temperature gauge	**c.**	how fast
____	**4.** fuel gauge	**d.**	how far

____	**5.** brake	**e.**	listen
____	**6.** gas pedal	**f.**	stop
____	**7.** door handle	**g.**	turn
____	**8.** steering wheel	**h.**	go
____	**9.** radio	**i.**	sit
____	**10.** seat	**j.**	open

G SAFETY FIRST!

air bags	flares	jack	jumper cables	seat belt	spare tire	trunk

As a good driver, you should always keep emergency equipment in the _____trunk_____ [1] of your car. When your battery doesn't work, you need to use _____ [2] and get help from another driver. In case of an emergency on the road, you can warn other drivers when you light your _____ [3] and put them in the road. When you have a flat tire, pull over, and make sure you stop in a safe area. Use a _____ [4] to lift the car, and replace the flat tire with your _____ [5]. Finally, even though some cars have _____ [6] to protect people in an accident, you and your passengers should always wear a _____ [7].

A WHICH WORD?

1. You didn't stop at the ((traffic)   speed limit) signal.
2. Make a right turn at the next (shoulder   intersection).
3. The (speed limit   route) sign says 55 miles per hour.
4. There's a (median   crosswalk) at the next intersection.
5. You have to pay one dollar at the (barrier   tollbooth).
6. You can get off the highway at the next (exit   entrance) ramp.
7. Meet me at the (overpass   corner) of Park Avenue and 10th Street.

B MATCHING

__f__ 1. You pay here.   a. left lane

____ 2. You can pass.   b. crosswalk

____ 3. You can't pass.   c. broken line

____ 4. You get on the highway here.   d. double yellow line

____ 5. You can walk here.   e. exit ramp

____ 6. You can get off the highway here.   f. tollbooth

____ 7. You pass other cars here.   g. on ramp

C WHAT ARE THEY TALKING ABOUT?

| bridge | one-way street | speed limit sign |
| exit sign | route sign | traffic light |

1. "Don't go so fast!"   ___speed limit sign___
2. "Cars can only go in one direction."   _____
3. "What road are we on?"   _____
4. "Slow down! It's turning yellow."   _____
5. "Which river are we crossing?"   _____
6. "We need to get off soon. Look for the right sign." _____

D ANALOGIES

| highway | intersection | overpass | right lane | traffic signal |

1. tunnel : underpass as bridge : _____overpass_____
2. street : road as interstate : _____
3. median : left lane as shoulder : _____
4. middle lane : center lane as traffic light : _____
5. tollbooth : exit ramp as traffic signal : _____

A WHICH WORD?

1. Go (into   (over)) the bridge.
2. Get (on   over) the train.
3. Go (down   through) the tunnel.
4. Go (into   across) South Street.
5. Get (off   out of) the taxi.
6. Get (off   into) the bus.
7. Turn left (into   onto) Grove Street.
8. Get (off   over) the highway at Exit 12.
9. Go (up   around) Bayside Boulevard.
10. Go (over   through) the Grant Bridge.

B CROSSWORD: *Pictures to Words*

Across

1.   3.   4.   7.

Down

2.   5.   6.

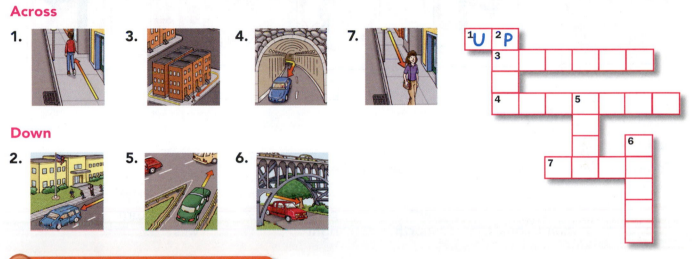

C HOW TO GET TO MY HOUSE

PARK ST

Here's how to get to my house for the party this Saturday. Get over (on) [1] the B Train and get through off [2] at Park Street. Walk off up [3] Park Street to Garden Street and turn right. Continue on Garden Street past over [4] the post office. When you get to the corner of Garden Street and Forest Street, walk across into [5] the street and turn left on Forest Street. Walk down over [6] Forest Street. My house is number 25, halfway down on the right.

See you on Saturday!

A WHICH WORD?

1. That's a (stop   (one way)) sign. You can't turn there!
2. We can't go left here. It says (left   right) turn only.
3. Let the other cars go. The sign says ("detour"   "yield").
4. We have to turn around. This is a (dead end   school crossing).
5. Stop at the (railroad   pedestrian) crossing and let the people cross.
6. You can't leave the car here. It's (right turn   handicapped parking) only.
7. Go slow! It's raining, and the sign says ("slippery when wet"   "merging traffic").

B LISTENING: *Traffic Signs*

Listen and write the number under the correct sign.

_____   _____   __1__   _____   _____

C ROAD TEST

Complete the road test instructions based on the diagram.

east	left	parallel park	3-point turn
hand signals	north	right	west

Go ____north____ ¹ on Main Street and turn _____ ² onto Second Avenue. Remember, always use _____ ³ when you make turns. Now, go _____ ⁴ on Second Avenue. When you get to the post office, make a _____ ⁵. Then go west on Second Avenue and take a right onto Elm Street. Go up Elm Street and turn _____ ⁶ onto First Avenue. Go _____ ⁷ to Center Street and turn right. Finally, _____ ⁸ in front of the library.

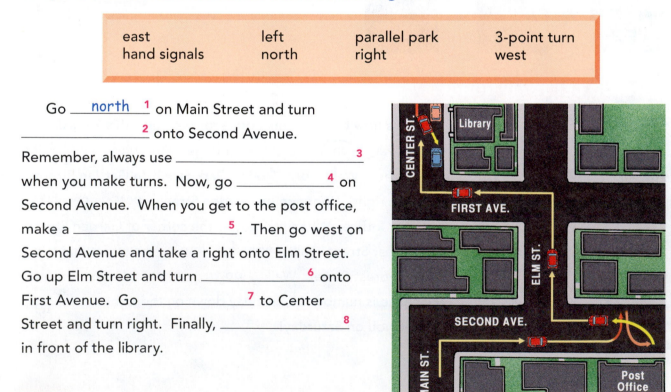

A WHICH WORD?

1. May I see your boarding (area   (pass))?
2. Do you need a (garment   baggage) cart?
3. Let me help you with that (suitcase   gate).
4. I packed three suits in my (carry-on   garment) bag.
5. Please fill out your customs (declaration form   officer).
6. Please take a seat in the (boarding area   metal detector).
7. Do you see your suitcase on the baggage (counter   carousel)?
8. All passengers have to go through the (metal   X-ray) detector.
9. Please pick up your luggage in the (baggage claim   check-in) area.
10. Show your ticket to the agent at the (luggage cart   check-in counter).

B WHICH WORD DOESN'T BELONG?

1. ticket agent   (luggage carrier)   security officer   customs officer
2. baggage   immigration   suitcase   carry-on bag
3. ticket   boarding pass   X-ray machine   baggage claim check
4. baggage claim   baggage   boarding area   security checkpoint
5. customs   visa   counter   passport
6. X-ray machine   metal detector   passport   security checkpoint

C FLYING INTERNATIONALLY

baggage claim	boarding pass	immigration	passport	ticket
boarding	customs	monitor	security	visa

When you fly to other countries, you should be ready to do many things. When you first get to the airport, you should go to the _____ticket_____ [1] counter to check your baggage and get your _____ [2]. Then, go to the _____ [3] area to wait for the flight. You should have your _____ [4] or other ID ready when you go through the _____ [5] checkpoint. On the way, you can check the departure _____ [6] to see the location of your gate. When you arrive at your destination, you'll have to go through _____ [7] to get your passport stamped, so make sure you have your _____ [8]. Then you have to go to the _____ [9] area to pick up your luggage. The last thing you need to do is go through _____ [10] to show what you're bringing into the country.

123

A WHAT DO THEY NEED?

1. Where can I put my carry-on bag?

   You can put it in the ((overhead compartment)   cockpit).

2. I feel nauseous. I think I'm going to be sick.

   Here. Use this (oxygen mask   air sickness bag).

3. Where can I wash my hands?

   The (lavatory   runway) is in the back of the plane.

4. I'm looking for the flight attendant.

   Press the (call button   middle seat).

5. Can I use the lavatory now?

   Not yet. The (Fasten Seat Belt   No Smoking) sign is on.

6. I'm having trouble breathing!

   Use this (emergency instruction card   oxygen mask) and breathe slowly.

B WHICH WORD?

1. The co-pilot and pilot are always in the ((cockpit)   aisle).

2. The sign says to fasten your (seat belt   air sickness bag).

3. Where is the emergency (compartment   exit)?

4. After the plane lands, it will go to the (lavatory   terminal).

5. If you want to see the city from the plane, sit in the (aisle   window) seat.

6. The workers in the (emergency exit   control tower) help the plane land.

C AIRPORT ACTIONS

_b_ **1.** Check in	**a.** your pockets.	**5.** Stow	**e.** your seat belt.
___ **2.** Take off	**b.** at the gate.	**6.** Find	**f.** the metal detector.
___ **3.** Board	**c.** the plane.	**7.** Walk through	**g.** your seat.
___ **4.** Empty	**d.** your shoes.	**8.** Fasten	**h.** your carry-on bag.

D LISTENING

Listen and put a check next to the words you hear.

✓	flight attendant	☐	emergency instruction card
☐	emergency exits	☐	overhead compartment
☐	life vest	☐	seat belts
☐	oxygen masks	☐	call button

A ASSOCIATIONS

_d_ 1. parking attendant
____ 2. room key
____ 3. desk clerk
____ 4. room service
____ 5. bellhop

a. guest room
b. luggage cart
c. restaurant
d. valet parking
e. front desk

B WHICH WORD DOESN'T BELONG?

1. bell captain	bellhop	(luggage cart)	guest
2. meeting	exercise	guest	service
3. guest	desk clerk	concierge	parking attendant
4. restaurant	room service	gift shop	hallway
5. desk clerk	doorman	housekeeper	pool

C WHICH WORD?

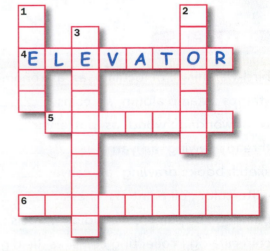

1. The ((doorman)   concierge) opened the door for the guest.
2. The guest used her room (service   key) to open her door.
3. You can find the bell captain in the (lobby   gift shop).
4. Does the hotel have a (pool   ice machine)? I love to swim.
5. The (housekeeper   concierge) can get theater tickets for you.
6. If you go to the (meeting   exercise) room, bring shorts and sneakers with you.
7. Please use the (ice machine   gift shop) as much as you like. It's free of charge.

D CROSSWORD

Across

4. This carries you and your luggage upstairs.
5. You walk through this to get to your room.
6. This person helps guests in many ways.

Down

1. This person stays at a hotel.
2. This person works at the hotel entrance.
3. You can eat all your meals here.

⁴E L E V A T O R

A WHAT'S THE WORD?

board games	knits	photography	surfing the net
draw	needlepoint	pottery	woodworking

1. Amanda takes wonderful pictures. She likes _____photography_____.
2. My son likes to build things with wood. His hobby is _____.
3. My aunt Judy made me this great sweater. She _____.
4. We bought our daughter a sketchbook. She loves to _____.
5. Do you like to play cards or _____?
6. What kind of clay do you use when you make _____?
7. My uncle is always online. He loves _____.
8. Look at this new pattern I'm doing. I love _____!

B ASSOCIATIONS

__c__ 1. knitting   **a.** airplanes
____ 2. photography   **b.** bowls
____ 3. build models   **c.** sweaters
____ 4. pottery   **d.** pictures

____ 5. stamp collecting   **e.** web browser
____ 6. painting   **f.** magnifying glass
____ 7. surfing the net   **g.** colored pencils
____ 8. drawing   **h.** canvas

C WHAT ARE THEY TALKING ABOUT?

__b__ 1. "Those feathers are beautiful!"   **a.** sewing
____ 2. "How do you spell this word?"   **b.** bird-watching
____ 3. "It's very rare. It's from 1909."   **c.** astronomy
____ 4. "Oh, no! My needle broke!"   **d.** Scrabble
____ 5. "Can you see the Big Dipper?"   **e.** coin collecting

D ANALOGIES

1. bird-watching : binoculars *as* astronomy : _____telescope_____
2. stamps : stamp album *as* coins : _____
3. woodworking : wood *as* pottery : _____
4. thread : sewing *as* yarn : _____
5. sketch book : drawing *as* canvas : _____
6. watercolor : oil paint *as* chess : _____
7. painting : oil paint *as* building models : _____
8. coin catalog : collecting coins *as* field guide : _____

acrylic paint
bird-watching
checkers
clay
coin collection
knitting
painting
telescope

A MATCHING

____c____ **1.** art   **a.** meet

_____ **2.** yard   **b.** gardens

_____ **3.** swap   **c.** gallery

_____ **4.** flea   **d.** site

_____ **5.** botanical   **e.** sale

_____ **6.** amusement   **f.** market

_____ **7.** historic   **g.** park

B WHERE SHOULD THEY GO?

1. My son loves animals.

Take him to the (flea market   zoo).

2. Do you want to go swimming?

Sure. Let's go to the (beach   mountains).

3. I'd love to listen to some live music.

There's a (concert   carnival) at 7:00 tonight.

4. Where did you go for your school trip?

We went to an interesting historic (sale   site).

5. We need to sell some of our old things.

There's a (flea market   yard sale) this weekend.

6. Where can I find beautiful hand-made jewelry?

You can usually find it at (an art gallery   a craft fair).

7. I like to look at paintings.

There's a wonderful exhibit at the (movies   museum).

8. I love to look at trees and flowers.

You should go to the (aquarium   botanical gardens).

9. I want to learn about the moon and the stars.

You should go to the (swap meet   planetarium).

10. Those rides were a lot of fun!

We should come back to this (national   amusement) park again!

C JOURNAL

Tell about your favorite places to go. Why are they your favorite places?

A WHICH WORD?

1. Let's rest for a minute on this (seesaw   (bench)).
2. Put your bicycle (on the grill   in the bike rack).
3. Please throw this away in the (sandbox   trash can).
4. We can cook our food on the (swings   grill).
5. Let's have lunch on this (picnic table   slide).
6. I'm going to run on the (merry-go-round   jogging path).
7. I'm going to get a drink at the (water fountain   carousel).
8. My children love to play in the (swings   sandbox).
9. Be careful, Billy! Don't fall into the (skateboard ramp   duck pond)!

B ANALOGIES

| ballfield | bikeway | carousel | playground | sandbox | skateboard |

1. water : duck pond *as* sand : _____sandbox_____
2. merry-go-round : carousel *as* bike path : _____
3. sit : bench *as* ride : _____
4. jog : jogging path *as* play baseball : _____
5. grill : picnic area *as* climber : _____
6. bicycle path : bicycle *as* skateboard ramp : _____

C WHAT ARE THEY TALKING ABOUT?

__b__ 1. "Don't climb up there so high!"
____ 2. "Let's get a drink here."
____ 3. "Make sure you wear a helmet!"
____ 4. "Up and down! Up and down!"
____ 5. "Have a seat and rest for a minute."
____ 6. "You can lock your bicycle here."
____ 7. "Ride the horse and go around!"

a. bench
b. climbing wall
c. carousel
d. water fountain
e. seesaw
f. skateboard ramp
g. bike rack

D LISTENING: *What Are They Talking About?*

Listen and circle the correct word.

1. (trash can)   water fountain
2. jogging path   tennis court
3. playground   merry-go-round
4. picnic area   bikeway

5. bike rack   sandbox
6. fountain   duck pond
7. grill   sand
8. ballfield   climber

A WHAT DO THEY DO?

<u>b</u> **1.** A lifeguard   **a.** sells drinks and snacks.

____ **2.** A sunbather   **b.** watches swimmers.

____ **3.** A vendor   **c.** rides the waves.

____ **4.** A surfer   **d.** sits in the sun.

____ **5.** A cooler   **e.** protect the eyes.

____ **6.** Suntan lotion   **f.** helps you stay above water.

____ **7.** Sunglasses   **g.** protects the skin.

____ **8.** A life preserver   **h.** keeps drinks cold.

B WHICH WORD?

1. Let's sit down on this beach ((chair)   ball)!

2. Use this (lifeguard   bucket) to make a sand castle.

3. Let's throw this (beach ball   kite) around!

4. Look at this pretty (sunblock   seashell)!

5. The sun is very bright! I need my (sunglasses   beach towel).

6. It's very windy today! It's a perfect day to fly a (sun hat   kite).

7. You have to be a strong (swimmer   sunbather) to be a lifeguard!

8. I'm going to get something to drink at the (snack bar   sand castle).

9. When I'm at the beach, I always sit under a (beach umbrella   cooler).

C ANALOGIES

boogie board   lifeguard stand   snack bar   sunscreen   surfboard

1. sunbather : beach blanket *as* surfer : _____<u>surfboard</u>_____

2. pail : bucket *as* refreshment stand : _____

3. wind : kite *as* wave : _____

4. sunbather : beach chair *as* lifeguard : _____

5. seashell : shell *as* suntan lotion : _____

D LISTENING: *What Are They Talking About?*

Listen and circle the correct word.

1. beach ball   (chair)   **5.** swimmer   sunscreen

2. beach umbrella   kite   **6.** vendor   surfer

3. life preserver   lifeguard   **7.** blanket   sun hat

4. shovel   towel   **8.** vendor   snack bar

OUTDOOR RECREATION

A WHICH WORD?

1. It's getting dark. Do you have a ((lantern)   hatchet)?
2. Tie a good knot with this (rope   tent).
3. I'm thirsty. Can you give me the (matches   thermos)?
4. I'm tired. This (backpack   Swiss army knife) is very heavy!
5. We need to get some (insect repellent   matches) to protect us.
6. Let's put up the tent. Where are the (thermos   stakes)?
7. Where's the picnic (blanket   basket) with our drinks and sandwiches?
8. We're going to be here all night. Did you bring your sleeping (bag   boots)?
9. I don't want to get lost. Where's the compass and the (harness   GPS device)?
10. You should always wear your helmet when you go (on a picnic   mountain climbing).

B MATCHING

__d__ 1. hiking
____ 2. camping
____ 3. rock climbing
____ 4. on a picnic

a. going up
b. eating outside
c. sleeping outside
d. walking

____ 5. camping stove
____ 6. canteen
____ 7. hatchet
____ 8. backpack

e. drinking
f. cooking
g. carrying
h. chopping

C MATCH AND WRITE

Draw a line to complete the word. Then write the word on the line.

1. sleeping — bike   __bag__
2. mountain   device   _____
3. trail   bag   _____
4. GPS   boots   _____
5. tent   climbing   _____
6. insect   map   _____
7. technical   repellent _____
8. hiking   stakes   _____

D LISTENING: Where Are They Going?

Listen and write the number next to the correct activity.

	camping		mountain biking
	hiking	1	rock climbing

A ASSOCIATIONS

__e__ 1. rowing machine
____ 2. black belt
____ 3. barbell
____ 4. reins
____ 5. balance beam
____ 6. bow and arrow

a. gymnastics
b. archery
c. martial arts
d. horseback riding
e. working out
f. weightlifting

B WHICH WORD?

1. Hit the (bowling   (ping pong)) ball over the net!
2. This new wrestling (mat   uniform) doesn't fit!
3. Put your feet in the (stirrups   knee pads).
4. Could you hand me the pool (table   stick)?
5. Protect your eyes with (reins   safety goggles).
6. Kevin likes to jump on the (trampoline   net).
7. Susan likes to practice with her bow and (target   arrow).
8. Put on your (saddle   bike helmet) before you go cycling.
9. You have to wear boxing (gloves   trunks) on both hands.
10. Jon works out on the (rowing machine   stirrups) every day.

C WHICH WORD DOESN'T BELONG?

1. golf ball   (barbell)   billiard ball   bowling ball
2. jogging shoes   running shoes   rollerblades   helmet
3. Frisbee   racquetball   birdie   saddle
4. cycling   tennis   ping pong   golf
5. pool stick   target   golf club   tennis racket
6. pool table   saddle   exercise bike   rowing machine
7. net   treadmill   universal   parallel bars

D ANALOGIES

| billiard ball | elbow pads | paddle | pool stick | shuttlecock | weightlifting |

1. tennis ball : tennis racket *as* ping pong ball : ____paddle____
2. tennis racket : tennis ball *as* badminton racket : _____
3. golf ball : golf club *as* billiard ball : _____
4. inline skating : knee pads *as* skateboarding : _____
5. trampoline : gymnastics *as* weights : _____
6. table tennis : ping pong ball *as* pool : _____

131

A WHICH SPORTS?

Look at the pictures on page 142 of the Picture Dictionary and answer these questions.

1. In which sports do players wear something on their head?

    _____baseball_____   _____

    _____   _____

    _____

2. What sport uses a ball that isn't round?

    _____

3. Which sports are played on a field?

    _____   _____

    _____   _____

    _____

4. Which sport is played on a rink?

    _____

B CROSSWORD: *Pictures to Words*

Across

3. 6.

7. 8.

Down

1. 2.

4. 5.

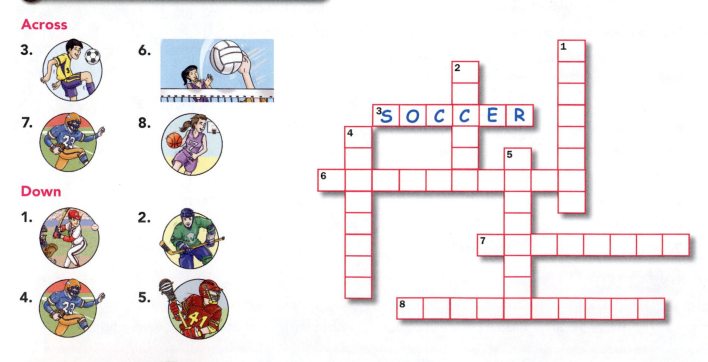

³S O C C E R

C LISTENING

Listen and circle the correct word to complete each sentence.

1. field   (court)   3. court   rink   5. court   field
2. player   field   4. lacrosse player lacrosse   6. field   player

132

A ASSOCIATIONS

_g_ **1.** softball   **a.** helmet, shoulder pads

____ **2.** football   **b.** net, volleyball

____ **3.** hockey   **c.** bat, helmet, glove

____ **4.** soccer   **d.** face guard, stick, ball

____ **5.** volleyball   **e.** hoop, backboard

____ **6.** lacrosse   **f.** shinguards, goal

____ **7.** basketball   **g.** glove, softball

____ **8.** baseball   **h.** skates, stick, mask

B WHICH WORD?

1. I'm batting next. Where's the batting (stick   (helmet))?
2. Put on the hockey (puck   mask) to protect your face.
3. That player isn't wearing hockey (skates   sticks)!
4. The basketball went through the (goal   hoop).
5. Football players must wear (helmets   mitts).
6. I can't find my softball (glove   shinguards).
7. Pass the ball with the (hockey   lacrosse) stick.
8. All the players on our team are wearing new (uniforms   nets).

C WHICH WORD DOESN'T BELONG?

1. catcher's mask   hockey mask   (shinguard)   face guard
2. bat   lacrosse ball   hockey puck   soccer ball
3. hockey stick   bat   backboard   lacrosse stick
4. baseball glove   shoulder pads   hockey glove   catcher's mitt
5. basketball   football   volleyball   hockey

D LISTENING: *Which Sport?*

Listen to the radio announcer. Write the number next to the correct picture.

____

____

____

_1_

A WHICH SPORTS?

Look at the pictures on page 144 of the Picture Dictionary and answer these questions.

1. Which sports do you do standing?

_____skiing_____   _____   _____

_____   _____

2. Which sports do you do sitting down?

_____   _____   _____

3. Which sports do you do on an ice rink?

_____   _____

4. For which sport do you use a gas-powered engine?

_____

B MATCHING

__e__ 1. downhill skiing   a. on an ice rink

_____ 2. cross-country skiing   b. down a hill, sitting down

_____ 3. skating   c. down a mountain, in a group

_____ 4. sledding   d. through a field or woods, on a vehicle

_____ 5. snowmobiling   e. down a mountain, standing up

_____ 6. bobsledding   f. through a field or woods, standing up

C WHICH WORD?

1. (Downhill   (Cross-country)) skiing is very calm and peaceful.
2. We go downhill skiing without (poles   bindings).
3. Our son practices figure (skating   skiing) every day.
4. Let's go down the hill together in this (snowboard   saucer)!
5. I have a friend on the Olympic (sledding   bobsledding) team.
6. I go through the woods quickly with my (snowmobile   skates).

D WHAT ARE THEY?

__c__ 1. We use these to protect the bottom of skates.   a. bindings

_____ 2. We use these to attach ski boots to skis.   b. snowmobile

_____ 3. This is a round sled.   c. skate guards

_____ 4. This is a vehicle with a motor.   d. poles

_____ 5. This is the part of the skate that touches the ice. e. saucer

_____ 6. We use these to help us keep balance.   f. blade

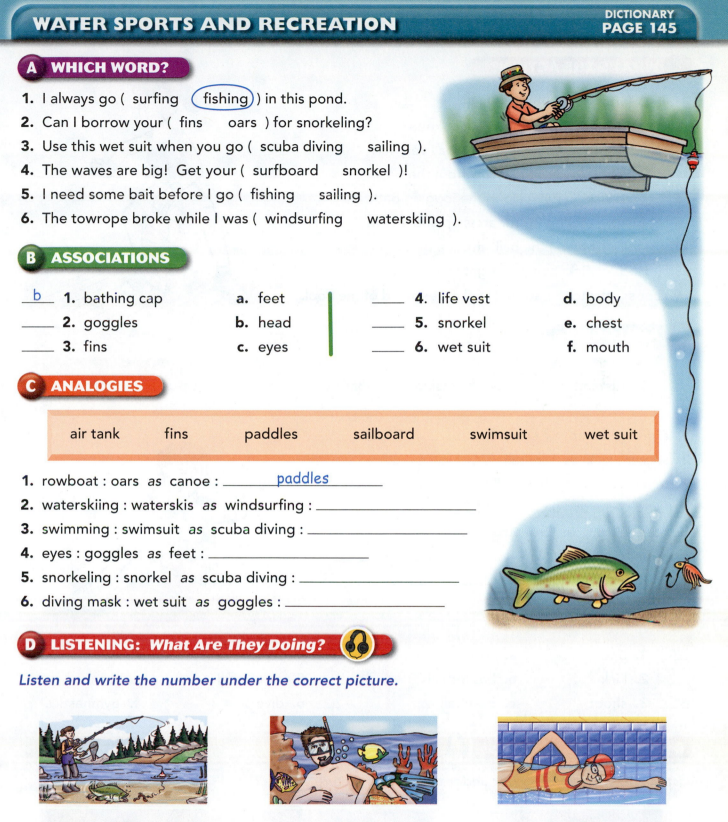

A WHICH WORD?

1. I always go (surfing (fishing)) in this pond.
2. Can I borrow your (fins   oars) for snorkeling?
3. Use this wet suit when you go (scuba diving   sailing).
4. The waves are big! Get your (surfboard   snorkel)!
5. I need some bait before I go (fishing   sailing).
6. The towrope broke while I was (windsurfing   waterskiing).

B ASSOCIATIONS

_b_ **1.** bathing cap   **a.** feet   ____ **4.** life vest   **d.** body

____ **2.** goggles   **b.** head   ____ **5.** snorkel   **e.** chest

____ **3.** fins   **c.** eyes   ____ **6.** wet suit   **f.** mouth

C ANALOGIES

air tank	fins	paddles	sailboard	swimsuit	wet suit

1. rowboat : oars *as* canoe : _____paddles_____
2. waterskiing : waterskis *as* windsurfing : _____
3. swimming : swimsuit *as* scuba diving : _____
4. eyes : goggles *as* feet : _____
5. snorkeling : snorkel *as* scuba diving : _____
6. diving mask : wet suit *as* goggles : _____

D LISTENING: *What Are They Doing?*

Listen and write the number under the correct picture.

____

____

____

____

_1_

____

____

A WHAT'S THE ACTION?

1. ((Dribble)   Reach) the ball!
2. Can you (bend   shoot) your knee?
3. He can (lift   pass) the football very far!
4. (Shoot   Pitch) the arrow from the bow.
5. Let's (kick   run) along the jogging path.
6. (Jump   Swing) your arms up and down!
7. (Hit   Throw) the ball with the bat!
8. (Hop   Kick) on your right foot ten times!
9. Let's (stretch   swim) to the deep end of the pool.

B ANALOGIES

| handstand | shoot | skip | hands | pitch | sit-up | throw |

1. arms : push-up *as* stomach : _____ sit-up _____
2. soccer : kick *as* football : _____
3. tennis : serve *as* baseball : _____
4. jump : hop *as* run : _____
5. baseball : hit *as* basketball : _____
6. hop : feet *as* cartwheel : _____
7. feet : jump *as* hands: _____

C ASSOCIATIONS

___c___ 1. pitch   **a.** soccer
_____ 2. kick   **b.** basketball
_____ 3. shoot   **c.** baseball

_____ 4. serve   **d.** swimming
_____ 5. cartwheel   **e.** tennis
_____ 6. dive   **f.** gymnastics

D LISTENING: *Aerobics*

Listen and write the number under the correct picture.

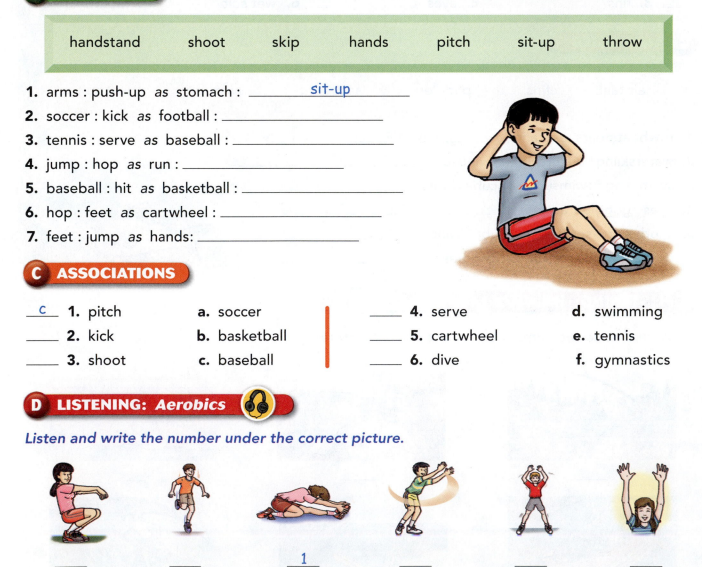

_____   _____   1   _____   _____   _____

A WHICH WORD?

1. If you like to laugh, you should go to a (music (comedy)) club.
2. I love that (actor   actress). She's in all my favorite movies.
3. Who is the (conductor   concert hall) for tonight's concert?
4. That (ballerina   comedian) dances very gracefully.
5. Let's change seats. I can't see the movie (theater   screen) from here.
6. Our favorite (actor   band) is performing in a concert this weekend.
7. The tickets for this (opera   play) are very expensive. Who is the singer?
8. Let's go to the theater tonight. They're performing a wonderful (play   movie).

B MATCH AND WRITE

Draw a line to complete the word. Then write the word on the line.

1. opera   screen   ___opera singer___
2. concert   club   _____
3. music   dancer   _____
4. movie   singer   _____
5. ballet   hall   _____

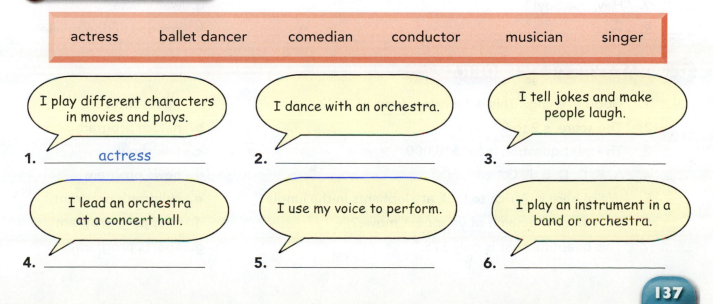

C WHICH WORD DOESN'T BELONG?

1. actor   (band)   actress   singer
2. theater   concert hall singer   comedy club
3. comedian   musician   orchestra   band
4. concert   ballet   opera   play
5. band   theater   music club   movie theater

D WHO IS TALKING?

actress   ballet dancer   comedian   conductor   musician   singer

I play different characters in movies and plays.

I dance with an orchestra.

I tell jokes and make people laugh.

1. ___actress___   2. _____   3. _____

I lead an orchestra at a concert hall.

I use my voice to perform.

I play an instrument in a band or orchestra.

4. _____   5. _____   6. _____

A WHO LIKES WHAT?

| movies | music | play | TV programs |

I like to go out on Friday and Saturday nights. I like to go to concerts to listen to _____music_____ [1] or go to the theater to see a _____ [2]. My brother doesn't like to go out on weekends. He likes to stay home, sit in the living room, and watch his favorite _____ [3]. My older sister likes to stay home, too. She rents _____ [4] and watches them on her DVD player. We never do anything together!

B LISTENING: *What Type of Music?*

Listen and write the number next to the type of music you hear.

| | classical | | hip hop | | rock | | gospel |
| **1** | reggae | | blues | | jazz | | country |

C WHAT TYPE OF MOVIE?

_e_ **1.** "This is the true story of what really happened."

_____ **2.** "The enemy is here. The fighting will begin soon."

_____ **3.** "Ha! Ha! Ha!"

_____ **4.** "Non possiamo vivere così. Scappiamo subito."

_____ **5.** "We are here from the planet Zorcon."

_____ **6.** "I'm gonna get that rabbit if it's the last thing I do!"

_____ **7.** "Hey, cowboy!"

_____ **8.** ♫♪

a. foreign film
b. western
c. cartoon
d. comedy
e. documentary
f. musical
g. war movie
h. science fiction movie

D WHAT TYPE OF TV PROGRAM?

_d_ **1.** "Good evening. This is Monday, June 19, 2012."

_____ **2.** "The score is 9 to 0."

_____ **3.** "The next question is for $10,000."

_____ **4.** "A, B, C, D, E, F, G."

_____ **5.** "We're here in Africa to look at elephants in the jungle."

_____ **6.** "So, what's the name of your next movie?"

_____ **7.** "This beautiful coat is only $75."

a. game show
b. nature program
c. talk show
d. news program
e. children's program
f. shopping program
g. sports program

A WHICH INSTRUMENT DOESN'T BELONG?

1. electric keyboard   (violin)   piano   organ
2. electric guitar   harp   banjo   trumpet
3. cello   piccolo   oboe   bassoon
4. trumpet   xylophone   tuba   trombone
5. tambourine   harmonica   drums   xylophone

B MUSIC ASSOCIATIONS

<u>b</u> 1. popular music   a. electric guitar
____ 2. rock   b. electric keyboard
____ 3. blues   c. acoustic guitar
____ 4. jazz   d. harmonica
____ 5. classical   e. violin
____ 6. folk   f. saxophone

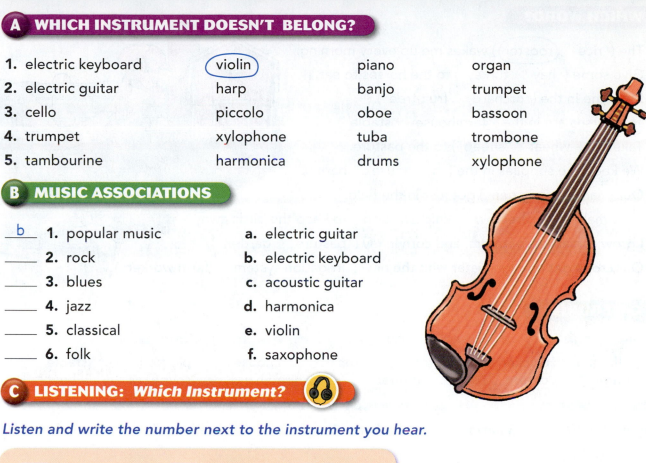

C LISTENING: Which Instrument?

Listen and write the number next to the instrument you hear.

☐ harmonica	☐ drum	☐ trumpet
☐ flute	☐ tuba	1 piano
☐ banjo	☐ harp	☐ guitar

D CROSSWORD: Pictures to Words

Across

1.    5. ╱   7. 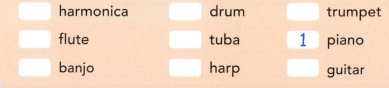   9.

Down

2.    3.    4.

6.   8.

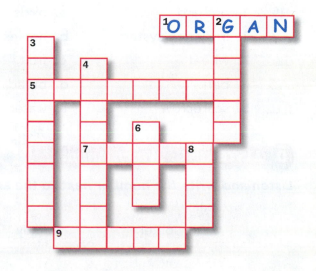

|¹O|R|²G|A|N|

A WHICH WORD?

1. The (rice **rooster**) wakes me up every morning.
2. Give some (hay   turkey) to the horses to eat.
3. Meet me in the (orchard   fruit tree).
4. The horses are in the (farmhouse   stable).
5. Take the (wheat   sheep) to the pasture.
6. We keep the supplies in the (hen house   barn).
7. Our (lamb   pig pen) got lost in the field.
8. Let's make a (scarecrow   chicken coop) to keep the birds away.
9. I grow tomatoes, peppers, and corn in my (pasture   garden).
10. Our crops get enough water with the new (irrigation system   farm worker).

B CATEGORIES

| alfalfa | chicken coop | farm worker | hen house | pig pen | stable |
| barn | cotton | farmer | hired hand | soybeans | wheat |

People Who Work on a Farm

farm worker
_____
_____

Farm Crops

_____
_____
_____

Places Where Animals Stay

_____
_____
_____
_____

C ASSOCIATIONS

_c_ 1. orchard
___ 2. irrigation system
___ 3. wheat
___ 4. barn
___ 5. scarecrow

a. birds
b. horses
c. fruit
d. bread
e. water

___ 6. barnyard
___ 7. cow
___ 8. sheep
___ 9. pig
___ 10. hired hand

f. wool
g. farm help
h. bacon
i. milk
j. animals

D LISTENING: Which Animal?

Listen and write the number next to the animal you hear.

___ rooster   ___ turkey   _1_ goat   ___ pig   ___ horse

A WHICH WORD?

1. We gave our daughter a (slug   (goldfish)) for her birthday.
2. Different zebras have different kinds of (stripes   horns).
3. Did you feed the (platypus   gerbil) today?
4. Can we take a ride on the (pony   coyote)?
5. Look at the (bison   squirrel) in that tree!
6. Let's go to see the (rats   monkeys) in the zoo!
7. I'm going to take the (dog   hamster) for a walk.
8. This sweater is made from the wool of a (llama   hippopotamus).

B WHICH ANIMAL?

_d_	**1.** kangaroo	**a.** It has sharp quills.
____	**2.** porcupine	**b.** It eats small insects.
____	**3.** anteater	**c.** It lives at the North Pole.
____	**4.** polar bear	**d.** Its kids are in its pouch.
____	**5.** worm	**e.** When it sleeps, it hangs upside down.
____	**6.** bat	**f.** It's small and lives in the ground.

____	**7.** platypus	**g.** It sprays a bad smell.
____	**8.** beaver	**h.** It laughs like a human.
____	**9.** chimpanzee	**i.** It has strong teeth and lives in a river.
____	**10.** skunk	**j.** It's from China.
____	**11.** hyena	**k.** It lays eggs.
____	**12.** panda	**l.** It uses its hands like a human.

C ANIMAL ANALOGIES

1. cat : kitten *as* _____dog_____ : puppy
2. elephant : tusk *as* _____ : horn
3. wolf : wolves *as* _____ : mice
4. leopard : spots *as* _____ : stripes
5. horse : tail *as* _____ : mane
6. camel : desert *as* _____ : river
7. hoof : deer *as* _____ : tiger
8. whiskers : cat *as* _____ : porcupine
9. mouse : hamster *as* _____ : baboon
10. cat : mouse *as* _____ : rabbit

> beaver
> dog
> gibbon
> lion
> mouse
> paw
> quills
> rhinoceros
> wolf
> zebra

(continued)

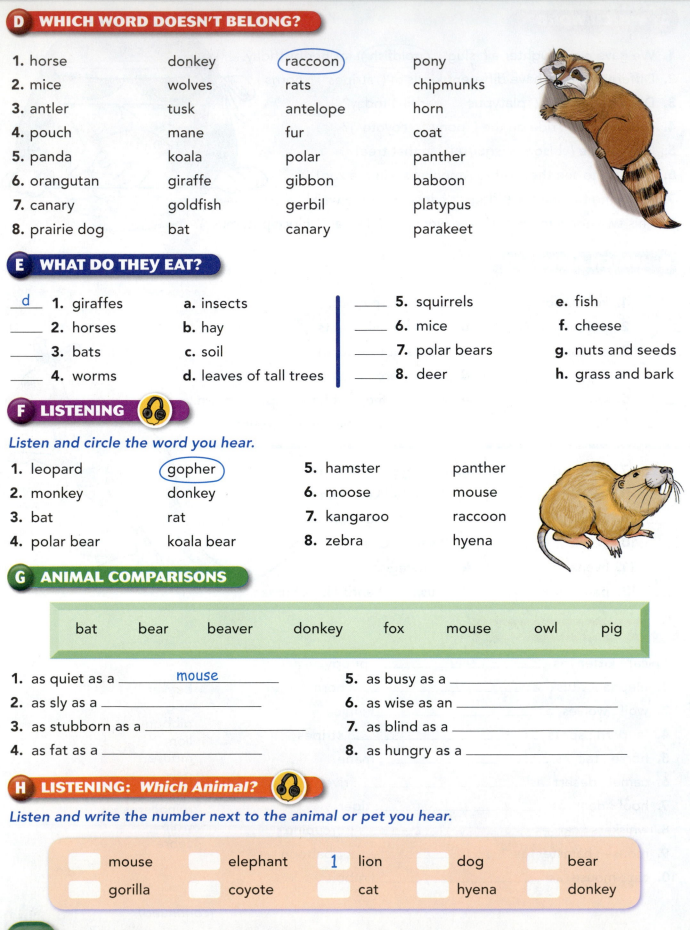

D WHICH WORD DOESN'T BELONG?

1. horse	donkey	(raccoon)	pony
2. mice	wolves	rats	chipmunks
3. antler	tusk	antelope	horn
4. pouch	mane	fur	coat
5. panda	koala	polar	panther
6. orangutan	giraffe	gibbon	baboon
7. canary	goldfish	gerbil	platypus
8. prairie dog	bat	canary	parakeet

E WHAT DO THEY EAT?

_d_ 1. giraffes	a. insects		___ 5. squirrels	e. fish
___ 2. horses	b. hay		___ 6. mice	f. cheese
___ 3. bats	c. soil		___ 7. polar bears	g. nuts and seeds
___ 4. worms	d. leaves of tall trees		___ 8. deer	h. grass and bark

F LISTENING

Listen and circle the word you hear.

1. leopard	(gopher)	5. hamster	panther
2. monkey	donkey	6. moose	mouse
3. bat	rat	7. kangaroo	raccoon
4. polar bear	koala bear	8. zebra	hyena

G ANIMAL COMPARISONS

bat	bear	beaver	donkey	fox	mouse	owl	pig

1. as quiet as a ____mouse____
2. as sly as a _____
3. as stubborn as a _____
4. as fat as a _____

5. as busy as a _____
6. as wise as an _____
7. as blind as a _____
8. as hungry as a _____

H LISTENING: *Which Animal?*

Listen and write the number next to the animal or pet you hear.

[ ] mouse	[ ] elephant	[1] lion	[ ] dog	[ ] bear
[ ] gorilla	[ ] coyote	[ ] cat	[ ] hyena	[ ] donkey

A WHICH BIRD?

1. A bird that can learn to speak is the (ostrich   (parrot)).
2. The smallest bird is the (goose   hummingbird).
3. A bird that can't fly is the (penguin   blue jay).
4. A bird that usually stands on one leg is the (crane   crow).
5. A bird that usually lives in the city is the (pigeon   pelican).
6. One of the most famous ballets is (Swan   Sparrow) Lake.
7. The (eagle   woodpecker) is the symbol of the United States.
8. The bird with feathers that look like many eyes is the (flamingo   peacock).
9. A bird with excellent eyesight that comes out at night is the (owl   sparrow).

B WHICH INSECT?

1. The insect that becomes a butterfly is the ((caterpillar)   centipede).
2. One of the most dangerous insects is the (dragonfly   scorpion).
3. The insect that shines a light at night is the (firefly   wasp).
4. An insect with eight legs is the (moth   spider).
5. (Beetle   Mosquito) bites are itchy.
6. An insect that drinks blood is the (moth   tick).
7. (Bees   Grasshoppers) are insects that make honey.
8. An insect that sings at night is the (dragonfly   cricket).

C ANALOGIES

bill	cocoon	feather	grasshopper	moth	nest

1. bee : beehive *as* robin : _____nest_____
2. woodpecker : beak *as* duck : _____
3. butterfly : wing *as* peacock : _____
4. eagle : hawk *as* butterfly : _____
5. bird : egg *as* butterfly : _____
6. sea : seagull *as* fields : _____

D LISTENING: *Which Bird or Insect?*

Listen and write the number next to the bird or insect you hear.

	parrot		owl		cricket		bee
	seagull		woodpecker		duck	1	crow

A CATEGORIES

bass	cod	newt	salamander	stingray	trout
cobra	frog	rattlesnake	shark	toad	tuna

Fish We Eat	Amphibians	Deadly Fish/Reptiles
bass		

B WHICH WORD?

1. (A starfish   (An octopus)) has eight tentacles.
2. A (turtle   crocodile) lives in a hard shell.
3. (Jellyfish   Dolphins) are very friendly animals.
4. Don't swim in that water! There are (swordfish   sharks) there!
5. A (squid   crab) releases black ink if it feels in danger.
6. (Sharks   Whales) are the largest animals on Earth.
7. Sea (horses   lions) are very small creatures.

C WHICH WORD DOESN'T BELONG?

1. fin   (seal)   gill   scale
2. rattlesnake   cobra   walrus   boa constrictor
3. squid   iguana   alligator   lizard
4. trout   jellyfish   cod   bass
5. tuna   squid   snail   iguana
6. salamander   frog   toad   flounder
7. ray   tusk   tentacle   shell

D ANALOGIES

1. fish : tuna *as* snake : _boa constrictor_
2. turtle : tortoise *as* frog : _____
3. octopus : tentacle *as* trout : _____
4. turtle : shell *as* fish : _____
5. dolphin : whale *as* lizard : _____
6. frog : toad *as* salamander : _____
7. eight : octopus *as* five : _____
8. dolphin : porpoise *as* seal : _____

boa constrictor
fin
iguana
newt
scales
sea lion
starfish
toad

A WHAT'S THE WORD?

branch	leaves	maple	palm	redwood	willow

1. I like the different colors of _____ leaves _____ in the fall.
2. The _____ leaf is the symbol on the Canadian flag.
3. The largest tree in North America is the _____.
4. Look at all the coconuts on that _____ tree!
5. Did you know that _____ trees love to grow near water?
6. During the storm, a big _____ from a tree fell on my car.

B WHERE DO THEY GROW?

__c__ 1. weeping willows   a. in the desert
____ 2. cacti   b. along walls and fences
____ 3. roses   c. near rivers
____ 4. vines   d. in California
____ 5. redwoods   e. in the garden
____ 6. palm trees   f. on mountains
____ 7. pine trees   g. in tropical areas

C WHICH WORD?

1. Many colorful types of (tulips   cacti) come from the Netherlands.
2. I gave my wife one dozen (bushes   roses) on our first anniversary.
3. Pine (needles   cones) are the leaves of pine trees.
4. Be careful! That plant has (bulbs   thorns)!
5. (Poinsettias   Carnations) are popular in the winter.
6. Trees and flowers drink water through their (roots   petals).
7. (Sunflowers   Crocuses) follow the sunshine during the day.
8. Some (twigs   berries) are very tasty, but others are poisonous.
9. My favorite flowers are (pansies and petunias   cherries and magnolias).

D ANALOGIES

1. flower : stem as tree: _____ trunk _____
2. oak : tree as lily : _____
3. tree : shrub as branch : _____
4. elm : root as tulip : _____
5. leaves : leaf as cacti : _____

| bulb |
| cactus |
| flower |
| twig |
| trunk |

A ASSOCIATIONS

_d_ **1.** solar energy   **a.** cars and factories

____ **2.** hydroelectric power   **b.** toxic waste

____ **3.** air pollution   **c.** radiation

____ **4.** nuclear energy   **d.** the sun

____ **5.** water pollution   **e.** waterfalls

B MATCH AND WRITE

Draw a line to complete the phrase. Then write the phrase on the line.

1. natural   waste   _natural gas_

2. acid   energy   _____

3. toxic   rain   _____

4. geothermal   gas   _____

5. global   power   _____

6. hydroelectric   warming   _____

C WHICH WORD?

1. The factory closed because of its (hazardous waste   solar energy).

2. (Global   Geothermal) energy comes from the earth's internal heat.

3. We should (recycle   conserve) plastic and paper products.

4. Burning (wind   coal) produces the most air pollution.

5. Do you heat your house with (oil   radiation)?

6. (Acid rain   Natural gas) destroyed the forests in this area.

7. If you drive your car less, you'll save (energy   water).

8. Let's (recycle   carpool) to save gas and help the environment.

D WHAT'S THE WORD?

air	carpool	conserve	global	recycle	save energy	solar

Our family is very concerned about water and ____air____[1] pollution and

_____[2] warming, so we started doing energy conservation in our house recently.

First, we started to _____[3] all our plastic bottles and newspapers. Next, my

father decided to _____[4] to work instead of driving by himself every day. Also,

we aren't going to water the lawn in the summer to _____[5] water. Another thing

we did is install a system to collect _____[6] energy from the sun. Finally, we added new

insulation to the walls and windows of the house, so that we can _____[7] in the

winter time.

A WHAT IS IT?

| blizzard | earthquake | forest fire | hurricane | tsunami | volcanic eruption |

1. strong winds, heavy rain _____ _hurricane_ _____

2. shaking earth, damage to buildings _____

3. huge waves, lots of water _____

4. burning trees, smoke damage _____

5. strong winds, heavy snow _____

6. shaking earth, fire and smoke from a mountain _____

B WHICH WORD?

1. Did you hear about the (wildfire ⟨typhoon⟩)?
   Yes. The winds were very strong.

2. I think there's a (tornado   blizzard) coming.
   Can you see it?

3. The town near the river had a (landslide   flood).
   Was there a lot of water damage?

4. Do you remember we're having a (mudslide   drought)?
   Yes, I remember. We need to conserve water.

5. The (forest fire   earthquake) caused a lot of damage!
   I know. All the trees burned down!

6. Our town is safe from (landslides   tsunamis).
   We're lucky. We're very far from the ocean.

C ANALOGIES

1. typhoon : hurricane *as* forest fire : _____ _wildfire_ _____

2. hurricane : blizzard *as* landslide : _____

3. landslide : mudslide *as* hurricane : _____

4. fire : volcanic eruption *as* water : _____

| avalanche |
| flood |
| typhoon |
| wildfire |

D WHAT ARE THEY TALKING ABOUT?

_e_ 1. "The wave is so big!"   **a.** earthquake

___ 2. "The water is rising very high!"   **b.** drought

___ 3. "Our crops are dying! They need water!"   **c.** hurricane

___ 4. "It snowed more than 30 inches!"   **d.** blizzard

___ 5. "The winds are very strong!"   **e.** tsunami

___ 6. "The ground is shaking!"   **f.** flood

ANSWER KEY AND LISTENING SCRIPTS

WORKBOOK PAGE 1

A. WHAT'S THE WORD?
1. family
2. first
3. phone
4. social security
5. apartment
6. zip
7. area

B. WHAT'S THE ANSWER?
1. d
2. c
3. a
4. b
5. h
6. e
7. g
8. f

WORKBOOK PAGE 2

A. WHICH GROUP?
daughter
mother
sister
wife
brother
father
husband
son

B. HIS NAME OR HER NAME?
1. Her
2. His
3. Her
4. His
5. His
6. Her

C. WHO IS WHO?
1. e
2. f
3. d
4. a
5. c
6. b

D. WHICH WORD DOESN'T BELONG?
1. son (The others are female.)
2. mother (The others are male.)
3. baby (The others are adults.)
4. wife (The others are siblings.)
5. husband (The others are children.)

WORKBOOK PAGES 3–4

A. WHICH GROUP?
aunt
niece
mother-in-law
daughter-in-law
sister-in-law
cousin
uncle
nephew
father-in-law
son-in-law
brother-in-law

B. WHO ARE THEY?
1. grandfather
2. uncle
3. cousin
4. mother-in-law
5. father
6. sister-in-law

C. WHICH WORD?
1. uncle, his
2. She's, she
3. His, nephew
4. niece, Her
5. uncle, cousin
6. he, wife

D. WHAT'S THE WORD?
1. sister
2. father
3. mother
4. brother
5. son
6. daughter

E. AT LINDA AND TOM'S WEDDING
1. wife
2. sister
3. husband
4. parents
5. father
6. mother
7. nephew
8. son
9. sister
10. niece
11. brother

WORKBOOK PAGE 5

A. MATCHING
1. d
2. e
3. f
4. c
5. b
6. a

B. WHAT DO YOU USE?
1. chalk
2. a pencil
3. a keyboard
4. a thumbtack
5. a ruler
6. a calculator

C. WHERE ARE THEY?
1. monitor
2. chalkboard
3. bookcase
4. pencil sharpener
5. table
6. desk

WORKBOOK PAGES 6–7

A. THE TEACHER'S INSTRUCTIONS
1. word
2. Look
3. paper
4. words
5. Correct
6. each other
7. name
8. Match
9. seat
10. group

B. WHAT'S THE WORD?
1. together
2. word
3. name
4. blank
5. dictionary
6. answer
7. work
8. answers
9. seat
10. lights
11. groups
12. paper

C. WHAT'S THE SEQUENCE?
1. 4   3. 4   5. 3
   1   3   4
   3   1   1
   2   2   2

2. 4   4. 2   6. 3
   3   1   2
   1   4   1
   2   3   4

D. WHAT ARE THEY DOING?
1. He's signing his name.
2. She's raising her hand.
3. He's collecting the tests.
4. They're sharing with the class.
5. He's doing his homework.
6. She's erasing the board.
7. They're working in a group.
8. She's lowering the shades.

E. LISTENING
Listen and choose the best word to complete the instructions.

1. Spell your . . . .
2. Go to the . . . .
3. Listen to the . . . .
4. Bring in your . . . .
5. Pronounce the . . . .
6. Break up into small . . . .
7. Work as a . . . .
8. Choose the correct . . . .
9. Fill in the . . . .

Answers
1. b   4. b   7. b
2. a   5. c   8. c
3. b   6. a   9. b

WORKBOOK PAGE 8

A. WHERE ARE THEY?
1. in
2. above
3. in front of
4. to the right of
5. between
6. on, under

B. LISTENING
Listen and write the number next to the correct item.

1. It's in the pencil sharpener.
2. It's above the globe.
3. It's on the dictionary.
4. It's to the right of the globe.
5. It's under the clock.
6. It's above the dictionary and the monitor.
7. It's below the bulletin board to the right of the dictionary.
8. It's above the pencil sharpener to the left of the clock.

Answers
2   5
4   3
8   1
7   6

C. LIKELY OR UNLIKELY?

	Likely	Unlikely
1.		✓
2.	✓	
3.	✓	
4.		✓
5.	✓	
6.		✓

WORKBOOK PAGE 9

A. EVERY MORNING
1. get
2. brushes
3. washes
4. puts on
5. takes
6. shaves
7. combs
8. get
9. have

B. MATCHING
1. f
2. a
3. e
4. d
5. c
6. b

C. CROSSWORD: What Do We Do?
(See page 169.)

D. WHAT'S THE SEQUENCE?
6
1
4
3
5
2

E. LISTENING: *Everyday Sounds*
Listen to the sounds. Write the number next to the activity you hear.

1. (sound: taking a shower)
2. (sound: shaving)
3. (sound: brushing teeth)
4. (sound: taking a bath)
5. (sound: making dinner)

2
3
5
1
4

WORKBOOK PAGE 10

A. CHOOSE THE RIGHT WORD

1. b   3. a   5. c
2. c   4. b   6. c

B. WHICH WORD DOESN'T BELONG?

1. b   3. b   5. c   7. a
2. a   4. a   6. b   8. c

C. A BUSY DAY

1. studying   4. take
2. feeding   5. do
3. go   6. iron

WORKBOOK PAGE 11

A. WHICH WORD?

1. TV   5. radio
2. letter   6. practicing
3. flowers   7. book
4. using   8. guitar

B. LISTENING

Listen to the sounds. Write the number next to the activity you hear.

1. (sound: swimming)
2. (sound: watching TV)
3. (sound: using a computer)
4. (sound: practicing the piano)
5. (sound: playing the guitar)
6. (sound: listening to music)

Answers

4   1
2   3
6   5

C. WHAT ARE THEY DOING?

1. He's swimming.
2. She's relaxing.
3. They're playing.
4. She's exercising.

WORKBOOK PAGE 12

A. WHAT'S THE RESPONSE?

1. e   3. a   5. b
2. d   4. c

B. WHAT'S THE ORDER?

1. Robert isn't here right now.
2. Can you please repeat that?
3. How are you doing?
4. I'd like to introduce my wife.
5. Can you please say that again?
6. Can I please speak to Maria?

C. WHICH WORD?

1. I'm   6. new
2. meet   7. speak
3. ask   8. say
4. understand 9. here
5. soon

D. LISTENING

Listen and choose the best response.

1. Good morning.
2. What's new with you?
3. Good night.
4. How are you?
5. Hi. I'm Tom.
6. Good afternoon.
7. Good-bye.
8. Hello.
9. Nice to meet you.
10. See you later.
11. Thank you.
12. May I please speak to Ron?

Answers

1. a   4. a   7. b   10. a
2. b   5. a   8. a   11. b
3. b   6. b   9. b   12. a

WORKBOOK PAGE 13

A. WHAT'S THE WORD?

1. sunny   4. windy
2. raining   5. smoggy
3. humid   6. foggy

B. ASSOCIATIONS

1. c   3. a   5. b   7. f
2. e   4. g   6. d

C. WHICH WORD?

1. temperature   4. thunderstorm
2. cool   5. dust storm
3. cloudy

D. FAHRENHEIT AND CELSIUS

1. a   3. a   5. b   7. a
2. b   4. a   6. a

WORKBOOK PAGE 14

A. WRITE THE NUMBERS

1. 14   6. seventeen
2. 25   7. thirty-three
3. 68   8. forty-six
4. 99   9. fifty-one
5. 110   10. eighty

B. MATCHING: *Cardinal and Ordinal Numbers*

1. d   3. e   5. f   7. h
2. g   4. a   6. c   8. b

C. WHICH NUMBER?

1. fifth   6. fourteenth
2. ten   7. fifty
3. sixth   8. eighteen
4. eighty-nine 9. twenty-one
5. second   10. thirtieth

D. LISTENING

Listen and circle the correct number.

1. Please read page five.
2. We live on the first floor.
3. There are thirty people in the class.
4. This lamp was sixty-two dollars.
5. My grandmother is seventy years old.
6. This is the second time I've seen this play.

7. That'll be nine dollars.
8. We've been married for forty years.

Answers

1. five   5. seventy
2. first   6. second
3. thirty   7. nine
4. sixty-two 8. forty

WORKBOOK PAGE 15

A. WHAT TIME IS IT?

1. 7:00   2. 7:30   3. 7:45
4. 7:15   5. 7:05   6. 7:50

B. MATCHING: *What's the Time?*

1. 6:30 .... six thirty
2. 6:40 .... twenty to seven
3. 5:45 .... five forty-five
4. 6:50 .... ten to seven
5. 6:15 .... six fifteen

C. LISTENING

Listen to the conversation and circle the correct time.

1. A. Excuse me. Can you tell me the time?
   B. Yes. It's exactly seven o'clock.
2. A. Pardon me. Do you have the time?
   B. Certainly. It's five minutes after nine.
3. A. What time does the movie begin?
   B. It begins at a quarter to eight.
4. A. What time will we arrive in Chicago?
   B. At ten oh five.
5. A. Excuse me. What time does the bus leave?
   B. At half past one.
6. A. What time will they arrive?
   B. Probably around midnight.

Answers

1. 7:00   3. 7:45   5. 1:30
2. 9:05   4. 10:05   6. 12:00 A.M.

D. WHEN IS IT?

1. A.M.   3. P.M.
2. midnight   4. noon

WORKBOOK PAGES 16–17

A. COINS

nickel, quarter, dime, penny, silver dollar, half-dollar

B. MATCHING

1. fifty cents .... half-dollar
2. twenty-five cents .... quarter
3. one cent .... penny
4. ten cents .... dime
5. one dollar .... silver dollar
6. five cents .... nickel

C. COUNTING COINS

1. 25¢ or $.25   4. 15¢ or $.15
2. 5¢ or $.05   5. 51¢ or $.51
3. 35¢ or $.35

D. COUNTING BILLS

1. $5.00   3. $30.00   5. $55.00
2. $10.00   4. $3.00

E. MAKING CHANGE

1. two dollars
2. twenty-five cents
3. five dollars
4. twenty dollars
5. five cents
6. one hundred dollars

F. LISTENING

Listen to the conversation and circle the correct amount.

1. A. How much does it cost?
   B. It costs one dollar.
2. A. Do you have any cash?
   B. Yes. I have twenty-five dollars.
3. A. Do you have enough money?
   B. Mmm. Let's see. I have seven fifty.
4. A. Do you have enough money to go to the store?
   B. Yes. I have forty dollars.
5. A. How much money do you have?
   B. I have three five-dollar bills, a quarter, and a dime.
6. A. What's the cost?
   B. Forty-seven dollars and sixty cents.
7. A. Do you have any change?
   B. I only have a half-dollar and a nickel.
8. A. How much is it?
   B. It's only ninety-nine ninety-nine.

Answers

1. $1.00   5. $15.35
2. $25.00   6. $47.60
3. $7.50   7. $.55
4. $40.00   8. $99.99

WORKBOOK PAGE 18

B. USING THE CALENDAR

1. Wednesday   4. Sunday
2. Friday   5. Thursday
3. Tuesday   6. Monday

C. DATES: *Words to Numbers*

1. 7/15/05   4. 5/2/08
2. 11/10/00   5. 1/19/11
3. 2/8/99   6. 10/31/03

D. DATES: *Numbers to Words*

1. March 3, 2003
2. June 11, 1995
3. September 20, 2006
4. April 14, 2004
5. August 29, 1966
6. December 16, 2012

E. WHAT'S THE SEQUENCE?

5	7	1	10
9	11	6	8
2	4	12	3

F. CROSSWORD

(See page 169.)

WORKBOOK PAGE 19

A. MATCHING

1. b   4. f   7. i
2. c   5. d   8. g
3. a   6. e   9. h

B. WHAT'S THE ORDER?

4
2
1
5
7
6
3

C. LISTENING

Listen and circle the correct words to complete the sentences.

1. His plane arrives this . . . .
2. I played basketball . . . .
3. Are you going to visit me . . .?
4. We call them twice a . . . .
5. I called you last . . . .
6. I'll be on vacation . . . .

Answers

1. evening   4. week
2. last night   5. night
3. this week   6. next week

D. WHICH WORD?

1. yesterday   5. once a
2. this   6. last
3. Winter   7. evening
4. tomorrow

E. WHAT'S THE SEASON?

1. winter   4. spring
2. summer   5. fall/autumn
3. fall/autumn   6. spring

WORKBOOK PAGE 20

A. COMPLETE THE SENTENCES

1. c   3. d   5. b   7. a
2. f   4. e   6. g

B. WHICH WORD?

1. in   4. suburbs
2. house   5. building
3. on   6. in

C. WHERE DO THEY LIVE?

1. b   3. a   5. b
2. a   4. b

WORKBOOK PAGE 21

A. CATEGORIES

3 Things You Can Sit on

loveseat
sofa/couch
armchair

6 Things You Plug in

DVD player
television/TV
VCR/video cassette recorder
stereo system
lamp
floor lamp

2 Things You Hang on the Wall

picture/photograph
painting

B. ANALOGIES

1. floor   4. end table
2. drapes   5. speaker
3. magazine holder

C. WHAT'S IN THE LIVING ROOM?

1. lamp   5. mantel
2. VCR   6. stereo
3. table   7. floor lamp
4. plant   8. fireplace

WORKBOOK PAGE 22

A. MATCHING

1. d   3. e   5. c
2. f   4. a   6. b

B. WHICH WORD DOESN'T BELONG?

1. pitcher (The others are used to put things on.)
2. napkin (The others are furniture.)
3. candle (The others are silverware.)
4. china (The others are for light.)
5. candlestick (The others are containers.)
6. knife (The others hold liquids.)
7. chandelier (The others go on a table.)

C. WHICH WORD?

1. vase   5. tablecloth
2. spoon   6. candlestick
3. buffet   7. tablecloth
4. fork

D. WORD SEARCH

(See page 169.)

WORKBOOK PAGE 23

A. MATCHING

1. b   3. a   5. g   7. h
2. d   4. c   6. e   8. f

B. WHICH WORD DOESN'T BELONG?

1. mirror (The others are bed coverings.)
2. clock radio (The others are bed coverings.)
3. curtains (The others are part of a bed.)
4. bedspread (The others are pieces of furniture.)
5. jewelry box (The others are electric.)
6. carpet (The others are bed coverings.)

C. MAKE THE BED!

4
6
3
5
1
2

D. WHAT'S IN THE BEDROOM?

1. pillow
2. carpet
3. jewelry box
4. clock radio
5. curtains
6. nightstand
7. bed frame
8. electric

WORKBOOK PAGE 24

A. COMPLETE THE SENTENCES

1. d
2. e
3. a
4. c
5. f
6. h
7. b
8. g

B. MATCH AND WRITE

1. dishwasher
2. placemat
3. cookbook
4. potholder
5. coffeemaker

C. WHAT'S IN THE KITCHEN?

1. coffeemaker
2. blender
3. canisters
4. spice rack
5. electric mixer, cabinet
6. microwave
7. tea kettle

D. CROSSWORD

(See page 169.)

WORKBOOK PAGE 25

A. MATCHING

1. d
2. a
3. e
4. c
5. b
6. g
7. j
8. i
9. h
10. f

B. WHICH WORD DOESN'T BELONG?

1. playpen (The others are toys.)
2. cradle (The others are for moving a baby.)
3. rattle (The others are for sitting.)
4. crib bumper (The others are pieces of furniture.)
5. mobile (The others are items a baby can sit in.)
6. intercom (The others are items a baby sits on.)

C. LISTENING

Listen and circle the word you hear.

1. My daughter loves her new doll.
2. Oh, no! I can't find the baby seat.
3. We're very happy with our new stroller.
4. High chairs are on sale this week.
5. I think we should buy a baby backpack.
6. The stretch suit is over there on the changing table.

Answers

1. doll
2. baby seat
3. stroller
4. high chairs
5. baby backpack
6. changing table

D. ASSOCIATIONS

1. c
2. e
3. d
4. b
5. a

E. WHICH WORD?

1. cradle
2. diaper pail
3. rattle
4. doll
5. toy chest
6. chest
7. night light
8. mobile
9. backpack

WORKBOOK PAGE 26

A. WHICH WORD?

1. scale
2. rubber mat
3. wastebasket
4. sponge
5. toothbrush
6. fan
7. plunger
8. washcloth
9. seat
10. soap

B. WHERE ARE THEY?

1. shelf
2. scale
3. vanity
4. mirror
5. hamper
6. air freshener
7. wastebasket

C. MATCHING

1. e
2. a
3. d
4. c
5. b
6. g
7. f
8. j
9. h
10. i

D. WHAT'S IN THE BATHROOM?

1. cup
2. mat
3. sink
4. shelf
5. fan
6. soap
7. drain
8. towel

WORKBOOK PAGE 27

A. HOME REPAIRS

1. roof
2. antenna
3. satellite
4. lamppost
5. back
6. doorknob
7. screens
8. garage
9. driveway
10. lawnmower
11. lawn chair
12. patio

B. ASSOCIATIONS

1. b
2. d
3. a
4. c
5. g
6. e
7. h
8. f

C. CROSSWORD

(See page 169.)

WORKBOOK PAGE 28

A. MATCHING

1. b
2. d
3. a
4. c
5. h
6. g
7. f
8. e

B. WHICH WORD?

1. key
2. elevator
3. trash chute
4. fire alarm
5. security deposit
6. lot
7. security gate
8. superintendent
9. classified ads
10. storage locker

C. OUR APARTMENT BUILDING

1. doorman
2. intercom
3. buzzer
4. lobby
5. stairway
6. trash
7. laundry
8. swimming
9. parking
10. lock
11. sprinkler
12. fire

WORKBOOK PAGE 29

A. SERVICE PEOPLE

1. painter
2. plumber
3. appliance repairperson
4. carpenter
5. exterminator
6. locksmith

B. HELP!

1. plumber
2. exterminator
3. electrician
4. roofer
5. chimneysweep
6. appliance repairperson
7. painter
8. carpenter

C. LOTS OF PROBLEMS!

1. broken
2. ring
3. peeling
4. leaking
5. loose
6. on
7. ants and rats

D. LISTENING

Listen and choose the best word to complete each sentence.

1. Call the plumber. We're having problems with our . . . .
2. Call the cable company. We're having problems with our . . . .
3. Call the exterminator! Our basement has a lot of . . . .
4. Call the electrician! There's a problem with our . . . .
5. We need an appliance repairperson. There's a problem with our . . . .
6. Can you recommend a good carpenter? We need someone who can fix our . . . .

Answers

1. a
2. b
3. a
4. b
5. b
6. a

WORKBOOK PAGE 30

A. WHICH WORD?

1. broom
2. bucket
3. scrub brush
4. vacuum cleaner
5. cleanser
6. feather duster
7. furniture polish
8. floor wax

B. WHICH WORD DOESN'T BELONG?

1. dust cloth (The others are for sweeping the floor.)
2. hand vacuum (The others are for washing the windows.)
3. vacuum (The others are for cleaning the bathroom.)
4. whisk broom (The others are for taking out the garbage.)
5. recycling bin (You hold the others in your hands for cleaning.)

6. feather (The others are types of mops.)

C. CROSSWORD: *Complete the Words*

(See page 169.)

D. LISTENING: *What Are They Doing?*

Listen to the sounds. Write the number next to the activity you hear.

1. (sound: mopping the floor)
2. (sound: vacuuming)
3. (sound: cleaning the bathroom)
4. (sound: sweeping)
5. (sound: taking out the garbage)
6. (sound: washing the windows)

Answers

4	6	3
2	1	5

E. LISTENING: *What Are They Going to Do?*

Listen to the conversation and choose the correct activity.

1. A. I can't find the vacuum cleaner.
   B. Look in the closet!
2. A. I can't find the sponge mop.
   B. Look over there!
3. A. Where's the recycling bin?
   B. Look in the hallway!
4. A. Where's the ammonia?
   B. It's in the cabinet.
5. A. I can't find the scrub brush.
   B. Look over there!
6. A. Where's the dustpan?
   B. It's in the closet.

Answers

1. b	3. a	5. b
2. a	4. b	6. a

WORKBOOK PAGE 31

A. WHICH WORD?

1. a flashlight
2. a mousetrap
3. yardstick
4. fly swatter
5. glue
6. work gloves
7. an extension cord
8. spray gun
9. roach killer
10. plunger

B. WHAT'S THE NEXT LINE?

1. c	3. a	5. h	7. d
2. g	4. f	6. b	8. e

C. MATCHING

1. b	6. i
2. e	7. f
3. d	8. j
4. c	9. h
5. a	10. g

D. LISTENING

Listen and circle the word you hear.

1. Where's the glue?
2. I can't find the paint pan.
3. Where's the plunger?
4. We need more paint thinner.

5. Can I have the spray gun?
6. I can't find the fly swatter!
7. Here's the paintbrush.
8. Where's the step ladder?
9. I can't find the masking tape.

Answers

1. glue	6. fly swatter
2. paint pan	7. paintbrush
3. plunger	8. step ladder
4. paint thinner	9. masking tape
5. spray gun	

WORKBOOK PAGE 32

A. MATCHING

1. c	3. a	5. g	7. f
2. d	4. b	6. h	8. e

B. HOW ARE THEY USED?

Tools that Cut	Power Tools
ax	electric drill
hacksaw	power sander
saw	router

Tools that Fasten Things

hammer
screwdriver
wrench

C. WHICH WORD?

1. hammer	4. ax
2. bit	5. a washer
3. hacksaw	6. power saw

D. WHICH WORD DOESN'T BELONG?

1. toolbox (The others are tools.)
2. saw (The others are for fastening things.)
3. scraper (The others are for cutting things.)
4. mallet (The others are for fastening things.)
5. hacksaw (The others are electric.)
6. wire (The others are tools.)

E. LISTENING

Listen to the sounds. Write the number next to the tool you hear.

1. (sound: electric drill)
2. (sound: hammer)
3. (sound: scraper)
4. (sound: ax)
5. (sound: power sander)
6. (sound: saw)

Answers

6	2	5	4	1	3

WORKBOOK PAGE 33

A. MATCHING

1. c	3. d	5. g	7. e
2. a	4. b	6. h	8. f

B. WHAT'S THE NEXT LINE?

1. f	3. h	5. a	7. d
2. c	4. g	6. e	8. b

C. CROSSWORD: *Complete the Actions*

(See page 169.)

D. LIKELY OR UNLIKELY?

	Likely	Unlikely
1.		✓
2.	✓	
3.	✓	
4.		✓
5.	✓	
6.		✓
7.		✓
8.	✓	

WORKBOOK PAGE 34

A. MAKE A LIST!

bakery
candy store
coffee shop
convenience store
delicatessen/deli
donut shop
fast-food restaurant
grocery store

B. MATCHING

1. d	6. h
2. a	7. j
3. e	8. g
4. c	9. f
5. b	10. i

C. WHICH PLACE?

1. flower	6. service
2. barber shop	7. donut shop
3. bakery	8. furniture
4. dry cleaners	9. fast-food
5. clinic	restaurant

D. WHAT'S THE PLACE?

1. drug store
2. eye-care center
3. grocery store
4. florist
5. child-care center
6. furniture store

WORKBOOK PAGE 35

A. GOING TO THE MALL

1. mall	5. photo
2. music	6. pizza
3. pet	7. restaurant
4. toy	8. theater

B. ANALOGIES

1. health club	4. restaurant
2. post office	5. library
3. jewelry store	6. travel agency

C. ASSOCIATIONS

1. c	3. g	5. f	7. d
2. a	4. h	6. e	8. b

D. LISTENING: *Where Are They?*

Listen to the conversation and circle the correct place.

1. A. I'd like to look at some earrings.
   B. Gold or silver?
   A. Silver, please.

2. A. I'd like to try on these shoes.
   B. Of course. What size do you wear?
   A. Size nine and a half.

3. A. May I help you?
   B. Yes, please. Where can I find hammers and screwdrivers?
   A. Look in Aisle Three.

4. A. I'd like to see a menu, please.
   B. Certainly. Can I get you something to drink?
   A. Yes. I'd like some water, please.

5. A. One ticket, please.
   B. For which movie?
   A. For "Springtime in Paris."

6. A. We need a room for two nights.
   B. For how many people?
   A. Two adults and one child.

7. A. I'd like two slices of pizza, please.
   B. Is that to go or to eat here?
   A. I'll take it to go.

8. A. I'd like the chocolate and vanilla, please.
   B. In a cone or a cup?
   A. In a cup.

Answers

1. jewelry store
2. shoe store
3. hardware store
4. restaurant
5. movie theater
6. motel
7. pizza shop
8. ice cream shop

WORKBOOK PAGE 36

A. WHERE ARE THEY?

1. intersection
2. courthouse
3. street
4. sidewalk
5. city hall
6. fire station
7. parking garage

B. WHICH WORD DOESN'T BELONG?

1. bus driver (The others are vehicles.)
2. sewer (The others are people.)
3. street sign (The others are part of the pavement.)
4. parking lot (The others are buildings.)
5. drive-through window (The others are part of a street.)

C. IN THE CITY

1. street sign
2. public telephone
3. street vendor
4. fire hydrant
5. intersection
6. bus stop
7. traffic light
8. crosswalk
9. parking lot
10. meter maid

WORKBOOK PAGE 37

A. WHICH WORD DOESN'T BELONG?

1. young
2. curly
3. tall
4. elderly
5. wavy
6. bald
7. pregnant

B. WHICH WORD?

1. blond
2. thin
3. height
4. gray
5. vision
6. teenager
7. tall
8. baby

C. CROSSWORD

(See page 169.)

D. TRUE OR FALSE?

	True	False
1.	✓	
2.		✓
3.		✓
4.	✓	
5.	✓	
6.	✓	

WORKBOOK PAGES 38–39

A. WHAT'S THE ANSWER?

1. cold
2. loose
3. married
4. dirty
5. wide
6. wet
7. poor
8. noisy/loud
9. high
10. uncomfortable
11. messy
12. rough

B. ANTONYMS

1. curly
2. crooked
3. heavy
4. dark
5. tall
6. long
7. young
8. new
9. easy
10. soft
11. shiny
12. sharp

C. MY HOUSE

1. new
2. old
3. neat
4. small
5. fancy
6. comfortable
7. quiet
8. low
9. inexpensive

D. CROSSWORD: *Opposites*

(See page 170.)

WORKBOOK PAGE 40

A. HAPPY OR SAD?

Happy Emotions	Sad Emotions
excited	disappointed
happy	frustrated
proud	homesick
	lonely
	miserable

B. WHICH WORD?

1. sick
2. cold
3. surprised
4. thirsty
5. lonely
6. frustrated
7. exhausted
8. angry
9. shocked

C. ANALOGIES

1. unhappy
2. sick
3. cold
4. tired
5. hungry

WORKBOOK PAGE 41

A. WHICH FRUIT DOESN'T BELONG?

1. lime
2. coconut
3. apricot
4. pineapple
5. strawberry
6. plantain

B. WHAT'S THE WORD?

1. banana
2. Prunes
3. nuts
4. coconut
5. grapes

C. CROSSWORD: *Pictures to Words*

(See page 170.)

D. LISTENING

Listen to the conversation and circle the word you hear.

1. A. These cherries are delicious.
   B. I like them, too.

2. A. I'm hungry. Do we have any fruit?
   B. Yes. We have apples.

3. A. Do we have any tangerines?
   B. No. I'll get some at the supermarket.

4. A. Would you like a plum?
   B. Yes. Plums are my favorite fruit.

5. A. Where did you get the papaya?
   B. At the supermarket.

6. A. Do we have any more grapes?
   B. No. I'll get some at the supermarket

Answers

1. cherries
2. apples
3. tangerines
4. plum
5. papaya
6. grapes

WORKBOOK PAGE 42

A. WHICH GROUP?

1. jalapeño
2. zucchini
3. yam
4. lima bean
5. bok choy

B. MATCHING

1. c
2. e
3. b
4. d
5. a

C. CROSSWORD: *Pictures to Words*

(See page 170.)

WORKBOOK PAGE 43

A. WHICH GROUP?

Meat	Poultry
bacon	chicken thighs
sausages	drumsticks
stewing beef	turkey
tripe	

Seafood

clams
flounder
lobster
mussels

B. WHAT'S THE WORD?

1. trout   4. scallops
2. drumsticks   5. ribs
3. lamb   6. ham

C. MATCHING

1. b   3. a   5. f
2. c   4. e   6. d

D. WHAT'S THE CATEGORY?

1. c   3. b   5. f
2. a   4. e   6. d

E. LISTENING

Listen to the conversation and circle the word you hear.

1. A. I'm going to the market.
   B. Could you get some steak?
2. A. Excuse me. Where can I find duck?
   B. Look in the poultry section.
3. A. Is there any fish on sale?
   B. Yes. Try the filet of sole.
4. A. How did you enjoy your meal at the new restaurant downtown?
   B. It was great. I ordered crabs, and they were delicious.
5. A. Let's have hamburgers tonight!
   B. Good idea. But we need ground beef.
6. A. What's your favorite part of the chicken?
   B. I like the wings.

Answers

1. steak   4. crabs
2. duck   5. ground beef
3. filet of sole 6. wings

WORKBOOK PAGE 44

A. WHICH GROUP?

Dairy   **Hot Drinks**

butter   cocoa
cheese   coffee
margarine   tea
yogurt

Cold Drinks

bottled water
grape juice
soda
tomato juice

B. WHICH WORD?

1. cream   6. punch
2. cheese   7. paks
3. milk   8. soda
4. Herbal   9. butter
5. juice

C. MATCH AND WRITE

1. chocolate milk
2. apple juice
3. instant coffee
4. bottled water
5. cream cheese

D. WHICH WORD DOESN'T BELONG?

1. soda (The others are hot drinks.)
2. herbal (The others are kinds of juices.)
3. tofu (The others are beverages.)
4. fruit punch (The others are dairy products.)
5. diet (The others are kinds of milk.)

WORKBOOK PAGE 45

A. WHICH GROUP?

1. potato chips   4. potato salad
2. ice cream   5. mozzarella
3. pastrami

B. MATCHING

1. c   3. d   5. f   7. e
2. a   4. b   6. h   8. g

C. WHICH WORD?

1. ham   4. Swiss
2. salad   5. orange juice
3. pretzels

D. CROSSWORD: *Pictures to Words*
(See page 170.)

WORKBOOK PAGE 46

A. WHICH GROUP?

Packaged Goods   **Canned Goods**

cereal   fruit
crackers   soup
macaroni   tuna fish
rice   vegetables

Condiments   **Baked Goods**

ketchup   bread
mayonnaise   cake
relish   English muffins
vinegar   rolls

B. WHICH WORD?

1. rolls   5. mayonnaise
2. sugar   6. spices
3. olives   7. noodles
4. fish

C. MATCHING

1. e   3. a   5. d   7. c
2. f   4. g   6. b

D. ASSOCIATIONS

1. b   3. e   5. d   7. a
2. f   4. g   6. c

WORKBOOK PAGE 47

A. WHICH WORD?

1. towels   5. formula
2. diapers   6. toilet
3. soap   7. foil
4. sandwich   8. plates

B. WHICH WORD DOESN'T BELONG?

1. baby food (The others are for pets.)
2. paper towels (The others are for eating.)
3. trash bags (The others are for wrapping foods.)
4. diapers (The others are for eating.)
5. sandwich bags (The others are for babies.)

C. ASSOCIATIONS

1. b   3. f   5. a
2. e   4. d   6. c

D. CROSSWORD
(See page 170.)

WORKBOOK PAGE 48

A. MATCHING

1. b   3. a   5. g   7. h
2. d   4. c   6. e   8. f

B. WHICH WORD?

1. basket   5. scanners
2. aisle   6. produce
3. bag   7. magazines
4. manager   8. coupons

C. TRUE OR FALSE?

1. T   3. F   5. F
2. F   4. T   6. F

D. ASSOCIATIONS

1. b   3. a   5. f
2. c   4. e   6. d

E. LISTENING

Listen and circle the word you hear.

1. This is a gigantic supermarket! Look at all the checkout lines!
2. Excuse me. Where can I find shopping carts?
3. How much money will we save with this coupon?
4. I think this cash register isn't working.
5. I'd like plastic bags, please.
6. Can you tell me where I can find the bottle-return machines?

Answers

1. checkout lines   4. cash register
2. shopping carts   5. plastic
3. coupon   6. bottle-return

WORKBOOK PAGE 49

A. WHAT'S THE CONTAINER?

1. box   3. roll   5. bag
2. bunch   4. can   6. jar

B. WHAT'S THE WORD?

1. pound   6. loaf
2. head   7. dozen
3. tube   8. box
4. gallon   9. six-pack
5. bottle   10. pack

C. WHICH WORD?

1. container
2. cans
3. pound
4. roll
5. head
6. half-gallon

D. LISTENING

Listen and circle the words you hear.

1. Please get two six-packs of soda when you go to the supermarket.
2. Don't forget to get a loaf of bread when you go to the store.
3. We only have a half-gallon of orange juice.
4. I'm looking for a package of rolls.
5. Where can I find a bottle of ketchup?
6. Can you get a few pints of ice cream when you go to the supermarket?
7. We need a quart of milk.
8. Get a few bunches of grapes in the produce section.

Answers

1. two six-packs
2. a loaf
3. a half-gallon
4. package
5. bottle
6. a few pints
7. quart
8. bunches

WORKBOOK PAGE 50

A. ABBREVIATIONS

1. b
2. a
3. d
4. e
5. c
6. h
7. j
8. i
9. g
10. f

B. WHICH IS EQUAL?

1. c
2. e
3. a
4. b
5. d

C. TRUE OR FALSE?

1. T
2. F
3. T
4. F
5. T

D. WHAT'S THE NUMBER?

1. 1
2. 2
3. 2
4. 64
5. 128
6. 1
7. 32
8. 2

E. WHICH WORD?

1. 3/4 lb.
2. teaspoon
3. tablespoons
4. cups
5. a gallon
6. cup

WORKBOOK PAGE 51

A. MATCHING

1. c
2. a
3. b
4. e
5. f
6. d

B. HELP IN THE KITCHEN

1. bake
2. beat
3. breaking
4. simmering
5. pour
6. slice
7. grill
8. boil

C. SPELLING RULE

1. slicing
2. baking
3. grating
4. combining

D. CROSSWORD

(See page 170.)

WORKBOOK PAGE 52

A. WHICH GROUP?

1. frying pan
2. pie plate
3. colander
4. ladle
5. knife

B. WHAT'S THE UTENSIL?

1. cookie cutter
2. bottle opener
3. can opener
4. grater
5. egg beater
6. vegetable peeler

C. WHICH WORD?

1. scoop
2. colander
3. whisk
4. roasting pan
5. wok
6. garlic press
7. cup
8. skillet
9. lid

D. ASSOCIATIONS

1. b
2. d
3. a
4. e
5. c

WORKBOOK PAGE 53

A. ORDERING FAST FOOD

1. f
2. e
3. a
4. g
5. c
6. d
7. b

B. WHICH GROUP?

1. hamburger
2. ice cream
3. plastic utensils
4. burrito
5. ketchup

C. CROSSWORD: *Pictures to Words*

(See page 170.)

WORKBOOK PAGE 54

A. WHICH WORD DOESN'T BELONG?

1. donut (The others are beverages.)
2. bacon (The others are forms of bread.)
3. iced tea (The others are sandwiches.)
4. danish (The others are types of bread.)
5. eggs (The others are forms of bread.)
6. biscuit (The others are types of bread.)
7. croissant (The others are beverages.)

B. LISTENING: *Taking Orders*

Listen to the order. Put a check next to the correct item.

1. I'll have a roast beef sandwich, please.
2. I'd like a biscuit, please.
3. I'd like an egg salad sandwich on rye bread, please.
4. I'll have a tuna fish sandwich on whole wheat bread.
5. Can I have a cup of tea?
6. I'd like an order of eggs and bacon.

Answers

1. ✓
2. ___ / ✓
3. ✓
4. ___ / ✓
5. ___ / ✓
6. ✓

C. WHICH WORD?

1. hot chocolate
2. roast
3. home
4. chicken
5. coffee
6. pita
7. tomato

WORKBOOK PAGE 55

A. MATCHING

1. c
2. a
3. b
4. e
5. f
6. d

B. WHAT ARE THEY DOING?

1. serving
2. seating
3. clearing
4. taking
5. leaving

C. WHICH WORD?

1. spoon
2. waitress
3. table
4. set
5. booth
6. dishwasher

D. THE PLACE SETTING

1. teaspoon
2. knife
3. napkin
4. butter knife
5. soup spoon
6. dinner fork
7. soup bowl

WORKBOOK PAGE 56

A. ORDERING DINNER

1. shrimp cocktail
2. antipasto
3. meatloaf
4. mixed vegetables
5. pudding

B. LISTENING: *Ordering at a Restaurant*

Listen to the order. Put a check next to the correct items.

A. May I take your order?
B. Yes, please. For the appetizer, I'd like the tomato juice.
A. And what kind of salad would you like?
B. I'll have the Caesar salad.
A. And for the main course?
B. I'd like the baked chicken, please.
A. And what side dish would you like with that?
B. Hmm. I think I'll have the rice.
A. Okay. And would you care for some dessert?
B. Yes. I'll have an ice cream sundae.

Answers

tomato juice
Caesar salad
baked chicken
rice
ice cream sundae

WORKBOOK PAGE 57

A. ASSOCIATIONS
1. b 3. a 5. g 7. d
2. f 4. e 6. c

B. WHICH COLORS?
1. gray 4. black
2. blue 5. Gold
3. green 6. red, white

WORKBOOK PAGE 58

A. WHAT'S THE WORD?
1. tie 4. suit
2. gown 5. shorts
3. coat 6. T-shirt

B. MATCH AND WRITE
1. necktie 3. turtleneck
2. jumpsuit 4. overalls

C. MAKING CLOTHES
1. vest 5. tie
2. dress 6. gown
3. jeans 7. jacket
4. coat 8. jumper

D. CROSSWORD: *Pictures to Words*
(See page 171.)

WORKBOOK PAGE 59

A. MATCHING
1. c 3. d 5. f 7. e
2. a 4. b 6. h 8. g

B. WHICH GROUP?

Jackets **Hats**

leather jacket cap
poncho rain hat
windbreaker ski hat

Accessories

earmuffs
gloves
sunglasses

C. WHAT DO WE USE?

. . . when it's raining

rain boots trench coat
raincoat umbrella

. . . when it's snowing

down jacket scarf
mittens ski mask

D. MATCHING: *Which Part of the Body?*
1. b 3. c 5. d
2. a 4. f 6. e

E. WHICH WORD?
1. an umbrella 4. ski
2. jacket 5. mittens
3. overcoat 6. parka

WORKBOOK PAGE 60

A. MATCHING
1. d 3. a 5. c 7. b
2. f 4. g 6. e

B. WHICH WORD?
1. pajamas 4. slippers
2. blanket sleeper 5. long
3. robe underwear

C. WHICH GROUP?
1. nightshirt 4. panties
2. knee-highs 5. boxer shorts
3. camisole

D. CROSSWORD: *Pictures to Words*
(See page 171.)

WORKBOOK PAGE 61

A. WHICH WORD?
1. sweatpants 4. boots
2. sandals 5. bathing
3. T-shirt 6. high-tops

B. WHICH WORD DOESN'T BELONG?
1. high-tops (The others are boots.)
2. leotard (The others are shoes.)
3. bike shorts (The others are tops.)
4. sweatshirt (The others are worn below the waist.)
5. tennis (The others are types of boots.)

C. WHAT DO WE WEAR?
1. e 3. f 5. b
2. a 4. c 6. d

D. WHAT'S THE SYNONYM?
1. high-top sneakers 4. flip-flops
2. bathing suit 5. running suit
3. bike shorts 6. athletic shoes

E. LISTENING

Listen to the conversation and circle the word you hear.

1. A. Are those new shoes?
   B. Yes. Do you like them?
2. A. I can't find my tank top.
   B. I think it's in the dryer.
3. A. Excuse me. Where can I find leotards?
   B. They're in the next aisle.
4. A. Is this your sweatband?
   B. No. Mine is at home.
5. A. I like your new jogging suit.
   B. Thanks.
6. A. I can't find my flip-flops.
   B. I think they're in the car.

Answers

1. shoes 4. sweatband
2. tank top 5. jogging suit
3. leotards 6. flip-flops

WORKBOOK PAGE 62

A. WHERE DO WE WEAR THEM?

Neck **Finger**

chain ring
locket wedding band
necklace

Wrist **Waist**

bracelet belt
watch

B. WHAT DO WE USE?
1. d 4. h 7. b
2. f 5. c 8. e
3. i 6. g 9. a

C. MATCH AND WRITE
1. pocketbook 4. backpack
2. handkerchief 5. briefcase
3. necklace 6. earring

D. WHICH WORD DOESN'T BELONG?
1. key chain (The others are worn around the neck.)
2. tote bag (The others are pieces of jewelry.)
3. wallet (The others hold books and other papers.)
4. bracelet (The others are pocketbooks.)
5. key ring (The others are rings.)

WORKBOOK PAGE 63

A. MATCHING
1. c 3. a 5. f
2. e 4. b 6. d

B. WHICH WORD?
1. turtleneck 5. extra-small
2. socks 6. polka-dotted
3. striped 7. leather
4. large 8. straw

C. LISTENING: *What Are They Describing?*

Listen and write the number next to the correct description.

1. How do you like this floral dress?
2. I prefer the paisley scarf.
3. Do you like this striped jersey?
4. How do you like this solid blue suit?
5. I really like this checked shirt.
6. I love that black and white polka-dotted tie.
7. I think you should wear your plaid skirt to the party.
8. I'm looking for a print dress.

Answers

6 8 7 3
2 5 1 4

D. WHICH WORD DOESN'T BELONG?
1. large (The others are types of material.)
2. denim (The others are types of sweaters.)
3. flowered (The others describe different types of shirt sleeves.)
4. V-neck (The others are types of socks.)
5. solid (The others are sizes.)
6. clip-on (The others are types of material.)

A. WHAT'S THE WORD?

1. wide
2. heavy
3. plain
4. light
5. tight
6. low

B. WHICH WORD?

1. missing
2. repair
3. take in
4. stained
5. shorten
6. let

C. WHICH WORD DOESN'T BELONG?

1. tight
2. short
3. fancy
4. long
5. dark
6. low

D. COMPLETE THE SENTENCES

1. e
2. a
3. f
4. c
5. d
6. b

A. DOING MY LAUNDRY

1. sort
2. load
3. unload
4. dryer
5. hang
6. iron
7. fold
8. put

B. MATCH AND WRITE

1. laundry basket
2. fabric softener
3. ironing board
4. spray starch
5. lint trap
6. wet clothing
7. static cling remover
8. washing machine

C. CROSSWORD

(See page 171.)

A. WHICH DEPARTMENT?

1. f
2. h
3. a
4. e
5. b
6. g
7. d
8. c

B. WHICH WORD?

1. escalator
2. elevator
3. water fountain
4. snack bar
5. directory
6. customer pickup area

C. LISTENING

Listen to the conversation. Write the number next to the correct place.

1. A. Those earrings are beautiful.
   B. Yes, they are. And we have a bracelet that goes very well with them.
2. A. I'll have a hamburger and a cup of coffee, please.
   B. Anything else?
3. A. What floor are you going to?
   B. The fourth floor. Could you push four for me, please?
4. A. My daughter usually wears a size 8 dress.
   B. Kids grow so fast. Maybe you should buy this dress in a size 9.
5. A. Which armchairs are on sale this week?
   B. The blue ones over there, next to the lamps.
6. A. Try this. I think you'll like the smell.
   B. Hmm. "Spring Breeze." How much does a bottle of this cost?
7. A. Watch your step, Jimmy! Put your hand on the railing!
   B. I like this better than the elevator, Mommy!
8. A. Excuse me. Are these DVD players on sale?
   B. Yes, they are. And VCRs are also on sale.

Answers

5	2
8	6
1	3
4	7

A. WHAT'S THE WORD?

1. label
2. size
3. receipt
4. discount
5. sale price
6. exchange

B. WHAT'S THE ANSWER?

1. f
2. h
3. a
4. d
5. c
6. g
7. i
8. e
9. b

C. WHICH WORD?

1. return
2. regular price
3. get
4. try
5. discount
6. price tag

A. ANOTHER WAY TO SAY IT

1. camcorder
2. compact disc
3. television
4. videocassette recorder
5. portable CD player
6. cassette deck
7. sound system
8. videocassette, videotape

B. ASSOCIATIONS

1. c
2. f
3. e
4. b
5. a
6. d

C. ANALOGIES

1. DVD
2. turntable
3. video game system
4. videotape
5. audiocassette
6. headphones

D. WHAT DO WE USE?

1. e
2. c
3. b
4. a
5. f
6. d

A. TELEPHONE OR CAMERA?

Telephone	Camera
cordless	film
answering machine	slide projector
fax machine	memory disk
cellular	lens

B. WHAT DO WE USE?

1. d
2. a
3. f
4. b
5. h
6. g
7. e
8. c

C. MATCHING

1. g
2. a
3. e
4. b
5. h
6. d
7. f
8. c

D. WHICH WORD?

1. adding
2. cell
3. tripod
4. film
5. answering

A. MATCHING

1. e
2. c
3. a
4. f
5. d
6. b

B. WHAT'S THE WORD?

1. mouse
2. disk drive
3. cable
4. joystick
5. modem
6. surge protector
7. scanner
8. notebook computer

C. CROSSWORD: *Pictures to Words*

(See page 171.)

A. TOYS

Toys We Use Inside

construction set
doll house
train set

Toys We Use Outside

pail and shovel
skateboard
tricycle

B. MATCHING

1. d
2. a
3. e
4. c
5. b
6. g
7. i
8. f
9. j
10. h

C. WHAT'S THE WORD?

1. inflatable pool
2. stuffed animal
3. coloring book
4. bicycle
5. rubber ball
6. paint set
7. doll house
8. construction set

WORKBOOK PAGE 72

A. MATCHING
1. c   3. a   5. g   7. d
2. f   4. b   6. e

B. WHICH WORD?
1. teller   5. credit card
2. check   6. officer
3. deposit   7. currency
4. withdrawal   8. traveler's checks

C. WHAT DO WE DO AT THE BANK?
1. e   3. f   5. b
2. c   4. a   6. d

D. WHICH WORD DOESN'T BELONG?
1. cash machine (The others are people.)
2. safe deposit box (The others are paper.)
3. teller (The others are objects in a bank.)
4. currency (The others are related to bank accounts.)
5. bank vault (The others are ways of paying for things.)

WORKBOOK PAGE 73

A. WHAT'S THE WORD?
1. checkbook   4. payment
2. monthly statement   5. cash
3. money order   6. bill

B. WHICH ONE DOESN'T BELONG?
1. gas bill (The others are methods of payment.)
2. checkbook (The others are bills.)
3. write a check (The others are steps for using an ATM machine.)
4. car payment (The others are utility bills.)
5. PIN number (The others are related to a checking account.)

C. WHICH WORD?
1. number   4. PIN
2. heating   5. checkbook
3. online   6. deposit

D. WHAT'S THE ORDER?
5
4
1
3
6
2

E. LISTENING
Listen and put a check next to the actions you hear.

I have a lot of bills, so I write checks all the time. Then I have to balance my checkbook. In addition, I use the ATM at my bank to make deposits into my account. I transfer funds very often.

Answers

__   ✓
✓   __
__   ✓
✓   __

WORKBOOK PAGE 74

A. MATCHING
1. c   3. d   5. g   7. h
2. a   4. b   6. e   8. f

B. SENDING MAIL
1. parcel post   8. postage
2. envelope   9. post
3. letter   10. truck
4. parcel   11. machine
5. stamps   12. change-of-
6. postcard   address
7. certified

C. WHICH WORD DOESN'T BELONG?
1. scale (The others appear on an envelope.)
2. mail truck (The others are people.)
3. mail slot (The others are things you mail.)
4. mail bag (The others are classes of mail service.)
5. roll of stamps (The others are things you mail.)
6. money order (The others are classes of mail service.)
7. letter carrier (The others appear on an envelope.)

WORKBOOK PAGE 75

A. WHERE WILL YOU FIND THESE?

Periodical Section
a journal
a magazine
a newspaper

Reference Section
an atlas
a dictionary
microfilm

Media Section
an audiotape
a CD
a DVD

B. AT THE LIBRARY
1. reference librarian
2. online catalog
3. author
4. title
5. shelves
6. magazines
7. periodical
8. microfilm reader
9. CDs
10. library card
11. clerk
12. checkout desk

C. LIBRARY ADVICE
1. e   4. a   7. h
2. f   5. d   8. b
3. i   6. c   9. g

WORKBOOK PAGE 76

A. MATCH AND WRITE
1. police officer
2. activities director
3. emergency operator
4. recycling center
5. swimming pool
6. town hall
7. sanitation worker
8. fire engine

B. WHICH WORD?
1. police station   6. meeting room
2. senior   7. emergency
3. center   8. sanitation
4. game   9. activities
5. recycling   director

C. CROSSWORD
(See page 171.)

WORKBOOK PAGE 77

A. MATCH AND WRITE
1. car accident
2. lost child
3. bank robbery
4. train derailment
5. chemical spill
6. downed power line
7. power outage
8. gang violence
9. drug dealing

B. WHAT HAPPENED?
1. d   2. g   3. b   4. a
5. c   6. e   7. f   8. h

C. ANALOGIES
1. blackout   4. mugging
2. drunk driving   5. vandalism
3. bank robbery   6. burglary

WORKBOOK PAGES 78–79

A. WHICH WORD DOESN'T BELONG?
1. nose (The others are part of the eye.)
2. gums (The others are part of the leg.)
3. tongue (The others are part of the skeletal system.)
4. hip (The others are part of the face.)
5. elbow (The others are part of the leg.)
6. armpit (The others are part of mouth.)

B. ASSOCIATIONS
1. e   3. f   5. d
2. a   4. b   6. c

C. WHERE DO THEY GO?
1. b   3. c   5. d
2. e   4. f   6. a

D. WHICH WORD?

1. shin
2. wrist
3. hip
4. chin
5. forehead
6. leg
7. knee
8. tongue

E. WHICH WORD DOESN'T BELONG?

1. bones (The others are internal organs.)
2. veins (The others are part of the hand.)
3. nerve (The others are external parts of the body.)
4. skin (The others are part of the foot.)
5. esophagus (The others relate to the circulation of blood.)
6. palm (The others are internal organs.)
7. muscle (The others are joints.)

F. ASSOCIATIONS

1. f
2. e
3. d
4. a
5. g
6. c
7. b

G. WHERE DO THEY GO?

1. d
2. c
3. e
4. b
5. a

H. WHICH WORD?

1. lungs
2. fingernails
3. bones
4. heart
5. stomach
6. throat

I. LISTENING

Listen to the conversation and circle the word you hear.

1. A. I have to see a doctor.
   B. Did you hurt your back?
2. A. What's wrong with your face?
   B. My nose is broken.
3. A. What's wrong?
   B. My stomach hurts.
4. A. What's the matter?
   B. I have a sore throat.
5. A. Does your mouth hurt?
   B. Yes. I think I broke my tooth.
6. A. Are you having trouble walking?
   B. Yes. I broke my hip.
7. A. What happened?
   B. I fell and cut my chin.
8. A. Did you hurt your tongue?
   B. No. My gums.

Answers

1. back
2. nose
3. stomach
4. throat
5. tooth
6. hip
7. chin
8. gums

WORKBOOK PAGES 80–81

A. MATCH THE AILMENTS

1. d
2. f
3. b
4. i
5. c
6. a
7. g
8. j
9. h
10. e

B. WHAT'S THE MATTER?

1. chills
2. stomachache
3. sore throat
4. sunburn
5. diarrhea
6. rash
7. backache
8. fever
9. cavity
10. stiff neck

D. FEELING TERRIBLE!

1. sprain
2. dislocate
3. itchy
4. congested
5. vomit
6. swollen
7. exhausted
8. burp
9. bleeding
10. coughing

E. CROSSWORD: *Pictures to Words*

(See p. 171.)

WORKBOOK PAGE 82

A. MATCHING

1. e
2. g
3. a
4. f
5. b
6. c
7. h
8. d

B. WHAT'S THE TREATMENT?

1. c
2. a
3. e
4. b
5. f
6. d

C. LISTENING

Listen and circle the word you hear.

1. Do we have a first-aid manual?
2. My friend is choking!
3. Do you have non-aspirin pain reliever?
4. I'm looking for an Ace bandage.
5. Do you know how to make a tourniquet?
6. I need some more elastic bandages.
7. Where are the sterile dressing pads?
8. Can I have an antiseptic cleansing wipe?

Answers

1. first aid manual
2. choking
3. pain reliever
4. Ace bandage
5. tourniquet
6. elastic
7. sterile
8. antiseptic

D. A CAR ACCIDENT

1. CPR
2. splint
3. gauze
4. adhesive
5. aspirin
6. rescue

WORKBOOK PAGE 83

A. MATCH AND WRITE

1. chicken pox
2. ear infection
3. strep throat
4. electric shock
5. allergic reaction
6. heart disease

B. ILLNESS OR EMERGENCY?

Illnesses	Emergencies
asthma	allergic reaction
chicken pox	fall
diabetes	frostbite
heart disease	heart attack
measles	heatstroke
mumps	unconscious

C. ASSOCIATIONS

1. c
2. a
3. b
4. e
5. f
6. d

D. WHICH WORD?

1. attack
2. in
3. injured
4. strep throat
5. allergic reaction
6. hypertension
7. asthma
8. diabetes

WORKBOOK PAGE 84

A. ASSOCIATIONS

1. d
2. a
3. f
4. g
5. c
6. e
7. b

B. WHAT WILL THEY USE?

1. scale
2. thermometer
3. table
4. eye chart
5. syringe
6. stethoscope
7. X-ray machine
8. room
9. gauge

C. THE MEDICAL EXAM

1. examined
2. measured
3. listen to
4. took
5. checked
6. drew
7. asked

WORKBOOK PAGE 85

A. MATCHING

1. d
2. e
3. a
4. b
5. f
6. c

B. WHAT DID THE DOCTOR DO?

1. cast, sling
2. alcohol, stitches
3. bandage, crutches
4. shot, prescription
5. medical history, examination

C. WHICH WORD?

1. dentist
2. alcohol
3. cast
4. hygienist
5. fillings
6. close
7. ice pack
8. examination
9. gloves
10. a mask

WORKBOOK PAGE 86

A. WHICH WORD?

1. fluids
2. work
3. acupuncture
4. surgery
5. Physical therapy
6. a cane
7. counselor
8. a walker

B. AT THE DOCTOR'S OFFICE

1. fluids
2. vitamins
3. exercise
4. bed
5. specialist
6. blood work
7. diet
8. acupuncture

C. GIVING ADVICE

1. a
2. b
3. a
4. a
5. b
6. a

A. SOLUTIONS

1. lozenge	6. antacid
2. cough	7. decongestant spray
3. vitamins	8. ointment
4. aspirin	9. cream
5. ointment	10. pain reliever

B. WHAT'S THE MEDICINE?

1. b	3. a	5. b	7. a
2. b	4. a	6. b	

C. LISTENING: *What's the Dosage?*

Listen to the directions. Circle the correct answer.

1. Take three tablespoons before breakfast.
2. Take two tablets every six hours.
3. Do not take more than four capsules.
4. Have one teaspoon with water.
5. Only take one pill.
6. Take five caplets every week.
7. Mix four teaspoons with warm water.
8. Never take more than seven caplets.

Answers

1. 3 tablespoons	5. 1 pill
2. 2 tablets	6. 5 caplets
3. 4 capsules	7. 4 teaspoons
4. 1 teaspoon	8. 7 caplets

A. WHO ARE THEY?

1. g	5. h	8. j
2. c	6. b	9. f
3. d	7. e	10. a
4. i		

B. WHAT DO THEY DO?

1. e	3. b	5. d
2. f	4. a	6. c

C. LISTENING: *What Kind of Doctor?*

Listen to the sentence and circle the correct answer.

1. I'm going to do some tests on your heart.
2. I recommend braces for your teeth.
3. I'm going to test for allergies.
4. Can you hear in your left ear?
5. I work with children.
6. I'm going to look at your stomach with this test.
7. Tell me your feelings about your mother.
8. Your vision is perfect. You don't need glasses.

Answers

1. cardiologist
2. orthodontist
3. allergist
4. audiologist
5. pediatrician
6. gastroenterologist
7. psychiatrist
8. ophthalmologist

A. WHICH WORD?

1. gown	6. a volunteer
2. I.V.	7. medical chart
3. pan	8. control
4. delivery	9. surgeon
5. X-ray	

B. WHAT DO THEY DO?

1. d	3. a	5. c	7. e
2. f	4. g	6. h	8. b

C. CROSSWORD

(See page 171.)

A. ASSOCIATIONS

1. b	3. f	5. a
2. c	4. d	6. e

B. WHAT DO I USE?

1. b	3. d	5. f	7. c
2. a	4. e	6. h	8. g

C. WHICH WORD DOESN'T BELONG?

1. mascara (The others have a scent and you put them on your skin.)
2. shower cap (The others are for washing your hair.)
3. nail polish (The others are for hair.)
4. hairspray (The others are for the mouth.)
5. styptic pencil (The others are for women.)
6. shoe polish (The others are for the nails.)

D. WHAT DO THEY NEED?

1. hair gel	6. eyebrow pencil
2. blow dryer	7. gargle
3. aftershave	8. polish
4. take a bath	9. moisturizer
5. hand lotion	

A. MATCH AND WRITE

1. baby food	4. rocking chair
2. diaper pin	5. cotton swab
3. child-care center	6. training pants
	7. disposable diaper

B. WHICH WORD?

1. teething ring	7. cotton swabs
2. vitamins	8. shampoo
3. play	9. rock
4. feed	10. disposable
5. nipple	11. change
6. formula	12. baby shampoo

C. CROSSWORD: *Pictures to Words*

(See page 172.)

A. WHICH TYPE OF SCHOOL?

1. elementary	6. an adult
2. medical	7. law
3. nursery	8. community
4. vocational	9. junior high
5. high	

B. ASSOCIATIONS

1. c	3. f	5. d
2. a	4. e	6. b

C. WHICH WORD DOESN'T BELONG?

1. college (The others are for young children.)
2. high school (The other schools are for students older than teenagers.)
3. law school (The others are schools for young children and teenagers.)
4. trade school (The others are schools you go to after college.)
5. community (The others are types of "schools.")

A. AT SCHOOL

1. locker	6. locker room
2. cafeteria	7. science lab
3. field	8. principal
4. nurse	9. guidance office
5. track	10. gymnasium

B. ASSOCIATIONS

1. c	3. d	5. g	7. h
2. a	4. b	6. e	8. f

C. MY SCHOOL

1. guidance office	5. science lab
2. library	6. track
3. nurse's office	7. main office
4. auditorium	

A. WHERE DO THESE SUBJECTS BELONG?

Sciences	Languages	Lifeskills
biology	English	driver's ed
chemistry	French	home economics
physics	Spanish	industrial arts

B. ASSOCIATIONS

1. d	3. f	5. c	7. e
2. a	4. h	6. g	8. b

C. LISTENING: *What Are They Talking About?*

Listen and circle the correct word.

1. That test was easy! I knew all the countries' names.
2. Oh, no! I forgot my paint and supplies.
3. Do you know how to use a mouse?
4. Volleyball is fun! I love to play it!
5. I like to learn about the past.
6. It's interesting to learn about how we elect our president.

Answers

1. geography
2. art
3. computer science
4. physical education
5. history
6. government

D. CROSSWORD: *Which Class?*

(See page 172.)

WORKBOOK PAGE 95

A. WHAT ACTIVITIES DO THEY DO?

1. c	6. b
2. a	7. d
3. j	8. f
4. i	9. e
5. h	10. g

B. WHICH ACTIVITY IS THE BEST?

1. international
2. football team
3. orchestra
4. yearbook
5. community service

C. WHICH ACTIVITY DOESN'T BELONG?

1. football (The others aren't a sport activity.)
2. student government (The others are music activities.)
3. drama (The others are related to sports.)
4. school newspaper (The others are related to theater production.)
5. choir (The others involve writing.)

D. LISTENING: *What Are They Talking About?*

Listen and circle the correct word.

1. I can't go to practice today. I have a sore throat. I can't sing.
2. We're having a meeting after school tomorrow. Bring the articles you wrote.
3. Six points! What a touchdown!
4. That was lovely. You played very well.
5. We're going to clean up the area around those apartment buildings.
6. This Korean food you brought today is delicious!

Answers

1. chorus
2. school newspaper
3. football
4. orchestra
5. community service
6. international club

WORKBOOK PAGES 96–97

A. MATH ASSOCIATIONS

1. b	3. d
2. a	4. c

B. SYMBOLS AND WORDS

1. d	3. c	5. g	7. h
2. a	4. b	6. e	8. f

C. MATH SENTENCES

1. $5 \times 4 = 20$
2. $24 - 10 = 14$
3. $16 \div 4 = 4$
4. $7 + 18 = 25$

D. WORDS AND FRACTIONS

1. c	3. e	5. d
2. a	4. b	

E. WORDS AND PERCENTS

1. d	3. e	5. c
2. a	4. b	

F. WHAT FRACTION IS IT?

1/3   2/3   1/2   1/4   3/4

G. LISTENING: *What's the Fraction?*

Listen and write the number under the correct fraction.

1. One quarter of the students in our class are from Asia.
2. They'll probably arrive in three quarters of an hour.
3. The gas tank is about two thirds full.
4. One third of the class is absent today.
5. This shirt is half off the regular price.

Answers

3   1   5   2   4

H. WHAT PERCENT IS IT?

50%   100%   10%   25%   75%

I. LISTENING: *What's the Percent?*

Listen and write the number under the correct percent.

1. She got seventy-five percent of the answers right.
2. This jacket is twenty-five percent off the regular price.
3. There's a fifty percent chance of rain.
4. He got fifteen percent of the answers wrong.
5. One hundred percent of the class is here today.

Answers

2   3   1   5   4

J. WHAT TYPE OF MATH?

1. calculus
2. statistics
3. geometry
4. algebra
5. trigonometry

WORKBOOK PAGE 98

A. ANALOGIES

1. wide
2. meter
3. cube
4. depth
5. diameter
6. ellipse
7. square
8. triangle

B. ABBREVIATIONS

1. b	4. f
2. c	5. d
3. a	6. e

C. WHICH HAS THE SAME MEANING?

1. b	3. e	5. a
2. d	4. c	

D. WHAT'S THE WORD?

1. long
2. high
3. height
4. width
5. feet
6. miles

WORKBOOK PAGE 99

A. WHICH PART OF SPEECH?

1. b	3. d	5. h	7. e
2. a	4. c	6. g	8. f

B. PUNCTUATION MATCH

1. c	3. d	5. h	7. g
2. a	4. b	6. e	8. f

C. THE WRITING PROCESS

1. final copy
2. organize
3. first draft
4. feedback
5. corrections
6. revise
7. brainstorm
8. title

WORKBOOK PAGE 100

A. WHICH WORD DOESN'T BELONG?

1. report (The others are forms of literature.)
2. essay (The others are things you send in the mail.)
3. fiction (The others are non-fiction.)
4. poetry (The others are things you send.)
5. fiction (The others aren't literary writing.)
6. non-fiction (The others are things you send.)

B. WHICH WORD?

1. e-mail
2. invitation
3. editorial
4. non-fiction
5. thank-you note
6. poems
7. biography

C. CROSSWORD

(See page 172.)

D. LISTENING: *What Are They Talking About?*

Listen and circle the correct word.

1. A. I love this book!
   B. What's the story about?
2. A. What does it say?
   B. It says we need to do something about the problems in our city.
3. A. Look! We got this from your parents.
   B. It looks like they're having a great vacation.
4. A. Do you want to come to lunch with us?
   B. Sorry. I can't. I have to finish this by five o'clock and give it to the boss.

5. A. You should read this.
   B. Are the characters interesting?
6. A. This says there's going to be a party on Saturday night.
   B. That's great! Let's go!
7. A. I have to send a message to my professor.
   B. You can use my computer.
8. A. What are you working on?
   B. I'm writing the story of my life.

Answers

1. novel	5. short story
2. editorial	6. invitation
3. postcard	7. e-mail
4. report	8. autobiography

WORKBOOK PAGE 101

A. WHICH WORD?

1. forest	6. seashore
2. river	7. island
3. brook	8. meadow
4. hill	9. valley
5. bay	

B. WHICH WORD DOESN'T BELONG?

1. forest (The others are bodies of water.)
2. shore (The others are types of land.)
3. canyon (The others are types of forests.)
4. rainforest (The others are bodies of water.)
5. valley (The others are "high.")
6. desert (The others are related to water.)

C. WHAT'S THE PLACE?

1. c	3. d	5. b	7. f
2. g	4. h	6. e	8. a

WORKBOOK PAGE 102

A. WHAT'S THE OBJECT?

1. cylinder	5. computer
2. Bunsen burner	6. magnet
3. microscope	7. scale
4. Petri dish	

B. WHICH WORD?

1. test tube	4. crucible tongs
2. microscope	5. slide
3. beaker	6. dropper

C. WHAT DO WE USE IT FOR?

1. b	3. a	5. f
2. e	4. c	6. d

D. THE SCIENTIFIC METHOD

1. state	4. make
2. form	5. doing
3. plan	6. draw

WORKBOOK PAGE 103

A. DO YOU REMEMBER?

Mercury	Mars	Uranus
Venus	Jupiter	Neptune
Earth	Saturn	Pluto

B. WHICH KIND OF MOON?

1. crescent	3. new
2. full	4. quarter

C. WHICH WORD?

1. Astronauts	5. comet
2. planet	6. sun
3. constellation	7. a telescope
4. lunar	

D. CROSSWORD: *Pictures to Words*
(See page 172.)

WORKBOOK PAGES 104–105

A. WHAT'S THE OCCUPATION?

1. bricklayer	6. assembler
2. carpenter	7. cashier
3. actress	8. chef
4. accountant	9. artist
5. architect	10. baker

B. WHAT DO THEY DO?

1. d	4. i	7. h
2. f	5. g	8. b
3. a	6. c	9. e

C. WHICH GROUP?

They cook.	They clean.
baker	custodian
chef	housekeeper

They cut hair.	They work with computers.
barber	data entry clerk
hairdresser	software engineer

They build things.	They work with money.
bricklayer	accountant
mason	cashier

D. MATCH AND WRITE

1. firefighter	5. homemaker
2. foreman	6. landscaper
3. dockworker	7. housekeeper
4. babysitter	

E. LISTENING: *What's the Job?*
Listen and circle the correct word.

1. I work outside with flowers and grass.
2. I work on a boat.
3. I design machines and tools.
4. I build things with wood. I use a hammer and nails.
5. I cut and prepare meat for my customers.
6. I serve meals and drinks.
7. I make clothes for men, women, and children.
8. I take care of sick people.

Answers

1. gardener
2. fisher
3. engineer
4. carpenter
5. butcher
6. food-service worker
7. garment worker
8. health-care aide

WORKBOOK PAGES 106–107

A. WHAT'S THE OCCUPATION?

1. messenger	6. photographer
2. receptionist	7. police officer
3. travel agent	8. pharmacist
4. sanitation worker	9. mechanic
5. musician	10. pilot

B. WHERE DO THEY WORK?

1. c	3. g	5. d	7. f
2. e	4. b	6. a	

C. ASSOCIATIONS

1. g	5. d	8. j
2. f	6. b	9. c
3. a	7. h	10. e
4. i		

D. WHAT'S THE WORD?

1. painter	7. owner
2. teacher	8. server
3. interpreter	9. manager
4. welder	10. carrier
5. reporter	11. mover
6. driver	12. waiter

E. CROSSWORD: *Pictures to Words*
(See page 172.)

WORKBOOK PAGES 108–109

A. WHAT DO THEY DO?

1. b	5. f	9. l	13. k
2. d	6. a	10. n	14. p
3. g	7. h	11. m	15. i
4. c	8. e	12. o	16. j

B. WHAT ARE THEIR SKILLS?

1. paint	5. sew
2. fix things	6. teach
3. play an instrument	7. assist patients
4. serve food	8. type

C. WHAT'S THE WORK ACTIVITY?

draw   type   manage   assemble   grow

D. ASSOCIATIONS

1. b	8. m
2. g	9. h
3. d	10. l
4. f	11. n
5. c	12. j
6. e	13. k
7. a	14. i

E. WHAT DOES IT MEAN?

1. c	3. e	5. d
2. a	4. f	6. b

F. LISTENING: *What Do They Do?*

Listen and put a check next to the correct sentence.

1. I'm an assembler at a factory.
2. I'm a secretary in an office.
3. I'm an English instructor at a school.
4. I'm an architect.
5. I'm a security guard. I usually work at night.
6. I grow vegetables and fruit and raise animals.
7. I play an instrument in a musical group. I work with other musicians.
8. I'm a salesperson in a department store.
9. I'm an actress.

Answers

1. __ / __   4. __ / __   7. __ / __
2. __ ✓ / __   5. __ / ✓   8. ✓ / __
3. __ / ✓   6. ✓ / __   9. __ / ✓

WORKBOOK PAGE 110

A. LOOKING FOR A JOB

1. f   3. a   5. c   7. b
2. h   4. d   6. g   8. e

B. WHICH WORD?

1. help   6. classified
2. experience   7. available
3. ad   8. excellent
4. required   9. time
5. interview

C. ABBREVIATIONS

1. b   3. g   5. d   7. c
2. h   4. f   6. a   8. e

D. LISTENING: *Requesting Information*

Listen and put a check next to the correct job description.

1. Hello. I'm calling about the part-time evening job.
2. The job requires previous experience.
3. Hello. Do you have any full-time evening jobs available?
4. The pay isn't very high, but there are very good benefits.
5. Can I have some information about the 30 hour-per-week job?
6. We have full-time positions available at thirteen dollars an hour.

Answers

1. ✓ / __   3. __ / ✓   5. ✓ / __
2. __ / ✓   4. ✓ / __   6. __ / ✓

WORKBOOK PAGE 111

A. WHICH WORD?

1. shredder   6. cubicle
2. a coffee   7. swivel chair
3. boss   8. reception area
4. supply   9. mailbox
5. manager

B. MATCHING

1. c   3. d   5. h   7. e
2. a   4. b   6. g   8. f

C. ROGER'S DAILY ROUTINE

1. secretary   5. coffee machine
2. coat closet   6. messages
3. mailboxes   7. letters
4. photocopier   8. presentations

D. WHERE IS THE CONVERSATION TAKING PLACE?

1. e   3. f   5. d
2. a   4. b   6. c

WORKBOOK PAGE 112

A. WHAT'S THE WORD?

1. letter tray   4. cellophane tape
2. glue stick   5. organizer
3. rotary card file   6. pencil sharpener

B. WHICH WORD?

1. stapler   6. ink
2. envelope   7. thumbtacks
3. cement   8. band
4. legal   9. Post-it note
5. ink   10. correction fluid

C. WHAT DO WE USE IT FOR?

1. b   3. d   5. f   7. a
2. e   4. g   6. c

WORKBOOK PAGE 113

A. WHICH WORD?

1. forklift
2. personnel office
3. payroll
4. freight elevator
5. fire extinguisher
6. line supervisor
7. locker

B. MATCHING

1. b   6. h
2. d   7. i
3. e   8. g
4. a   9. j
5. c   10. f

C. WHAT DO THEY DO?

1. e   3. b   5. c
2. a   4. f   6. d

D. CROSSWORD

(See page 172.)

WORKBOOK PAGE 114

A. WHICH GROUP?

Building Materials	Tools
brick	jackhammer
cement	pickax
lumber	shovel
plywood	sledgehammer

Vehicles

bulldozer
crane
dump truck
pickup truck

B. WHICH WORD?

1. wheelbarrow   6. insulation
2. blueprints   7. toolbelt
3. trowel   8. shingles
4. ladder   9. concrete mixer
5. front-end loader

C. MATCH AND WRITE

1. backhoe   4. drywall
2. blueprints   5. plywood
3. bulldozer   6. jackhammer

D. LISTENING

Listen and circle the word you hear.

1. The construction workers will bring the beam in the pickup truck.
2. Could you get me that trowel?
3. Be careful when you use the crane!
4. Do you need help with the cement mixer?
5. Dig a twelve-foot hole with this backhoe.
6. We need a tape measure to see how long this beam is.
7. We can't reach that height without a cherry picker.
8. We need to lift this girder.
9. Without insulation, this building will be very cold.
10. We have to use a lot of wire to provide electricity to this house.

Answers

1. beam   6. tape measure
2. trowel   7. cherry picker
3. crane   8. girder
4. cement mixer 9. insulation
5. backhoe   10. wire

WORKBOOK PAGE 115

A. WHAT DO THEY PROTECT?

1. g   3. e   5. d   7. f
2. a   4. b   6. c

B. MATCH AND WRITE

1. fire extinguisher
2. hard hat
3. electrical hazard
4. emergency exit

C. WHAT'S THE WORD?

1. electrical hazard   4. defibrillator
2. first-aid kit   5. emergency exit
3. biohazard   6. fire extinguisher

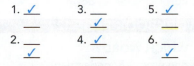

D. WHICH WORD?

1. back support
2. respirator
3. poisonous
4. hairnet
5. corrosive
6. earplugs
7. dangerous
8. radioactive
9. flammable

WORKBOOK PAGE 116

A. JUST IN TIME!

1. train station
2. information
3. timetable
4. train
5. ticket window
6. arrival and departure
7. track
8. baggage
9. platform
10. conductor

B. WHICH WORD DOESN'T BELONG?

1. taxi (The others are things you pay.)
2. meter (The others are people.)
3. schedule (The others allow you to be a passenger.)
4. ferry (The others are places passengers wait.)
5. bus route (The others are places in bus or train stations.)

C. WHICH WORD?

1. platform
2. stand
3. station
4. timetable
5. fare
6. luggage
7. transfer
8. window
9. token, turnstile

D. LISTENING: *Where Are They?*

Listen to the conversations and decide where the passengers are.

1. Excuse me. Where's track 14?
2. Buy a token and go through the turnstile.
3. Can I please have a transfer?
4. It's cold out here on this boat!
5. The meter says you owe me fifteen dollars.
6. Look! Here comes the bus.

Answers

6	2	4
5	1	3

WORKBOOK PAGE 117

A. WHAT KIND OF CAR?

1. tow truck
2. mini
3. pickup
4. a hybrid
5. bicycle
6. R.V.
7. sports car
8. limousine

B. MATCH AND WRITE

1. pickup truck
2. tractor trailer
3. moving van
4. station wagon
5. sports car
6. motor scooter
7. recreational vehicle

C. WHICH VEHICLE DOESN'T BELONG?

1. sports car (The others are trucks.)
2. minivan (The others have two wheels.)
3. sedan (The others are long vehicles.)
4. semi (The others are small vehicles.)
5. jeep (The others are long/large vehicles.)

WORKBOOK PAGES 118–119

A. WHAT SHOULD THEY USE?

1. c
2. g
3. e
4. d
5. f
6. h
7. a
8. b

B. MATCH AND WRITE

1. windshield
2. headlight
3. gearshift
4. tailpipe
5. armrest
6. hubcap
7. sunroof

C. WHICH WORD?

1. signal
2. plate
3. tire
4. belt
5. seat belt
6. mirror
7. navigation
8. a CD player

D. LISTENING: *Checklist*

Listen to the car dealers. Put a check next to the items each car has.

1. A. This is a very nice car.
   B. I like the sunroof. Tell me, does the car come with automatic transmission?
   A. No, it has manual transmission. But look! It has a navigation system.
   B. Yes. I see. I have a few more questions.
   A. Certainly. I'll be glad to answer them.
   B. Does the car have a roof rack?
   A. No, it doesn't. But it has a very large trunk.
   B. Oh yes, I see. Tell me, does the car come with a spare tire and air bags?
   A. Yes. It has both.
   B. And finally, does the car have a CD player?
   A. No, but it has an excellent radio.

2. A. I'm interested in this car.
   B. Yes, sir. This is a nice car. But I should tell you that this car doesn't have certain features like a sunroof or a navigation system.
   A. I understand. Does it at least have a spare tire?
   B. Yes. And also an air bag for the driver.
   A. I see. Tell me, is there a CD player?
   B. No, but we can install one for you.
   A. Does the car have a big trunk?
   B. No, but there's a roof rack.

Answers

1.	✓		2.		
		✓		✓	✓
	✓	✓	✓		

E. WHICH WORD?

1. visor
2. ignition
3. conditioner
4. glove compartment
5. fender
6. gauge
7. horn
8. stickshift

F. ASSOCIATIONS

1. c
2. d
3. b
4. a
5. f
6. h
7. j
8. g
9. e
10. i

G. SAFETY FIRST!

1. trunk
2. jumper cables
3. flares
4. jack
5. spare tire
6. air bags
7. seat belt

WORKBOOK PAGE 120

A. WHICH WORD?

1. traffic
2. intersection
3. speed limit
4. crosswalk
5. tollbooth
6. exit
7. corner

B. MATCHING

1. f
2. c
3. d
4. g
5. b
6. e
7. a

C. WHAT ARE THEY TALKING ABOUT?

1. speed limit sign
2. one-way street
3. route sign
4. traffic light
5. bridge
6. exit sign

D. ANALOGIES

1. overpass
2. highway
3. right lane
4. traffic signal
5. intersection

WORKBOOK PAGE 121

A. WHICH WORD?

1. over
2. on
3. through
4. across
5. out of
6. off
7. onto
8. off
9. up
10. over

B. CROSSWORD: *Pictures to Words*

(See page 172.)

C. HOW TO GET TO MY HOUSE

1. on
2. off
3. up
4. past
5. across
6. down

WORKBOOK PAGE 122

A. WHICH WORD?

1. one way
2. right
3. "yield"
4. dead end
5. pedestrian
6. handicapped parking
7. "slippery when wet"

B. LISTENING: *Traffic Signs*

Listen and write the number under the correct sign.

1. Careful! You can't turn left here.
2. We can't turn onto this street. It says, "Do Not Enter."
3. Didn't you see that sign? You were supposed to stop.
4. Keep going straight. We can't turn right here.
5. That sign says we can't make a U-turn here.

Answers

2 5 1 3 4

C. ROAD TEST

1. north
2. right
3. hand signals
4. east
5. 3-point turn
6. left
7. west
8. parallel park

WORKBOOK PAGE 123

A. WHICH WORD?

1. pass
2. baggage
3. suitcase
4. garment
5. declaration form
6. boarding area
7. carousel
8. metal
9. baggage claim
10. check-in counter

B. WHICH WORD DOESN'T BELONG?

1. luggage carrier (The others are people.)
2. immigration (The others are for garments.)
3. X-ray machine (The others are paper.)
4. baggage (The others are areas in an airport.)
5. counter (The others are related to customs.)
6. passport (The others are related to security.)

C. FLYING INTERNATIONALLY

1. ticket
2. boarding pass
3. boarding
4. passport
5. security
6. monitor
7. immigration
8. visa
9. baggage claim
10. customs

WORKBOOK PAGE 124

A. WHAT DO THEY NEED?

1. overhead compartment
2. air sickness bag
3. lavatory
4. call button
5. Fasten Seat Belt
6. oxygen mask

B. WHICH WORD?

1. cockpit
2. seat belt
3. exit
4. terminal
5. window
6. control tower

C. AIRPORT ACTIONS

1. b
2. d
3. c
4. a
5. h
6. g
7. f
8. e

D. LISTENING

Listen and put a check next to the words you hear.

Good morning passengers, and welcome to flight 959 to Los Angeles. This is your flight attendant, Joan Mendez. Let me go over a few safety instructions. In case of emergency, oxygen masks will appear from above your seat. Please put the mask over your nose and mouth and breathe normally. Also, please take a minute to look at the emergency instruction card, which shows the location of the emergency exits on both sides of the plane. We'll be taking off shortly, so please fasten your seat belts.

Answers

✓	✓
✓	—
—	✓
✓	—

WORKBOOK PAGE 125

A. ASSOCIATIONS

1. d
2. a
3. e
4. c
5. b

B. WHICH WORD DOESN'T BELONG?

1. luggage cart (The others are people.)
2. service (The others are kinds of "rooms" in a hotel.)
3. guest (The others are hotel employees.)
4. room service (The others are places in a hotel.)
5. pool (The others are people.)

C. WHICH WORD?

1. doorman
2. key
3. lobby
4. pool
5. concierge
6. exercise
7. ice machine

D. CROSSWORD

(See page 172.)

WORKBOOK PAGE 126

A. WHAT'S THE WORD?

1. photography
2. woodworking
3. knits
4. draw
5. board games
6. pottery
7. surfing the net
8. needlepoint

B. ASSOCIATIONS

1. c
2. d
3. a
4. b
5. f
6. h
7. e
8. g

C. WHAT ARE THEY TALKING ABOUT?

1. b
2. d
3. e
4. a
5. c

D. ANALOGIES

1. telescope
2. coin collection
3. clay
4. knitting
5. painting
6. checkers
7. acrylic paint
8. bird-watching

WORKBOOK PAGE 127

A. MATCHING

1. c
2. e
3. a
4. f
5. b
6. g
7. d

B. WHERE SHOULD THEY GO?

1. zoo
2. beach
3. concert
4. site
5. flea market
6. a craft fair
7. museum
8. botanical gardens
9. planetarium
10. amusement

WORKBOOK PAGE 128

A. WHICH WORD?

1. bench
2. in the bike rack
3. trash can
4. grill
5. picnic table
6. jogging path
7. water fountain
8. sandbox
9. duck pond

B. ANALOGIES

1. sandbox
2. bikeway
3. carousel
4. ballfield
5. playground
6. skateboard

C. WHAT ARE THEY TALKING ABOUT?

1. b
2. d
3. f
4. e
5. a
6. g
7. c

D. LISTENING: *What Are They Talking About?*

Listen and circle the correct word.

1. Throw this away over there.
2. Do you and your friends play there very often?
3. Look at the swings and the slide!
4. Let's go over there. There are tables and a grill.
5. The children love to play in it.
6. Look at all the ducks!
7. We can cook our food on this.
8. Don't go so high! Be careful! You'll fall!

Answers

1. trash can
2. tennis court
3. playground
4. picnic area
5. sandbox
6. duck pond
7. grill
8. climber

WORKBOOK PAGE 129

A. WHAT DO THEY DO?

1. b
2. d
3. a
4. c
5. h
6. g
7. e
8. f

B. WHICH WORD?

1. chair
2. bucket
3. beach ball
4. seashell
5. sunglasses
6. kite
7. swimmer
8. snack bar
9. beach umbrella

C. ANALOGIES

1. surfboard
2. snack bar
3. boogie board
4. lifeguard stand
5. sunscreen

D. LISTENING: *What Are They Talking About?*

Listen and circle the correct word.

1. Would you like to sit down?
2. Look how high it's going!
3. Use this if you can't swim.
4. You can make a sand castle with this.
5. Put this on so you don't get a sunburn.
6. Wait a minute! I have to get my surfboard.
7. I'll put this down and we can sit on it.
8. He's selling ice cream and other snacks.

Answers

1. chair
2. kite
3. life preserver
4. shovel
5. sunscreen
6. surfer
7. blanket
8. vendor

WORKBOOK PAGE 130

A. WHICH WORD?

1. lantern
2. rope
3. thermos
4. backpack
5. insect repellent
6. stakes
7. basket
8. bag
9. GPS device
10. mountain climbing

B. MATCHING

1. d
2. c
3. a
4. b
5. f
6. e
7. h
8. g

C. MATCH AND WRITE

1. sleeping bag
2. mountain bike
3. trail map
4. GPS device
5. tent stakes
6. insect repellent
7. technical climbing
8. hiking boots

D. LISTENING: *Where Are They Going?*

Listen and write the number next to the correct activity.

1. A. Great idea! Let's go this weekend!
   B. But I don't have a harness!
   A. No problem. I have a rope and harness you can use.
2. A. Let's ride over that hill!
   B. Okay. I'm glad I wore my helmet.
3. A. Which way do we go now?
   B. I don't know. Let's look at the GPS device.
4. A. Here are the sleeping bags. Where are the tent stakes?
   B. Over there. Do you have the insect repellent?

Answers

4	2
3	1

WORKBOOK PAGE 131

A. ASSOCIATIONS

1. e
2. c
3. f
4. d
5. a
6. b

B. WHICH WORD?

1. ping pong
2. uniform
3. stirrups
4. stick
5. safety goggles
6. trampoline
7. arrow
8. bike helmet
9. gloves
10. rowing machine

C. WHICH WORD DOESN'T BELONG?

1. barbell (The others are kinds of balls.)
2. helmet (The others are for the feet.)
3. saddle (The others are things you throw or hit.)
4. cycling (The others are sports in which you hit a ball.)
5. target (The others are implements you hold.)
6. pool table (The others are things you sit on.)
7. net (The others are exercise equipment.)

D. ANALOGIES

1. paddle
2. shuttlecock
3. pool stick
4. elbow pads
5. weightlifting
6. billiard ball

WORKBOOK PAGE 132

A. WHICH SPORTS?

1. baseball, softball, football, lacrosse, hockey
2. football
3. baseball, softball, football, lacrosse, soccer
4. hockey

B. CROSSWORD: *Pictures to Words*

(See page 172.)

C. LISTENING

Listen and circle the correct word to complete each sentence.

1. All the players are on the volleyball . . . .
2. He's an excellent football . . . .
3. We play hockey on a hockey . . . .
4. My favorite sport is . . . .
5. She's over there on the basketball . . . .
6. Who is your favorite soccer . . . ?

Answers

1. court
2. player
3. rink
4. lacrosse
5. court
6. player

WORKBOOK PAGE 133

A. ASSOCIATIONS

1. g
2. a
3. h
4. f
5. b
6. d
7. e
8. c

B. WHICH WORD?

1. helmet
2. mask
3. skates
4. hoop
5. helmets
6. glove
7. lacrosse
8. uniforms

C. WHICH WORD DOESN'T BELONG?

1. shinguard (The others are worn on the head.)
2. bat (The others are hit during the game.)
3. backboard (The others are used for hitting.)
4. shoulder pads (The others are worn on the hand.)
5. hockey (The others are played on a field or court, not on ice.)

D. LISTENING: *Which Sport?*

Listen to the radio announcer. Write the number next to the correct picture.

1. Good pass! He shoots the puck! Goal!
2. Nice pass! He's going toward the basket. He misses! He gets the rebound. It's in!
3. The ball is hit into left field. The left fielder is running. He catches it! Oh! The ball falls out of his glove!
4. Nice serve. The forward players set up the ball. It goes over the net. It comes back fast! Score! Nice volley that time!
5. It's a long pass! He caught it! He's going for the touchdown!
6. The center is running down the field. He passes the ball. The player kicks it—and it's a goal!

Answers

5	3	2
6	1	4

WORKBOOK PAGE 134

A. WHICH SPORTS?

1. skiing, cross-country skiing, ice skating, figure skating, snowboarding
2. sledding, bobsledding, snowmobiling
3. ice skating, figure skating
4. snowmobiling

B. MATCHING

1. e
2. f
3. a
4. b
5. d
6. c

C. WHICH WORD?

1. Cross-country
2. poles
3. skating
4. saucer
5. bobsledding
6. snowmobile

D. WHAT ARE THEY?

1. c	3. e	5. f
2. a	4. b	6. d

WORKBOOK PAGE 135

A. WHICH WORD?

1. fishing	4. surfboard
2. fins	5. fishing
3. scuba diving	6. waterskiing

B. ASSOCIATIONS

1. b	3. a	5. f
2. c	4. e	6. d

C. ANALOGIES

1. paddles	4. fins
2. sailboard	5. air tank
3. wet suit	6. swimsuit

D. LISTENING: *What Are They Doing?*

Listen and write the number under the correct picture.

1. A. Can you show me how to use them?
   B. You don't know how to use paddles?
2. A. Is this your first time?
   B. Yes. It's fun to use the snorkel and flippers.
3. A. The ocean looks calm.
   B. I think the waves are big enough.
4. A. I brought my towel and bathing suit.
   B. Great! Let's go to the pool!
5. A. Here's the towrope.
   B. Thanks. I'm ready. Start the boat!
6. A. I got one!
   B. Look how big it is!

Answers

6	2	4
1	5	3

WORKBOOK PAGE 136

A. WHAT'S THE ACTION?

1. Dribble	6. Swing
2. bend	7. Hit
3. pass	8. Hop
4. Shoot	9. swim
5. run	

B. ANALOGIES

1. sit-up	5. shoot
2. throw	6. hands
3. pitch	7. handstand
4. skip	

C. ASSOCIATIONS

1. c	3. b	5. f
2. a	4. e	6. d

D. LISTENING: *Aerobics*

Listen and write the number under the correct picture.

1. Okay, everybody! I want you all to stretch! Stretch those muscles! Stretch! Stretch!
2. Okay, now bend! Bend to the floor! Bend! Bend!
3. Okay. Now I want you to jump in place. Up and down! Jump! Jump!
4. Now one foot at a time! Hop, left! Hop, right! Hop! Hop!
5. Now reach to the ceiling! As high as you can! Reach! Reach!
6. Now swing those arms! To the left, to the right! Swing! Swing!

Answers

2	4	1	6	3	5

WORKBOOK PAGE 137

A. WHICH WORD?

1. comedy	5. screen
2. actress	6. band
3. conductor	7. opera
4. ballerina	8. play

B. MATCH AND WRITE

1. opera singer	4. movie screen
2. concert hall	5. ballet dancer
3. music club	

C. WHICH WORD DOESN'T BELONG?

1. band (The others are performers.)
2. singer (The others are places.)
3. comedian (The others are related to music.)
4. play (The others have music.)
5. band (The others are places.)

D. WHO IS TALKING?

1. actress	4. conductor
2. ballet dancer	5. singer
3. comedian	6. musician

WORKBOOK PAGE 138

A. WHO LIKES WHAT?

1. music	3. TV programs
2. play	4. movies

B. LISTENING: *What Type of Music?*

Listen and write the number next to the type of music you hear.

1. (sound: reggae music)
2. (sound: classical music)
3. (sound: country music)
4. (sound: jazz)
5. (sound: rock music)
6. (sound: blues)
7. (sound: hip hop)
8. (sound: gospel music)

Answers

2	7	5	8
1	6	4	3

C. WHAT TYPE OF MOVIE?

1. e	3. d	5. h	7. b
2. g	4. a	6. c	8. f

D. WHAT TYPE OF TV PROGAM?

1. d	3. a	5. b	7. f
2. g	4. e	6. c	

WORKBOOK PAGE 139

A. WHICH INSTRUMENT DOESN'T BELONG?

1. violin (The others are keyboard instruments.)
2. trumpet (The others are string instruments.)
3. cello (The others are woodwind instruments.)
4. xylophone (The others are brass instruments.)
5. harmonica (The others are percussion instruments.)

B. MUSIC ASSOCIATIONS

1. b	3. d	5. e
2. a	4. f	6. c

C. LISTENING: *Which Instrument?*

Listen and write the number next to the instrument you hear.

1. (sound: piano)
2. (sound: flute)
3. (sound: harp)
4. (sound: harmonica)
5. (sound: trumpet)
6. (sound: tuba)
7. (sound: banjo)
8. (sound: drum)
9. (sound: guitar)

Answers

4	8	5
2	6	1
7	3	9

D. CROSSWORD: *Pictures to Words*

(See page 172.)

WORKBOOK PAGE 140

A. WHICH WORD?

1. rooster	6. barn
2. hay	7. lamb
3. orchard	8. scarecrow
4. stable	9. garden
5. sheep	10. irrigation system

B. CATEGORIES

People Who Work on a Farm

farm worker
farmer
hired hand

Farm Crops

alfalfa
cotton
soybeans
wheat

Places Where Animals Stay

barn
chicken coop
hen house
pig pen
stable

C. ASSOCIATIONS

1. c	6. j
2. e	7. i
3. d	8. f
4. b	9. h
5. a	10. g

D. LISTENING: *Which Animal?*

Listen and write the number next to the animal you hear.

1. (sound: goat)
2. (sound: rooster)
3. (sound: horse)
4. (sound: turkey)
5. (sound: pig)

Answers

2   4   1   5   3

WORKBOOK PAGES 141–142

A. WHICH WORD?

1. goldfish	5. squirrel
2. stripes	6. monkeys
3. gerbil	7. dog
4. pony	8. llama

B. WHICH ANIMAL?

1. d	4. c	7. k	10. g
2. a	5. f	8. i	11. h
3. b	6. e	9. l	12. j

C. ANIMAL ANALOGIES

1. dog	6. beaver
2. rhinoceros	7. paw
3. mouse	8. quills
4. zebra	9. gibbon
5. lion	10. wolf

D. WHICH WORD DOESN'T BELONG?

1. raccoon (The others are horses.)
2. wolves (The others are rodents.)
3. antelope (The others are parts that grow on certain animals.)
4. pouch (The others are external parts of animals.)
5. panther (The others are types of bears.)
6. giraffe (The others are types of monkeys.)
7. platypus (The others are common pets.)
8. prairie dog (The others fly.)

E. WHAT DO THEY EAT?

1. d	3. a	5. g	7. e
2. b	4. c	6. f	8. h

F. LISTENING

Listen and circle the word you hear.

1. Is that a gopher?
2. Look at that monkey!

3. I wasn't happy to see a rat yesterday!
4. They went to the zoo and saw a koala bear.
5. Look at that hamster!
6. We heard a moose last night.
7. What a big raccoon!
8. Look at that zebra!

Answers

1. gopher	5. hamster
2. monkey	6. moose
3. rat	7. raccoon
4. koala bear	8. zebra

G. ANIMAL COMPARISONS

1. mouse	5. beaver
2. fox	6. owl
3. donkey	7. bat
4. pig	8. bear

H. LISTENING: *Which Animal?*

Listen and write the number next to the animal or pet you hear.

1. (sound: lion)
2. (sound: cat)
3. (sound: donkey)
4. (sound: dog)
5. (sound: coyote)
6. (sound: hyena)
7. (sound: gorilla)
8. (sound: mouse)
9. (sound: elephant)
10. (sound: bear)

Answers

8	9	1	4	10
7	5	2	6	3

WORKBOOK PAGE 143

A. WHICH BIRD?

1. parrot	6. Swan
2. hummingbird	7. eagle
3. penguin	8. peacock
4. crane	9. owl
5. pigeon	

B. WHICH INSECT?

1. caterpillar	5. Mosquito
2. scorpion	6. tick
3. firefly	7. Bees
4. spider	8. cricket

C. ANALOGIES

1. nest	4. moth
2. bill	5. cocoon
3. feather	6. grasshopper

D. LISTENING: *Which Bird or Insect?*

Listen and write the number next to the bird or insect you hear.

1. (sound: crow)
2. (sound: seagull)
3. (sound: cricket)
4. (sound: woodpecker)
5. (sound: duck)
6. (sound: parrot)
7. (sound: bee)
8. (sound: owl)

Answers

6	8	3	7
2	4	5	1

WORKBOOK PAGE 144

A. CATEGORIES

Fish We Eat	Amphibians
bass	frog
cod	newt
trout	salamander
tuna	toad

Deadly Fish/Reptiles

cobra
rattlesnake
shark
stingray

B. WHICH WORD?

1. An octopus	5. squid
2. turtle	6. Whales
3. Dolphins	7. horses
4. sharks	

C. WHICH WORD DOESN'T BELONG?

1. seal (The others are parts of fish.)
2. walrus (The others are snakes.)
3. squid (The others are amphibians.)
4. jellyfish (The others are fish.)
5. iguana (The others live in water.)
6. flounder (The others are amphibians.)
7. ray (The others are parts of animals.)

D. ANALOGIES

1. boa constrictor	5. iguana
2. toad	6. newt
3. fin	7. starfish
4. scales	8. sea lion

WORKBOOK PAGE 145

A. WHAT'S THE WORD?

1. leaves	4. palm
2. maple	5. willow
3. redwood	6. branch

B. WHERE DO THEY GROW?

1. c	3. e	5. d	7. f
2. a	4. b	6. g	

C. WHICH WORD?

1. tulips	6. roots
2. roses	7. Sunflowers
3. needles	8. berries
4. thorns	9. pansies and petunias
5. Poinsettias	

D. ANALOGIES

1. trunk	4. bulb
2. flower	5. cactus
3. twig	

WORKBOOK PAGE 146

A. ASSOCIATIONS

1. d	3. a	5. b
2. e	4. c	

B. MATCH AND WRITE
1. natural gas
2. acid rain
3. toxic waste
4. geothermal energy
5. global warming
6. hydroelectric power

C. WHICH WORD?
1. hazardous waste
2. Geothermal
3. recycle
4. coal
5. oil
6. Acid rain
7. energy
8. carpool

D. WHAT'S THE WORD?
1. air
2. global
3. recycle
4. carpool
5. conserve
6. solar
7. save energy

WORKBOOK PAGE 147

A. WHAT IS IT?
1. hurricane
2. earthquake
3. tsunami
4. forest fire
5. blizzard
6. volcanic eruption

B. WHICH WORD?
1. typhoon
2. tornado
3. flood
4. drought
5. forest fire
6. tsunamis

C. ANALOGIES
1. wildfire
2. avalanche
3. typhoon
4. flood

D. WHAT ARE THEY TALKING ABOUT?
1. e
2. f
3. b
4. d
5. c
6. a

WORKBOOK PAGE 9

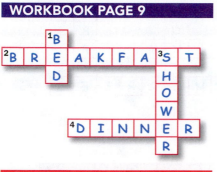

WORKBOOK PAGE 18

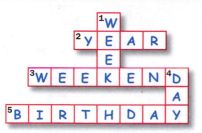

WORKBOOK PAGE 22

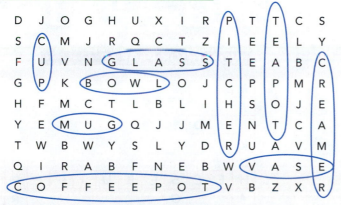

WORKBOOK PAGE 24

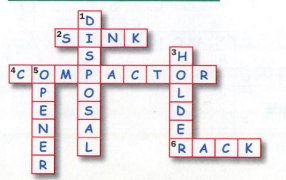

WORKBOOK PAGE 27

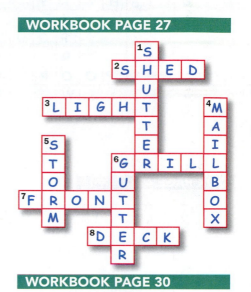

WORKBOOK PAGE 30

WORKBOOK PAGE 33

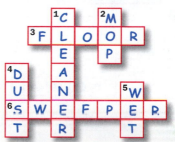

WORKBOOK PAGE 37

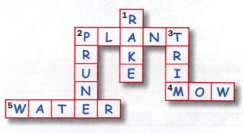

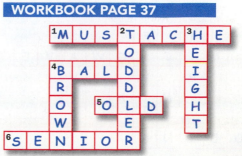

WORKBOOK PAGE 39

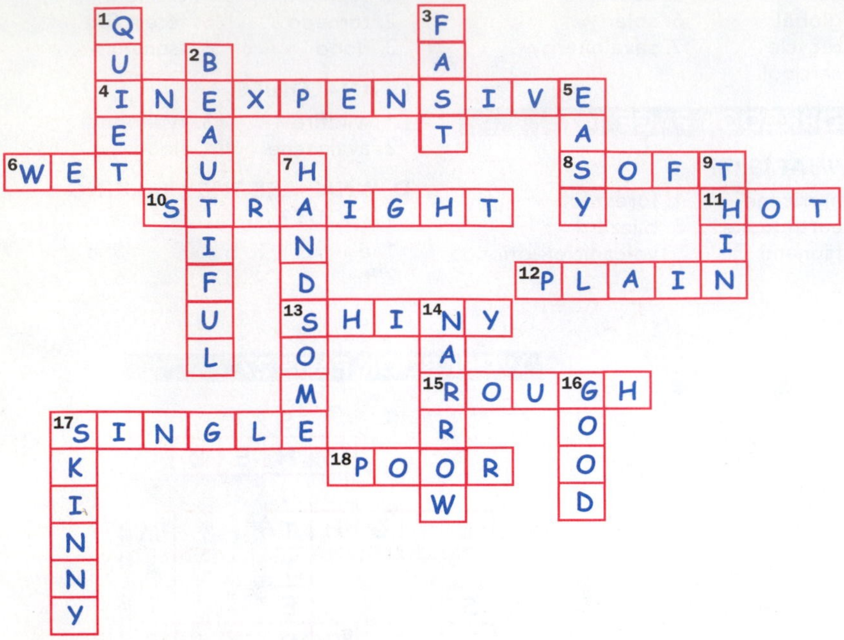
1 QUIET
2 BEAUTIFUL
3 FAST
4 INEXPENSIVE
5 EASY
6 WET
7 HANDSOME
8 SOFT
9 THIN
10 STRAIGHT
11 HOT
12 PLAIN
13 SHINY
14 NARROW
15 ROUGH
16 GOOD
17 SINGLE
SKINNY
18 POOR

WORKBOOK PAGE 41

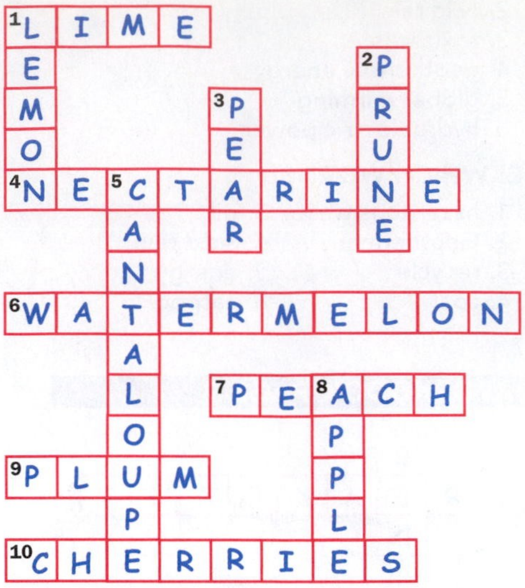
1 LIME
LEMON
2 PRUNE
3 PEAR
4 NECTARINE
5 CANTALOUPE
6 WATERMELON
7 PEACH
8 APPLE
9 PLUM
10 CHERRIES

WORKBOOK PAGE 42

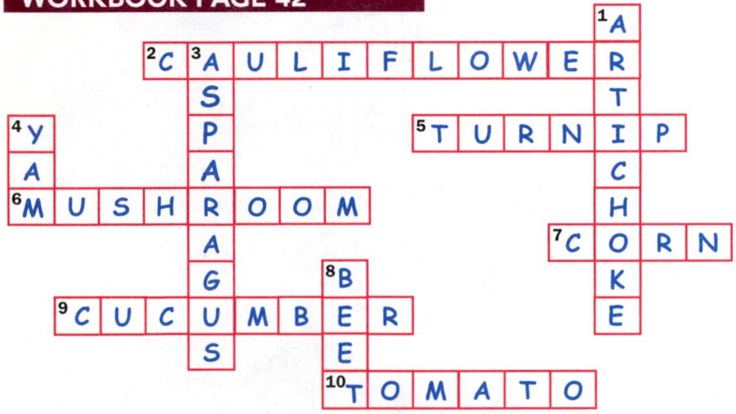
1 ARTICHOKE
2 CAULIFLOWER
3 ASPARAGUS
4 YAM
5 TURNIP
6 MUSHROOM
7 CORN
8 BEET
9 CUCUMBER
10 TOMATO

WORKBOOK PAGE 45

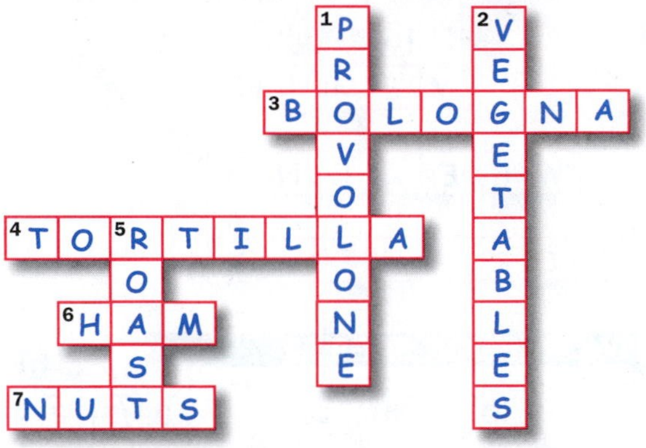
1 PROVOLONE
2 VEGETABLES
3 BOLOGNA
4 TORTILLA
5 ROAST
6 HAM
7 NUTS

WORKBOOK PAGE 47

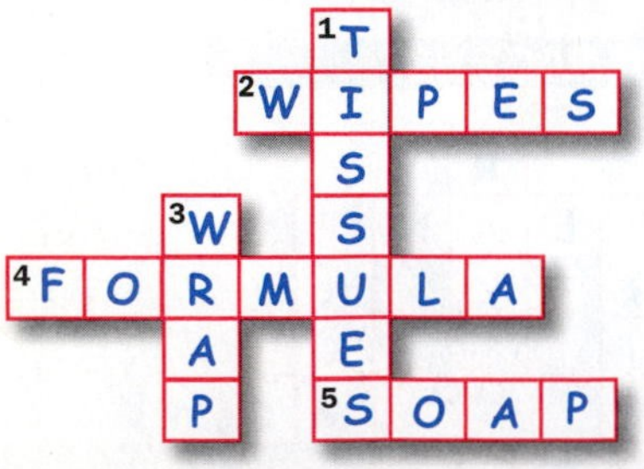
1 TISSUE
2 WIPES
3 WRAP
4 FORMULA
5 SOAP

WORKBOOK PAGE 51

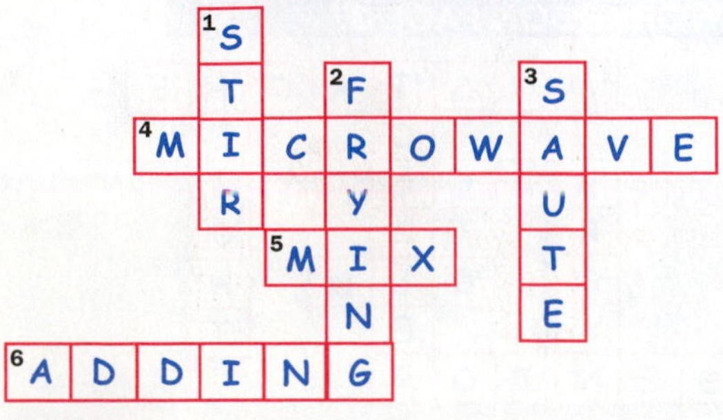
1 STIR
2 FRYING
3 SAUTE
4 MICROWAVE
5 MIX
6 ADDING

WORKBOOK PAGE 53

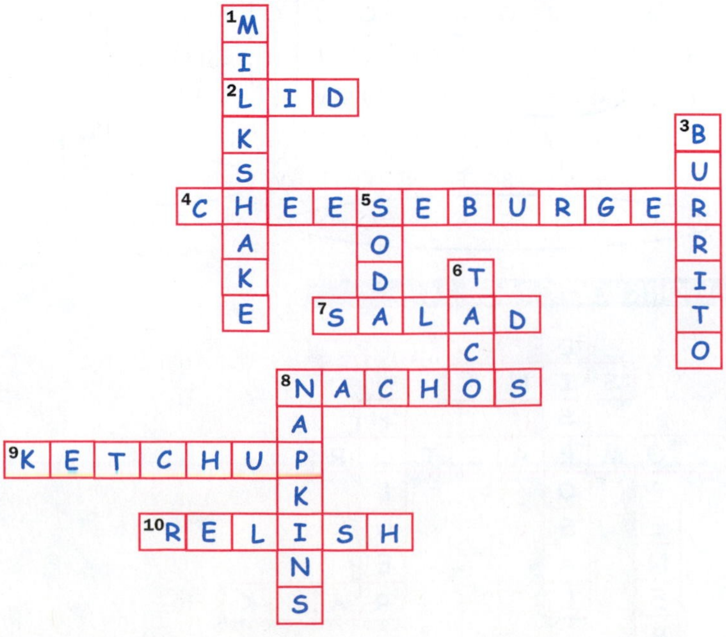
1 MILKSHAKE
2 LID
3 BURRITO
4 CHEESEBURGER
5 SODA
6 TACO
7 SALAD
8 NACHOS
NAPKINS
9 KETCHUP
10 RELISH

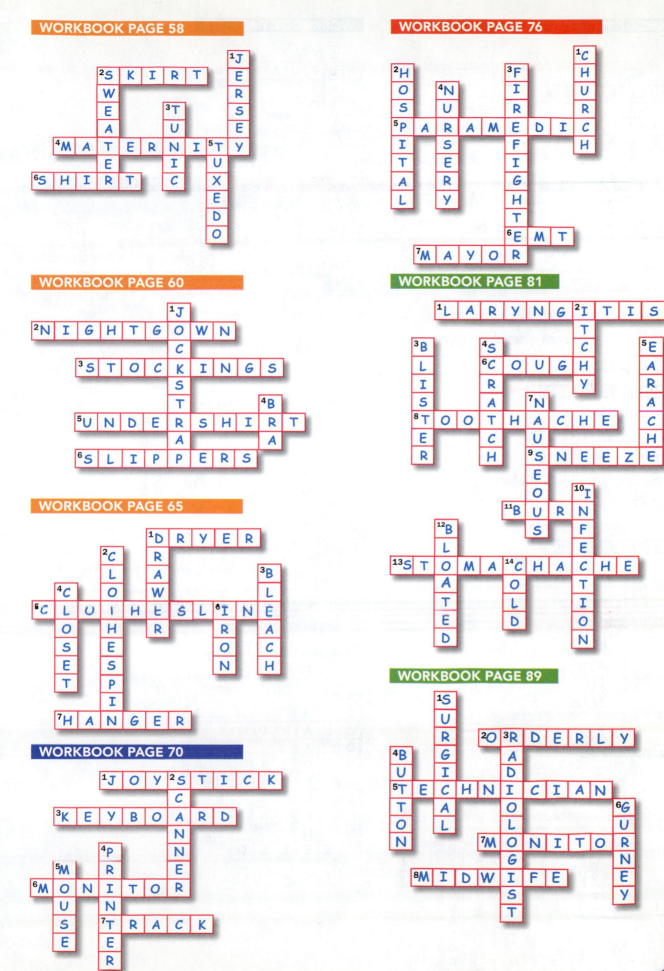

WORKBOOK PAGE 58

Across: SKIRT, TUNIC, MATERNITY, SHIRT
Down: JERSEY, SWEATER, TUXEDO

WORKBOOK PAGE 60

NIGHTGOWN, STOCKINGS, UNDERSHIRT, SLIPPERS
JOCKSTRAP, BRA

WORKBOOK PAGE 65

DRYER, DRAWER, CLOSET, CLOTHESPI, CLOTHESLINE, IRON, BLEACH, HANGER

WORKBOOK PAGE 70

JOYSTICK, SCANNER, KEYBOARD, PRINTER, MONITOR, MOUSE, TRACK

WORKBOOK PAGE 76

CHURCH, HOSPITAL, NURSERY, FIREFIGHT, PARAMEDIC, EMT, MAYOR

WORKBOOK PAGE 81

LARYNGITIS, BLISTER, SCRATCH, COUGH, ITCHY, EARACHE, NAUSEOUS, TOOTHACHE, SNEEZE, BURN, INFECTION, BLOATED, STOMACHACHE, COLD

WORKBOOK PAGE 89

SURGICAL, ORDERLY, RADIOLOGIST, BUTTON, TECHNICIAN, GURNEY, MONITOR, MIDWIFE

WORKBOOK PAGE 91

- BOTTLE
- FORMULA
- DIAPER
- BIB
- OINTMENT
- PACIFIER
- WIPES

WORKBOOK PAGE 113

- CLERK
- DOCK
- ELEVATOR
- ROOM

WORKBOOK PAGE 94

- GOVERNMENT
- SHOP
- SCIENCE
- ENGLISH
- MATH
- SPANISH
- HEALTH
- MUSIC
- HISTORY

WORKBOOK PAGE 121

- UP
- PAST
- AROUND
- THROUGH
- OUT
- UNDER
- DOWN

WORKBOOK PAGE 125

- GUEST
- DOORMAN
- RESTAURANT
- ELEVATOR
- HALLWAY
- CONCIERGE

WORKBOOK PAGE 100

- POETRY
- ESSAY
- NOVEL
- LETTER
- EDITORIAL
- NOTE
- REPORT

WORKBOOK PAGE 132

- BASEBALL
- HOCKEY
- SOCCER
- FOOTBALL
- LACROSS
- VOLLEYBALL
- FOOTBALL
- BASKETBALL

WORKBOOK PAGE 103

- METEOR
- SATELLITE
- PLANET
- OBSERVATORY
- UFO
- ASTEROID

WORKBOOK PAGE 139

- ORGAN
- GUITAR
- ACCORDION
- SAXOPHONE
- CLARINET
- BASS
- PIANO
- OBOE
- CELLO

WORKBOOK PAGE 107

- PILOT
- SHOPKEEPER
- COURIER
- TAILOR
- TELEMARKETER
- LAWYER
- MOVER
- TRANSLATOR
- WELDER
- PAINTER

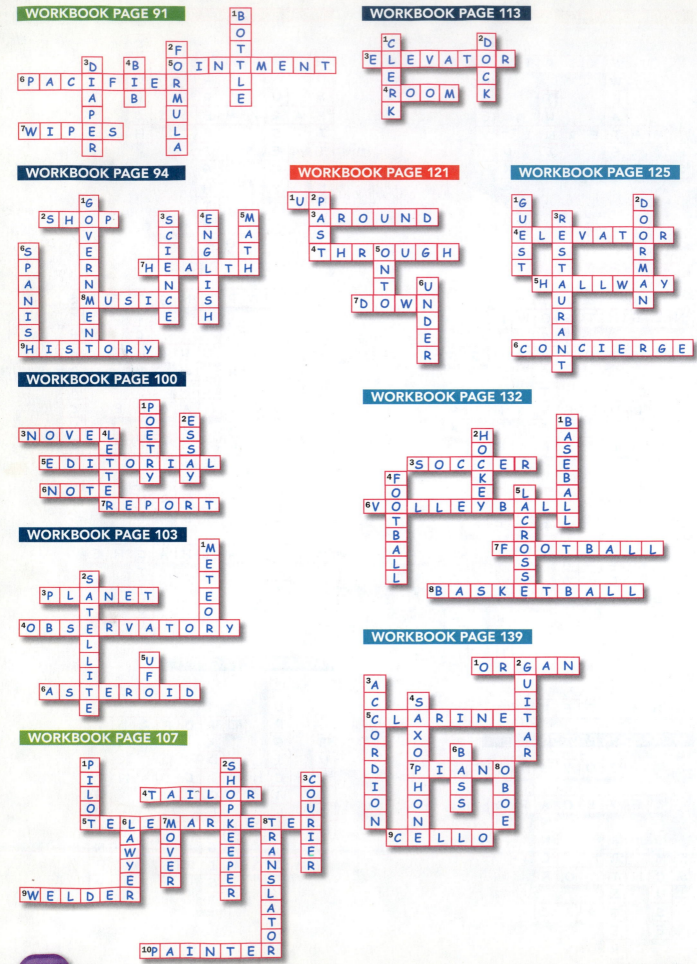